高等职业教育"十二五"精品课程规划教材

电子信息专业英语

（第 2 版）

主　编　庄朝蓉
副主编　余小川　任　敬
参　编　施　艳　赵李春
主　审　李开柱

北京邮电大学出版社
www.buptpress.com

内 容 简 介

电子信息英语作为电子信息类专业的一门专业基础课,很好地突出了高职高专的教学实用性。本书共16个单元,内容包括电子技术、通信和计算机3大板块,涉及电气元件、测量工具、电子器件、集成电路、数字信号处理器、电源、同步数字系列、密集波分复用系统、嵌入式系统、可编程逻辑控制器、第三代移动通信技术、非对称数字用户环路、无线网络技术、无线局域网、网络实用技术和微波通信等,基本覆盖了目前电子信息业的技术或业务领域。在构架上,每个单元包含2篇课文,按难易程度和篇幅分为 Text A 和 Text B,2篇课文后均配以生词短语及课文注释。在练习的设计上,Text A 注重短语、句子及段落的翻译,Text B 侧重阅读理解。每个单元还包括科技英语翻译技巧及实践。附录包括电子信息常用专业英语缩略语表、课文参考译文、练习参考答案和参考文献,以方便教师在教学中选用和学生自学。

本书除适用于信息通信类高职高专学生外,还可以作为其他电子信息类学生或英语爱好者从英语角度学习和了解电子信息技术或业务的参考书。

图书在版编目(CIP)数据

电子信息专业英语 / 庄朝蓉主编. —2版. —北京:北京邮电大学出版社,2013.6(2020.7重印)
ISBN 978-7-5635-3324-4

Ⅰ.①电… Ⅱ.①庄… Ⅲ.①电子技术—英语 Ⅳ.①H31

中国版本图书馆 CIP 数据核字(2012)第 283444 号

书　　名:电子信息专业英语(第2版)
主　　编:庄朝蓉
责任编辑:彭　楠　马晓仟
出版发行:北京邮电大学出版社
社　　址:北京市海淀区西土城路10号(邮编:100876)
发 行 部:电话:010-62282185　传真:010-62283578
E-mail:publish@bupt.edu.cn
经　　销:各地新华书店
印　　刷:北京九州迅驰传媒文化有限公司
开　　本:787 mm×1 092 mm　1/16
印　　张:17
字　　数:419
版　　次:2009年1月第1版　2013年6月第2版　2020年7月第4次印刷

ISBN 978-7-5635-3324-4　　　　　　　　　　　　　　　定　价:35.00元

・ 如有印装质量问题,请与北京邮电大学出版社发行部联系 ・

前　言

随着科技的进步和经济全球化的到来，社会对专业人才的外语能力要求越来越高。电子信息是当今国际、国内发展最迅速、技术更新最活跃的领域之一。

本书为电子信息类高职高专学生进行专业英语学习而编写，其目的在于使学生通过电子信息专业英语的学习，扩展其在电子信息专业方面的英语词汇量，熟悉该领域的专业术语，了解科技英语的表达特点及掌握专业英语翻译技巧，从而大大提高他们的业务素质并有利于增强学生在电子信息专业领域内的英语应用能力和职业能力，为学生在今后的学习和工作中阅读和翻译电子信息类相关英文专业技术资料作准备。

本书可作为高职高专电子信息、通信、计算机等专业的教材，也可作为其他电子信息类学生或英语爱好者从英语角度学习和了解电子信息技术或业务的参考书。

本书主要选取国内外优秀教材及专业网站相关英文原文及电子信息新技术、新业务介绍的科普文章，这些文章难度适中，语言流畅，具有较强的专业性和可读性。在选材上，广泛借鉴了传统的相关书籍和教材，并充分考虑到电子信息技术日新月异的发展趋势，选用了与新技术、新业务有关的时文，突出了选材的新颖性。

本次改版结合电子信息专业的最新发展状况以及高职高专注重实践能力锻炼的特点，在原版基础上对内容进行了增删，使得全书涉及更广泛，内容更丰富，知识更实用。改版后，本书共16个单元，内容包含电子技术、通信和计算机3大板块，涉及电气元件、测量工具、电子器件、集成电路、数字信号处理器、电源、同步数字系列、密集波分复用系统、嵌入式系统、可编程逻辑控制器、第三代移动通信技术、非对称数字用户环路、无线网络技术、无线局域网、网络实用技术和微波通信等，基本覆盖了目前电子信息业的技术或业务领域。本教材可作为电子信息类高职、高专各专业学生学习专业英语时的教学用书及参考资料。结合编者多年的专业英语教学实践，本教材练习设计更实用、内容更翔实；考虑到高职高专学生英语水平差异，各单元课后生词罗列大量词条，加注音标，在给出专业词汇含义的同时保留部分词条的普通释义，以方便学生温故知新；每个单元配以科技英语翻译技巧及实践,突出教学内容的实用性和针对性,满足高职高专"实用为主,够用为度"的需要。为便于教师教学和读者自学,每篇文章都附课文注释和参考译文,所有练习配参考答案。

参加本书编写的教师有四川邮电职业技术学院的庄朝蓉、余小川、任敬、赵李春和防灾科技学院的施艳老师,本书编写分工如下。

庄朝蓉负责本书的策划和架构设计,并且编写第1、2、3、4、6单元,并对全书进行统稿、校对、修订和排版;余小川编写第7、11、12单元以及缩略语的整理;任敬编写第13、14、15单元;施艳编写第5、9、10、16单元;赵李春编写第8单元。全书的翻译技巧部分由5位老师共同完成。四川财经职业学院李开柱副教授对全书进行了审阅。

本书是集体智慧的结晶。选材上参照并借鉴了笔者主持的2006年四川省省级精品课程《通信英语》的相关资料和选材思路,为了确保本书内容的翔实丰富和相关技术知识的时效性,笔者编写过程中参考了大量的国内外书籍和专业网站内容,在此对"精品课程"课题组的相关老师、国内外相关资料和网站的文献作者表示由衷的感谢。

在成书过程中得到笔者单位相关领导的支持和李媛、阳旭艳等专业课老师无私帮助,在此一并表示衷心的感谢!

由于编者的水平与实践经验有限,书中疏漏和错误之处敬请专家和读者批评指正。

编　者

目 录

Unit 1　Circuits and Electrical Components ……………………………………… 1
Text A　Circuits ……………………………………………………………………… 1
Text B　Electrical Components …………………………………………………… 6
Translating Skill 1　派生词的翻译(一) …………………………………………… 9

Unit 2　Instruments for Measurement ……………………………………………… 11
Text A　What Do Meters Measure? ……………………………………………… 11
Text B　Oscilloscope ……………………………………………………………… 15
Translating Skill 2　派生词的翻译(二) …………………………………………… 20

Unit 3　Electronic Components …………………………………………………… 21
Text A　Electronic Components ………………………………………………… 21
Text B　Semiconductor Diode …………………………………………………… 25
Translating Skill 3　Tele-和-Phone 的译法 ……………………………………… 30

Unit 4　Integrated Circuits ………………………………………………………… 33
Text A　Integrated Circuits ……………………………………………………… 33
Text B　Application of Chips …………………………………………………… 37
Translating Skill 4　广告的翻译 …………………………………………………… 41

Unit 5　Digital Signal Processor …………………………………………………… 44
Text A　Digital Signal Processor (DSP) ………………………………………… 44
Text B　Architecture of the Digital Signal Processor ………………………… 49
Translating Skill 5　专业术语翻译 ………………………………………………… 52

Unit 6　Power Supply ……………………………………………………………… 55
Text A　Power Supply …………………………………………………………… 55
Text B　Types of Power Supply ………………………………………………… 59
Translating Skill 6　新词的翻译 …………………………………………………… 62

Unit 7　Synchronous Digital Hierarchy ……………………………………………… 65

　　Text A　Synchronous Digital Hierarchy ………………………………………… 65
　　Text B　The Architecture of SDH ……………………………………………… 69
　　Translating Skill 7　缩略词的翻译（一） ……………………………………… 73

Unit 8　DWDM ………………………………………………………………………… 76

　　Text A　DWDM …………………………………………………………………… 76
　　Text B　DWDM—Wavelength Converting Transponders, Muxponder and the
　　　　　　Reconfigurable Optical Add-Drop Multiplexer ……………………… 82
　　Translating Skill 8　缩略词的翻译（二） ……………………………………… 86

Unit 9　Embedded System …………………………………………………………… 90

　　Text A　Overview of an Embedded System …………………………………… 90
　　Text B　Regulated Power Supply for Embedded Systems …………………… 95
　　Translating Skill 9　数量词的翻译 …………………………………………… 100

Unit 10　PLC ………………………………………………………………………… 103

　　Text A　Ladder Logic …………………………………………………………… 103
　　Text B　PLC Programming ……………………………………………………… 109
　　Translating Skill 10　长句的翻译 ……………………………………………… 113

Unit 11　3G …………………………………………………………………………… 117

　　Text A　IMT-2000 Global 3G Standard ………………………………………… 117
　　Text B　Implementation and History of 3G …………………………………… 121
　　Translating Skill 11　被动句 …………………………………………………… 125

Unit 12　ADSL ………………………………………………………………………… 128

　　Text A　ADSL …………………………………………………………………… 128
　　Text B　Application for ADSL ………………………………………………… 133
　　Translating Skill 12　专有名词的翻译（一） ………………………………… 136

Unit 13　The Wireless Web ………………………………………………………… 139

　　Text A　Second-Generation Wireless Web …………………………………… 139
　　Text B　I-Mode …………………………………………………………………… 145
　　Translating Skill 13　专有名词的翻译（二） ………………………………… 148

Unit 14　WLAN 151
Text A　Wireless LANs：802.11 151
Text B　New Wireless LAN Standard 156
Translating Skill 14　否定的处理 159

Unit 15　Networks Applied Technology 162
Text A　Home Networking 162
Text B　E-Mail 167
Translating Skill 15　And 引导的句型（一） 170

Unit 16　Microwave Communication 172
Text A　Networking Microwave Communication 172
Text B　Understanding Microwave Communication Frequencies 177
Translating Skill 16　And 引导的句型（二） 181

附录1　电子信息常用缩略语 183

附录2　课文参考译文 189

附录3　练习参考答案 232

参考文献 260

Unit 1 Circuits and Electrical Components

This unit introduces you to electronic circuits and explains what is meant by current, voltage and resistance. You can also find out about the important types of components used in building electronic circuits. [1]

本单元介绍电路并解释什么是电流、电压和电阻。读者也可以了解用于构成电子电路的重要电气元件类型。

Text A

Circuits

Current

An electric current is a flow of charged particles. Inside a copper wire, current is carried by small negatively-charged particles, called electrons. The electrons drift in random directions until a current starts to flow. When this happens, electrons start to move in the same direction. [2] The size of the current depends on the number of electrons passing per second.

Current is represented by the symbol I, and is measured in amperes, "amps", or A. One ampere is a flow of 6.24×10^{18} electrons per second past any point in a wire. That's more than six million million million electrons passing per second.

In electronic circuits, currents are most often measured in milliamps, mA, that is, thousandths of an amp.

Voltage

In the torch circuit, what causes the current to flow? The answer is that the cells provide a "push" which makes the current flow round the circuit. [3]

Each cell provides a push, called its potential difference, or voltage. This is represented by the symbol U, and is measured in volts, or V.

Typically, each cell provides 1.5 V. Two cells connected one after another, in series, provide 3 V, while three cells would provide 4.5 V, shown in Fig. 1-1.

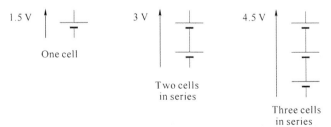

Fig. 1-1 Cells in Series

Cells connected in series

Which arrangement would make the lamp glow most brightly? Lamps are designed to work with a particular voltage, but, other things being equal, the bigger the voltage, the brighter the lamp.[4]

Strictly speaking, a battery consists of two or more cells. These can be connected in series, as is usual in a torch circuit, but it is also possible to connect the cells in parallel, like Fig. 1-2.

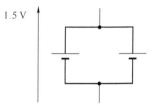

Fig. 1-2 Cells in Parallel

Cells connected in parallel

A single cell can provide a little current for a long time, or a big current for a short time. Connecting the cells in series increases the voltage, but does not affect the useful life of the cells. On the other hand, if the cells are connected in parallel, the voltage stays at 1.5 V, but the life of the battery is doubled.

A torch lamp which uses 300 mA from C-size alkaline cells should operate for more than 20 hours before the cells are exhausted.

Resistance

Part of the torch circuit limits, or resists the flow of current. Most of the circuits consist of thick metal conductors which allow current to flow easily. These parts, including the spring, switch plates and lamp connections, have a low resistance. The lamp filament, on the other hand, is made up of very thin wire. It conducts much less easily than the rest of the circuit and has a higher resistance.[5]

The resistance, R, of the filament is measured in ohms, or Ω. If the battery voltage is 3 V (2 C-size cells in series) and the lamp current is 300 mA, or 0.3 A, what is the resistance of the filament? This is calculated from

$$R = \frac{U}{I} = \frac{3}{0.3} = 10 \ \Omega$$

where R is resistance, U is the voltage across the lamp, and I is current. In this case, 10 Ω is the resistance of the lamp filament once it has heated up.

Resistance values in electronic circuits vary from a few ohms, or Ω to values in kilohms, or kΩ (thousands of ohms) and megohms, or MΩ (millions of ohms). Electronic components designed to have particular resistance values are called resistors.

Words and Expressions

component [kəmˈpəunənt] *n.* 零件，元件；成分
circuit [ˈsəːkit] *n.* 电路，巡回，一圈
current [ˈkʌrənt] *n.* 流动，气流，水流；电流
voltage [ˈvəultidʒ] *n.* 电压

resistance [riˈzistəns] *n.* 电阻
electric [iˈlektrik] *adj.* 导电的，电动的，电的
charge [tʃɑːdʒ] *v.* 充电，使带电；收费 *n.* 费用；电荷
particle [ˈpɑːtikl] *n.* 粒子，极小量，点
negative [ˈnegətiv] *adj.* 否定的；负的；消极的 *n.* 否定，负数
drift [drift] *n.* 漂流；漂移 *v.* 漂，漂流；漂移
random [ˈrændəm] *adj.* 任意的，随便的
symbol [ˈsimbl] *n.* 符号，象征，记号
ampere [ˈæmpeə] *n.* 安培
tiny [ˈtaini] *adj.* 很少的，微小的
switch [switʃ] *n.* 开关，转换；电闸 *v.* 转换，转变，变换
terminal [ˈtəːminl] *n.* 终端，末端 *adj.* 终端的，末端的
flow [fləu] *n.* 水流，电流，气流；流动 *v.* 流动
filament [ˈfiləmənt] *n.* 细丝，灯丝
blow [bləu] *n.* 吹动，吹气 *v.* 吹，刮；随风飘动
potential [pəuˈtenʃl] *n.* 潜在性，可能性 *adj.* 有潜力的，潜在的，可能的
difference [ˈdifrəns] *n.* 差异；分歧；差别
double [ˈdʌbl] *n.* 两倍 *v.* 使加倍；加倍 *adj.* 两倍的；双重的 *adv.* 双倍地；双重地
exhaust [igˈzɔːst] *v.* 用尽；抽完；耗尽
positive [ˈpɔzətiv] *n.* 正面；正数 *adj.* 肯定的，积极的；正极的
resist [riˈzist] *v.* 抵抗，抗拒，反抗
design [diˈzain] *n.* 设计 *v.* 设计；计划
glow [gləu] *v.* 发红光，发热，发亮
vary [ˈveri, ˈveər-] *v.* 改变，变更；变化
find out 找出，发现，揭示；了解
make up 弥补；形成
in series 串联
in parallel 平行，并联
strictly speaking 严格地说
consist of 由……组成
be made up of 由……组成
depend on 取决于

Notes

[1] You can also find out about the important types of components used in building electronic circuits.

此句可译为：你也可以了解用于构成电子电路的重要电气元件类型。

此句是简单句，"used in building electronic circuits"为过去分词做后置定语修饰 components。在科技英语中，此类分词短语用作后置定语的情况较为频繁。

［2］When this happens, electrons start to move in the same direction.

此句可译为：当电流流动时，电子开始朝一个相同的方向移动。

句中 When this happens 意指上句中的 a current starts to flow，即"当电流流动时"。

［3］The answer is that the cells provide a "push" which makes the current flow round the circuit.

此句可译为：答案是电池单元提供一个"推力"让电流在电路中环行。

句中 that 引导表语从句，which makes the current flow round the circuit 为定语从句，修饰先行词 push。

［4］Lamps are designed to work with a particular voltage, but, other things being equal, the bigger the voltage, the brighter the lamp.

此句可译为：灯泡是设计成工作在特定电压下的，但是当其他条件相同时，电压越高，灯泡就越亮。

句中"other things being equal"为分词的独立主格结构做状语，"the bigger the voltage, the brighter the lamp."可译为"电压越高，灯泡越亮。"英语中"the more…, the more…"结构用于表示随着前事物的变化，后事物呈相应的变化，翻译为"越……，越……"。

［5］It conducts much less easily than the rest of the circuit and has a higher resistance.

此句可译为：它（灯泡的灯丝）比电路的其他部分更不容易传导电流，也具有更高的电阻。

句中 it 指代上句中提到的 the lamp filament。

Exercises

1. Put the following phrases into English.

(1) 电气元件

(2) 电子电路

(3) 随机漂移

(4) 度量单位为安培

(5) 带电荷的粒子流

(6) 电势差

(7) 金属导体

(8) C-型碱性电池

(9) 串联

(10) 并联

2. Put the following phrases into Chinese.

(1) components used in building electronic circuits

(2) small negatively-charged particles

(3) represented by the symbol I

(4) move in the same direction

(5) the number of electrons passing per second

(6) makes the current flow round the circuit

(7) work with a particular voltage

(8) strictly speaking

(9) connecting the cells in series

(10) switch plates

3. Translate the following sentences into Chinese.

(1) You can also find out about the important types of components used in building electronic circuits.

(2) An electric current is a flow of charged particles.

(3) The electrons drift in random directions until a current starts to flow.

(4) The size of the current depends on the number of electrons passing per second.

(5) Other things being equal, the bigger the voltage, the brighter the lamp.

(6) Strictly speaking, a battery consists of two or more cells.

(7) Connecting the cells in series increases the voltage, but does not affect the useful life of the cells.

(8) Most of the circuits consist of thick metal conductors which allow current to flow easily.

(9) Electronic components designed to have particular resistance values are called resistors.

(10) It conducts much less easily than the rest of the circuit and has a higher resistance.

4. Translate the following paragraphs into Chinese.

(1) Series and parallel connections

There are two ways of connecting components.

In series, each component has the same current. The battery voltage is divided between the two lamps. Each lamp will have half the battery voltage if the lamps are identical.

In parallel, each component has the same voltage. Both lamps have the full battery voltage across them. The battery current is divided between the two lamps.

(2) Resistance values in electronic circuits vary from a few ohms, or Ω to values in kilohms, kΩ (thousands of ohms) and megohms, MΩ (millions of ohms). Electronic components designed to have particular resistance values are called resistors.

Text B

Electrical Components

Resistors

A resistor is an electrical component that resists the flow of electrical current. The amount of current (I) flowing in a circuit is directly proportional to the voltage across it and inversely proportional to the resistance of the circuit.[1] This is Ohm Law and can be expressed as a formula: $I = \dfrac{U_R}{R}$. The resistor is generally a linear device and its characteristics form a straight line when plotted on a graph.

Resistors are used to limit current flowing to a device, thereby preventing it from burning out, as voltage dividers to reduce voltage for other circuits, as transistor biasing circuits, and to serve as circuit loads.[2]

Capacitors

Electrical energy can be stored in an electric field. The device capable of doing this is called a capacitor or a condenser.

A simple condenser consists of two metallic plates separated by a dielectric. If a condenser is connected to a battery, the electrons will flow out of the negative terminal of the battery and accumulate on the condenser plate connected to that side. At the same time, the electrons will leave the plate connected to the positive terminal and flow into the battery to make the potential difference just the same as that of the battery.[3] Thus the condenser is said to be charged.

To discharge the condenser, the external circuit of these two plates is completed by joining terminals together with a wire. The electrons start moving from one plate to the other through the wire to restore electrical neutrality.

Inductors

An inductor is an electrical device, which can temporarily store electromagnetic energy in the field about it as long as current is flowing through it.[4] Also, inductor are wound with various sizes of wire and in varying numbers of trunks which affect the DC (direct current) resistance of the coil. Later, you will study how the resistance affects inductor operation in certain AC (alternating current) circuit applications.

Excellent information is available about the details of winding coils to desired specifications in *The Radio Amateur's Handbook* published by the American Radio Relay League (ARRL).[5] Also there are numerous inexpensive special slide rules that allow you to establish required parameters and to read the number of turns, coil length, coil diameter, and so on, needed for the desired results.

Words and Expressions

resistor [riˈzistə(r)] *n.* 电阻器
electrical [iˈlektrikl] *adj.* 与电有关的,电气科学的;电的
proportional [prəˈpɔːʃnəl] *adj.* 比例的,成比例的
directly proportional [数] 成正比(的)
inversely proportional [数] 成反比(的)
formula [ˈfɔːmjulə] *n.* 公式;规则
linear [ˈliniə(r)] *adj.* 线的,线性的,直线的
device [diˈvais] *n.* 装置;图案;设计
characteristics [ˌkærəktəˈristik] *n.* [数] 特征,特征线
form [fɔːm] *n.* 形状,形式;表格 *v.* 形成,构成
plot [plɔt] *n.* 图,地区图 *v.* 划分;绘图
graph [grɑːf] *n.* 图;图表 *v.* 用图表表示
limit [ˈlimit] *n.* 界限;限制;限度 *v.* 限制;限定
thereby [ˈðeəˈbai] *adv.* 因此,从而
load [ləud] *n.* 负荷;装载量 *v.* 装载;负载
capacitor [kəˈpæsitə] *n.* 电容器
condenser [kənˈdensə] *n.* 电容器;冷凝器
metallic [miˈtælik] *adj.* 金属的,含金属的
plate [pleit] *n.* 图版,金属板
dielectric [daiiˈlektrik] *n.* 电介质;绝缘体 *adj.* 非传导性的
negative terminal [电] 负端
accumulate [əˈkjuːmjuleit] *v.* 积聚,累积;积攒
positive terminal [电] 正端
discharge [disˈtʃɑːdʒ] *n.* 卸货;放电 *v.* 卸下,卸货;放电
external [eksˈtəːnl] *n.* 外部;外面 *adj.* 外部的,表面的
restore [riˈstɔː] *v.* 恢复;使复原;修复
neutrality [nuːˈtræləti/njuː-] *n.* 中立,中间状态
inductor [inˈdʌktə(r)] *n.* 电感器,感应器
temporarily [ˌtempəˈreəli] *adv.* 暂时地,临时地
field [fiːld] *n.* 领域,范围 *adj.* 田间的;野外的
wound [waund, wuːnd] (wind 的过去分词) 上发条,缠绕
coil [kɔil] *n.* 卷,圈;线圈 *v.* 卷,盘绕;把……卷成圈
application [æpliˈkeiʃn] *n.* 申请;要求;运用;适用
available [əˈveiləbl] *adj.* 有空的;有用的
specification [ˌspesifiˈkeiʃn] *n.* 规格;详细说明书;详述
slide [slaid] *n.* 滑,滑道 *v.* 滑,滑落;使滑动,使滑行
parameter [pəˈræmitə(r)] *n.* 参数,参量;界限;因素

Notes

[1] The amount of current (I) flowing in a circuit is directly proportional to the voltage across it and inversely proportional to the resistance of the circuit.

此句可译为：在电阻器中流过的电流与加在电阻两端的电压成正比，与电阻的阻值成反比。

此句是简单句，"flowing in a circuit"为现在分词做后置定语修饰 current。

directly proportional to 成正比(的)；inversely proportional to 成反比(的)。

[2] Resistors are used to limit current flowing to a device, thereby preventing it from burning out, as voltage dividers to reduce voltage for other circuits, as transistor biasing circuits, and to serve as circuit loads.

此句可译为：电阻器常用作限流器，限制流过器件的电流以防止器件因流过的电流过大而烧坏。电阻器也可用作分压器，以减小其他电路的电压，如晶体管偏置电路。电阻器还可用作电路的负载。

此句是简单句，谓语部分采用了动词的被动语态。科技英语中大量使用被动语态。

are used to 在此处指"被用于做什么"；as 表示"用于，作为"。

[3] At the same time, the electrons will leave the plate connected to the positive terminal and flow into the battery to make the potential difference just the same as that of the battery.

此句可译为：同时与电源正极相接的极板上的电子将离开极板流入电池正极，这样两极板上就产生了与电池上相等的电位差。

句中"connected to the positive terminal"为过去分词短语做后置定语，修饰 plate，"just the same as that of the battery"中的"that"在此处替代的是"potential difference"。

[4] An inductor is an electrical device, which can temporarily store electromagnetic energy in the field about it as long as current is flowing through it.

此句可译为：当电流流过电感器时，电感器周围就有电磁场，电感器是以电磁场的形式暂时储存电磁能量的电子器件。

此句为复合句，句中 which 引导了一个非限制性定语从句，对前面内容进行解释说明；"as long as"意思是"只要"，引导条件状语从句。

[5] Excellent information is available about the details of winding coils to desired specifications in *The Radio Amateur's Handbook* published by the American Radio Relay League (ARRL).

此句可译为：在《业余无线电手册》中有满足所需的技术条件绕制线圈的详尽资料。

句中"of winding coils to desired specifications"为介词后跟动名词短语，在句中修饰 details。

The Radio Amateur's Handbook published by the American Radio Relay League (ARRL):《业余无线电手册》。

Exercises

Mark the following statements with T(true) or F (false) according to the text.

(1) The amount of current flowing in a circuit is inversely proportional to the voltage across it and directly proportional to the resistance of the circuit.　　　　　　　　　　(　　)

(2) Resistors are used to limit current flowing to a device. ( )
(3) Electrical energy cannot be stored in an electric field. ( )
(4) A simple condenser consists of two metallic plates separated by a dielectric. ( )
(5) If a condenser is connected to a battery, the electrons will flow out of the positive terminal of the battery and accumulate on the condenser plate connected to that side. ( )
(6) To discharge the condenser the external circuit of these two plates is completed by joining terminals together with a wire. ( )
(7) The electrons start moving from one plate to the other through the wire to restore electrical neutrality. ( )
(8) An inductor is an electrical device, which can permanently store electromagnetic energy in the field about it as long as current is flowing through it. ( )
(9) Excellent information is available about the details of winding coils to desired specifications in *The Radio Amateur's Handbook* published by the American Radio Relay League (ARRL). ( )
(10) A resistor is an electrical component that enhances the flow of electrical current. ( )

Translating Skill 1

派生词的翻译(一)

电子信息专业英语词汇有相当一部分以派生词法构成。所谓派生词法这里指词根加上前缀和后缀形成的词。大部分词缀都源于拉丁语和希腊语。掌握词缀及其派生词的翻译要点,对准确迅速地译出电子信息类专业原文有很大帮助。

本单元和下单元的翻译技巧将分别介绍电子信息工作人员必须掌握的主要词缀和汉译。

1. 形容词词缀

词缀	译义	词例	译义
in-	不,非	insufficient	不足的
im-	不,非	imcompatible	不兼容的
un-	不,非	unstable	不稳定的
super-	上,超,过	supersonic	超音速的
-ive	……的,有……作用的	reactive	电抗性的
-ar	……状的,……特性的	linear	线性的
-ic	具有……性质的	electronic	电子的
-ous	有……特性,像……的	synchronous	同步的
-proof	防……的	fireproof	防火的

2. 动词词缀

词缀	译义	词例	译义
re-	再,反复	reuse	再使用,多次利用
over-	过分,额外	overload	过载
under-	不足,低于	under-load	欠载
dis-	相反,除去	discharge	放电
de-	取消,降低,离开	demagnetise	去磁
trans-	横穿,通过	transform	变换,使改变性质
-fy	使……	electrify	使带电
-ise	……化	normalise	正常化
-ate	使……形成	integrate	使成一体,使结合

Exercises to Translating Skill

Translate the following words or expressions into Chinese.

(1) incoherent
(2) incomplete matrix
(3) incorrect block
(4) immobile
(5) imperfect contact detector
(6) improper function
(7) uncommitted logic array
(8) unblocking signal
(9) unprotected cable terminal
(10) supergroup translating equipment
(11) super-regenerative reception
(12) super-synchonomous satellite
(13) recycling circuit breaker
(14) reconditioned-carrier reception
(15) redirectioned-to-new-address signal
(16) overcoupling
(17) overlay method
(18) overtime charge
(19) undervoltage alarm
(20) undercurrent relay
(21) underground cable rack
(22) disconnect command
(23) disengagement time
(24) discontinuity
(25) depolarization
(26) demultiplexer
(27) decentralized computer network
(28) transposition system
(29) trans-horizon propagation
(30) transfer of technology

Unit 2　Instruments for Measurement

In electronics, a meter is an instrument for displaying the magnitude of one of a wide variety of quantities in electrical circuits. The term can refer to either an electronic component that is part of a larger device, or a free-standing test instrument. [1]

在电子学中,仪表是用来显示电子电路中某种变量程度的仪器。它可以是大型设备当中的一个电子部件,也可以是独立的测试单元。

Text A

What Do Meters Measure?

A meter is a measuring instrument. An ammeter measures current, a voltmeter measures the potential difference (voltage) between two points, and an ohmmeter measures resistance. A multimeter combines these functions, and possibly some additional ones as well, into a single instrument.

Analogue multimeters

An analogue meter moves a needle along a scale. Switched range analogue multimeters are very cheap but are difficult for beginners to read accurately, especially on resistance scales. The meter movement is delicate and dropping the meter is likely to damage it. [2]

Each type of meter has its advantages. Used as a voltmeter, a digital meter is usually better because its resistance is much higher, 1 MΩ or 10 MΩ, compared to 200 kΩ for an analogue multimeter on a similar range. On the other hand, it is easier to follow a slowly changing voltage by watching the needle on an analogue display.

Used as an ammeter, an analogue multimeter has a very low resistance and is very sensitive, with scales down to 50 μA. [3] More expensive digital multimeters can equal or better this performance. [4]

Most modern multimeters are digital and traditional analogue types are destined to become obsolete.

Digital multimeters

Multimeters are designed and mass produced for electronics engineers. Even the simplest and cheapest types may include features which you are not likely to use. Digital meters give an output in numbers, usually on a liquid crystal display.

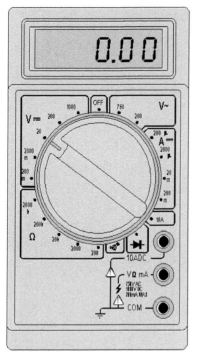

Fig. 2-1 Switched Range Multimeter

The diagram in Fig. 2-1 shows a switched range multimeter.

The central knob has lots of positions and you must choose which one is appropriate for the measurement you want to make.[5] If the meter is switched to 20 V DC, for example, then 20 V is the maximum voltage which can be measured. This is sometimes called 20 V fsd, where fsd is short for full scale deflection.

For circuits with power supplies of up to 20 V, which includes all the circuits you are likely to build, the 20 V DC voltage range is the most useful. DC ranges are indicated by "V=" on the meter. Sometimes, you will want to measure smaller voltages, and in this case, the 2 V or 200 mV ranges are used.

Words and Expressions

instrument ['instrəmənt] n. 仪表，仪器，工具
measurement ['meʒə(r)mənt] n. 测量法；尺寸；度量
electronics [ilek'trɔniks] n. 电子学
meter ['mi:tə(r)] n. 米；仪表 v. 用仪表测量
display [di'splei] n. [计]显示，屏幕；监控器 v. 陈列；显示
magnitude ['mægnitju:d] n. 大小；光度；重要；幅度
variety [və'raiəti] n. 变化，多样性
quantity ['kwɔntiti] n. [科]大量
refer to 提到，参考，参照；与……关联
electronic component [电] 电子元件
free-standing adj. 独立的
ammeter ['æmitə] n. 安培计
voltmeter ['vəult,mi:tə(r)] n. 伏特计
ohmmeter ['əum,mi:tə(r)] n. 欧姆计；电阻表
combine [kəm'bain] v. 使结合，使联合；兼备
function ['fʌŋkʃn] n. 功能；函数 v. 行使职责；运行
analogue ['ænəlɔg] n. 模拟，相似物，类似情况
multimeter [mʌlti'mitə] n. 万用表

scale [skeil] *n.* 刻度；尺度
accurately ['ækjərətli] *adv.* 准确地，精确地
delicate ['delikət] *adj.* 细致优雅的；精密的
range [reindʒ] *n.* 量程，范围 *v.* 排列，使并列，归类于
sensitive ['sensitiv] *adj.* 敏感的
performance [pə'fɔːməns] *n.* 性能；成绩；履行，执行
destined ['destind] *adj.* 命中注定的；预定的
obsolete ['ɔbsəliːt] *adj.* 荒废的，陈旧的
mass [mæs] *n.* 块；大多数 *v.* 集中；聚集 *adj.* 大规模的
feature ['fiːtʃə(r)] *n.* 特征，特点 *v.* 是……的特色；特写
liquid crystal display 液晶显示器
diagram ['daiəgræm] *n.* 图表 *v.* 用图解法表示，图示
knob [nɔb] *n.* 把手，旋钮
appropriate [ə'prəupriət] *adj.* 适当的，恰当的，相称的
maximum (max.) ['mæksiməm] *adj.* 最高的，最多的；最大极限的
full scale deflection [电] 满刻度偏转
power supply 电力供应；动力供应，电源
indicate ['indikeit] *v.* 指出；象征；显示

Notes

[1] The term can refer to either an electronic component that is part of a larger device, or a free-standing test instrument.

此句可译为：该术语可以指大型设备当中的一个电子部件，也可以是独立的测试单元。

本句中 refer to 后面带的宾语由 either…or 连接，that 引导定语从句限定 electronic component。

refer to 提到，谈论；参考，参照；与……关联。

[2] The meter movement is delicate and dropping the meter is likely to damage it.

此句可译为：万用表的移动非常精密，所以摔万用表就很容易造成损坏。

delicate 在此句中可译为精密的。

be likely to 极有可能。

[3] Used as an ammeter, an analogue multimeter has a very low resistance and is very sensitive, with scales down to 50 μA.

此句可译为：作为安培表使用的时候，一个模拟万用表的电阻非常低，因此很敏感，可以量至 50 微安。

此句中"Used as an ammeter"为过去分词做状语，"with scales down to 50 μA"可理解为"可以量至 50 微安"，down to 表示一种程度。

[4] More expensive digital multimeters can equal or better this performance.

此句可译为：更昂贵的数字万用表能够大于或等于这个性能。

此句中 equal or better 为形容词活用作动词，译为等于或大于。

[5] The central knob has lots of positions and you must choose which one is appropriate for the measurement you want to make.

此句可译为：中间的旋钮有很多个位置，你必须选择一个来匹配你的测量。

此句中"which one is appropriate for the measurement you want to make."为宾语从句，"you want to make"前省略了which，此句为定语从句，限定measurement。

appropriate 适当的，恰当的，相称的，此处可译为匹配。

Exercises

1．Put the following phrases into English.

（1）测量仪器

（2）两点间的电势差

（3）模拟万用表

（4）在类似的量程

（5）跟踪缓慢的电压变化

（6）更昂贵的数字万用表

（7）批量生产

（8）可变量程的万用表

（9）与测量相匹配

（10）测量更低的电压

2．Put the following phrases into Chinese.

（1）free-standing test instrument

（2）combines these functions into a single instrument

（3）moves a needle along a scale

（4）watching the needle on an analogue display

（5）equal or better this performance

（6）destined to become obsolete

（7）liquid crystal display

（8）full scale deflection

（9）give an output in numbers

（10）electronics engineers

3．Translate the following sentences into Chinese.

（1）A meter is an instrument for displaying the magnitude of one of a wide variety of quantities in electrical circuits.

（2）Switched range analogue multimeters are very cheap but are difficult for beginners to read accurately.

（3）Each type of meter has its advantages.

（4）More expensive digital multimeters can equal or better this performance.

（5）Traditional analogue types are destined to become obsolete.

(6) Multimeters are designed and mass produced for electronics engineers.

(7) Even the simplest and cheapest types may include features which you are not likely to use.

(8) You must choose which one is appropriate for the measurement you want to make.

(9) It is easier to follow a slowly changing voltage by watching the needle on an analogue display.

(10) The meter movement is delicate and dropping the meter is likely to damage it.

4. Translate the following paragraphs into Chinese.

(1) A meter is a measuring instrument. An ammeter measures current, a voltmeter measures the potential difference (voltage) between two points, and an ohmmeter measures resistance. A multimeter combines these functions, and possibly some additional ones as well, into a single instrument.

(2) Multimeters are designed and mass produced for electronics engineers. Even the simplest and cheapest types may include features which you are not likely to use. Digital meters give an output in numbers, usually on a liquid crystal display.

Text B

Oscilloscope

An oscilloscope (commonly abbreviated to scope or O-scope) is a type of electronic test equipment that allows signal voltages to be viewed, usually as a two-dimensional graph of one or more electrical potential differences (vertical axis) plotted as a function of time or of some other voltage (horizontal axis).[1] The oscilloscope is one of the most versatile and widely-used electronic instruments.

Oscilloscopes are widely used when it is desired to observe the exact wave shape of an electrical signal.[2] In addition to the amplitude of the signal, an oscilloscope can measure the frequency, show distortion, and show the relative timing of two related signals. Oscilloscopes are used in the science, medicine, engineering, telecommunications, and industry. General-purpose instruments are used for maintenance of electronic equipment and laboratory work. Special-purpose oscilloscopes may be used for such purposes as adjusting an automotive ignition system, or to display the waveform of the heartbeat.

Originally all oscilloscopes used cathode ray tubes as their display element, but modern digital oscilloscopes use high-speed analog-to-digital converters and computer-like display screens and processing of signals.[3] Oscilloscope peripheral modules for general purpose laptop or desktop personal computers can turn them into useful and flexible test instruments.

Examples of use

Fig. 2-2 shows Lissajous figures on an oscilloscope, with 90 degrees phase difference between x and y inputs.

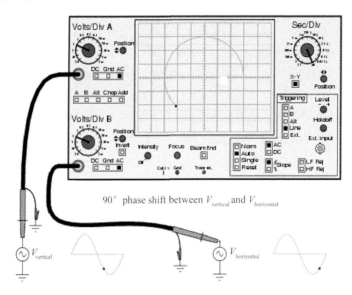

Fig. 2-2 Lissajous Figures on an Oscilloscope with 90 Degrees Phase Difference between x and y Inputs

One of the most frequent uses of scopes is troubleshooting malfunctioning electronic equipment.[4] One of the advantages of a scope is that it can graphically show signals: where a voltmeter may show a totally unexpected voltage, a scope may reveal that the circuit is oscillating. In other cases the precise shape of a pulse is important.

In a piece of electronic equipment, for example, the connections between stages (e. g. electronic mixers, electronic oscillators, amplifiers) may be "probed" for the expected signal, using the scope as a simple signal tracer. If the expected signal is absent or incorrect, some preceding stage of the electronics is not operating correctly. Since most failures occur because of a single faulty component, each measurement can prove that half of the stages of a complex piece of equipment either work, or probably did not cause the fault.

Once the faulty stage is found, further probing can usually tell a skilled technician exactly which component has failed.[5] Once the component is replaced, the unit can be restored to service, or at least the next fault can be isolated.

Another use is to check newly designed circuitry. Very often a newly designed circuit will misbehave because of design errors, bad voltage levels, electrical noise etc. Digital electronics usually operate from a clock, so a dual-trace scope which shows both the clock signal and a test signal dependent upon the clock is useful. "Storage scopes" are helpful for "capturing" rare electronic events that cause defective operation.

Another use is for software engineers who must program electronics. Often a scope is the only way to see if the software is running the electronics properly. Fig. 2-3 is the use of oscilloscope.

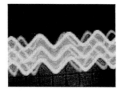 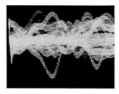 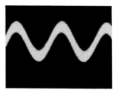

Heterodyne　　　　AC hum on sound　　　　AM signal

Fig. 2-3　Pictures of Use

Words and Expressions

oscilloscope [əˈsiləuskəup] n. 示波器
abbreviate [əˈbriːvieit] v. 缩写，使……简略；缩短
signal [ˈsignl] n. 信号；暗号；交通指示灯 v. 发信号，打信号
view [vjuː] n. 视野；见解；风景 v. 看，视察；考虑
two-dimensional 二维的；没有深度感觉的
vertical [ˈvəːtikl] n. 垂直线，竖向，垂直面 adj. 垂直的；顶点的
axis [ˈæksis] n. 轴；轴线；光轴
versatile [ˈvəːsətail] adj. 通用的，万能的
amplitude [ˈæmplitjuːd] n. 幅度，振幅；射程
frequency [ˈfriːkwənsi] n. 频率；发生次数
distortion [diˈstɔːʃn] n. 失真，扭曲；变形
engineering [ˈendʒiˈniriŋ] n. 工程
telecommunications [ˌtelikəˌmjuːniˈkeiʃnz] n. 电信，通信，电信学
adjust [əˈdʒʌst] v. 调节；校正；调整，适应于；校准
ignition [igˈniʃn] n. 点火，点燃
waveform [ˈweivfɔːm] n. 波形
cathode ray tubes [计]阴极射线管
analog-to-digital converter [计]模-数转换器，模拟-数字转换器
peripheral [pəˈrifrəl] adj. 周边的，周围的
module [ˈmɔdjuːl] n. 模数；组件；单元；子系统
laptop [ˈlæptɔp] n. 手提式电脑
desktop [ˈdesktɔp] n. [计]桌面
flexible [ˈfleksəbl] adj. 柔软的，灵活的
troubleshooting [ˈtrʌblʃuːtiŋ] n. 排故，发现并修理故障
malfunction [mælˈfʌŋkʃn] n. 故障 v. 发生故障；机能失常
graphically [ˈɡræfikli] adv. 通过图表；轮廓分明地；生动地
reveal [riˈviːl] v. 露出；透露；显示

precise [pri'sais] *adj.* 精确的，严谨的
probe [prəub] *n.* 探针，探测针；调查 *v.* 详细调查；探测
tracer ['treisə(r)] *n.* 跟踪器；追踪者
preceding [pri'si:diŋ] *adj.* 在前的，在先的；前面的
failure ['feiljə(r)] *n.* 错误，失误；失败；失败者
faulty ['fɔ:lti] *adj.* 有过失的；不完美的；有缺点的
replace [ri'pleis] *v.* 把……放回；以……代替；取代；归还
isolate ['aisəleit] *v.* 使隔离；使绝缘；使孤立；排查
circuitry ['sə:kitri] *n.* 电路；线路
misbehave [,misbi'heiv] *v.* 工作、表现不正常
error ['erə] *n.* 错误，失误，过失
dual-trace scope [电] 双迹示波器
storage scope 存储示波器
defective [di'fektiv] *adj.* 有缺陷的；欠缺的
software ['sɔftweə(r)] *n.* 软件；程序材料
program (Amer.) ['prəugræm] *n.* 节目；计划；程序 *v.* 编程；规划

Notes

[1] An oscilloscope (commonly abbreviated to scope or O-scope) is a type of electronic test equipment that allows signal voltages to be viewed, usually as a two-dimensional graph of one or more electrical potential differences (vertical axis) plotted as a function of time or of some other voltage (horizontal axis).

此句可译为：示波器(通常缩写成 scope 或 O-scope)是一种看见信号电压的电子测试设备。通常显示一个或多个电势差(纵轴)对时间或者其他电压(横轴)的二维图像。

请注意分析长句的结构。主语为 An oscilloscope，谓语为一系表结构，其中 that 引导定语从句修饰先行词 electronic test equipment。句中 two-dimensional graph 译为二维图像。

[2] Oscilloscopes are widely used when it is desired to observe the exact wave shape of an electrical signal.

此句可译为：示波器被广泛使用在需要观察电子信号的准确波形的情况下。

此句中使用了动词的被动语态。如前所述，科技英语中，被动语态的使用频率非常高，分析和翻译时要进行必要的转换，以符合汉语表达习惯。

[3] Originally all oscilloscopes used cathode ray tubes as their display element, but modern digital oscilloscopes use high-speed analog-to-digital converters and computer-like display screens and processing of signals.

此句可译为：一开始所有的示波器用阴极射线管显示器作为显示单元，但是现代的数字示波器使用高速的数-模转换器和计算机化的显示屏和信号处理。

used cathode ray tubes as their display element：用阴极射线管显示器作为显示单元。

use… as… 把……用作……。

cathode ray tubes,阴极射线管,常缩略为 CRT。

[4] One of the most frequent uses of scopes is troubleshooting malfunctioning electronic equipment.

此句可译为:示波器一个最常用的用途是解决电子设备的故障。

troubleshooting,排除故障;malfunctioning 故障,发生故障;机能失常。其中,构词法中前缀 mal 表示"坏、非、不良",如 mal-condition 表示[化]恶劣条件;maladjustment 失调;不平衡;不适应环境。

[5] Once the faulty stage is found, further probing can usually tell a skilled technician exactly which component has failed.

此句可译为:一旦故障器件被发现,进一步的探测通常可以告诉有经验的技术人员具体哪一个元件出错。

此句中 Once 引导时间状语从句,主句主语为 further probing,谓语动词 can tell 后接双宾语,which component has failed 为宾语从句。

Exercises

Mark the following statements with T (true) or F (false) according to the text.

(1) The oscilloscope is not one of the most versatile and widely-used electronic instruments. ( )

(2) Oscilloscopes are widely used when it is desired to observe the exact wave shape of an electrical signal. ( )

(3) General-purpose instruments are only used for maintenance of electronic equipment. ( )

(4) Modern digital oscilloscopes use high-speed analog-to-digital converters and computer-like display screens. ( )

(5) Oscilloscope peripheral modules for general purpose laptop or desktop personal computers cannot turn them into useful and flexible test instruments. ( )

(6) One of the most frequent uses of scopes is troubleshooting malfunctioning electronic equipment. ( )

(7) Once the faulty stage is found, further probing can usually tell a skilled technician exactly which component has failed. ( )

(8) Very often a newly designed circuit will not misbehave even if there exist design errors, bad voltage levels, electrical noise etc. ( )

(9) Oscilloscope can be used for software engineers who must program electronics. ( )

(10) The oscilloscope is one of the most versatile and widely-used electronic instruments. ( )

Translating Skill 2

派生词的翻译(二)

如 Unit 1 翻译技巧所述,掌握派生词的构词法对准确迅速地译出电子信息类专业原文有很大帮助。

本单元介绍电子信息工作人员必须掌握的名词词缀和汉译。

3. 名词词缀

词缀	译义	词例	译义
inter-	互相,在……中间	interface	界面,接口
counter-	反,对应	counterpart	对应部分,副本
in-	在……内部	inlet	入口
out-	在外	output	输出
di-	二	diode	二极管
tele-	远	teleconference	远程电信会议
photo-	光	photosphere	光球
micro-	微,小	microwave	微波
ultra-	超	ultra-high-frequency	超高频

Exercises to Translating Skill

Translate the following words or expressions into Chinese.

(1) interactive data transaction
(2) intermachine trunk
(3) intermodulation distortion
(4) counter-clockwise polarized wave
(5) counter-EMF cell
(6) counterpoise
(7) input
(8) injection laser diode
(9) insertion loss
(10) outboard channel
(11) outdoor telephone
(12) outgoing traffic
(13) dichotomizing search
(14) digram coding
(15) diphase line codes
(16) telecommunications
(17) teledata
(18) teleprocessing
(19) photoconductive cell
(20) photoelectric effect
(21) photosensitive record
(22) microwave relay system
(23) microvolts per meter
(24) microcomputer
(25) ultrasonic leak detector
(26) ultraviolet degradation
(27) ultra high frequency band

Unit 3 Electronic Components

An electronic component is a basic electronic element usually packaged in a discrete form with two or more connecting leads or metallic pads.

电子器件是基本的电子元件,通常单体封装,并带有两个或者更多的连接引线或者金属连接片。

Text A

Electronic Components

Electronic circuits consist of interconnections of electronic components. Components are classified into two categories—active and passive. Passive elements never supply more energy than they absorb; active elements can supply more energy than they absorb. [1]

Vacuum tubes

A vacuum tube consists of an air-evacuated glass envelope that contains several metal electrodes. A simple, two-element tube (diode) consists of a cathode and an anode that is connected to the positive terminal of a power supply. The cathode—a small metal tube heated by filament-frees electrons, which migrate to the anode—a metal cylinder around the cathode (also called the plate). [2] If an alternating voltage is applied to the anode, electrons will only flow to the anode during the positive half-cycle. During the negative cycle of the alternating voltage, the anode repels the electrons, and no current passes through the tube. Diodes connected in such a way that only the positive half-cycles of an alternating current (AC) are permitted to pass are called rectifier tubes, these are direct current (DC). By inserting a grid, consisting of a spiral of metal wire, between the cathode and the anode and applying a negative voltage to the grid, the flow of electrons can be controlled. [3] When the grid is negative, it repels electrons, and only a fraction of the electrons emitted by the cathode can reach the anode. Such a tube, called a triode, can be used as an amplifier. Small variations in voltage at the grid, such as can be produced by a ratio or audio signal, will cause large variations in the flow of electrons from the cathode to the anode and hence, in the circuitry connected to the anode.

Transistors

Transistors are made from semiconductors. These are materials, such as silicon or germanium, that are "doped" (have minute amounts of foreign elements added) so that either an abundance or a lack of free electrons exists.[4] In the former case, the semiconductor is called N-type, and in the latter case, P-type. By combining N-type and P-type materials, a diode can be produced. When this diode is connected to a battery so that the P-type material is positive and the N-type negative, electrons are repelled from the negative battery reversed, the electrons arriving in the P-material can pass only with difficulty to the N-material, which is already filled with free electrons, and the current is almost zero. The bipolar transistor was invented in 1948 as a replacement for the triode vacuum tube. It consists of three layers of doped material, forming two P-N (bipolar) junctions with configurations of P-N-P or N-P-N, one junction is connected to a battery so as to allow current flow (forward bias), and the other junction has a battery connected in the opposite direction (reverse bias). If the current in the forward-biased junction is varied by the addition of a signal, the current in the reverse-biased junction of the transistor will vary accordingly. The principle can be used to construct amplifiers in which a small signal applied to the forward-biased junction causes a large change in current in the reverse-biased junction.

Another type of transistor is the field-effect transistor (FET). Such a transistor operates on the principle of repulsion or attraction of charges due to a superimposed electric field. Amplification of current is accomplished in a manner similar to the grid control of a vacuum tube. Field-effect transistors operate more efficiently than bipolar types, because a large signal can be controlled by a very small amount of energy.[5]

Words and Expressions

interconnection [ˌintəkəˈnekʃn] n. 互相连接；互相联络
category [ˈkætigəri] n. 种类；范畴
active [ˈæktiv] adj. 有源
passive [ˈpæsiv] adj. 无源
absorb [əbˈsɔːb] v. 吸收；汲取
vacuum tube 真空管；电子管
evacuate [iˈvækjueit] v. 抽真空；撤离；从……撤退；排空
envelope [ˈenvələup] n. 膜，信封；封袋；封套
electrode [iˈlektrəud] n. 电极
diode [ˈdaiəud] n. 二极管
cathode [ˈkæθəud] n. 阴极
anode [ˈænəud] n. 阳极，正极
migrate [maiˈgreit] v. 移动；移植；移往；迁移
cylinder [ˈsilində] n. 圆筒，圆筒状之物；[计]硬盘里有形存储单位
half cycle [电] 半周期
repel [riˈpel] v. 击退；拒绝；排斥；抵抗；相互排斥
rectifier tube [电]整流管

insert [in'sərt /-'səːt] n. 插入物 v. 插入；嵌入
grid [grid] n. 栅格，格子；烤架；铁丝网；极板网栅
spiral ['spaiərəl] n. 螺旋；螺旋形的东西 adj. 螺旋的；蜷线的 v. 盘旋；不断加剧地增加；使成螺旋形
fraction ['frækʃn] n. 分数；破片；小部分
triode ['traiəud] n. 三极管
variation [ˌveri'eiʃn /ˌveər-] n. 变更；变种；变化
ratio ['reiʃəu /-ʃiəu] n. 比，比率
audio ['ɔːdiəu] adj. 声音的，听觉的；音的；音频的
hence [hens] adv. 因此；从此
transistor [træn'sistə(r),-z-] n. 晶体管
semiconductor [ˌsemikən'dʌktə] n. 半导体
silicon ['silikən] n. 硅，硅元素
germanium [dʒər'meiniəm /dʒəː'm-] n. 锗
doped [dəupt] adj. [电]掺杂质的
abundance [ə'bʌndəns] n. 丰富；充足；充裕
reverse [ri'vərs /-'vəːs] n. 相反；反面，背面 v. 颠倒，翻转；使反向；倒退 adj. 颠倒的；反向的；相反的；背面的，反面的
bipolar [ˌbai'pəulə] adj. 有两极的；双极的
junction ['dʒʌŋkʃn] n. 结，连接；交叉点，会合处
configuration [kənˌfigju'reiʃn] n. 结构；形态；表面配置
bias ['baiəs] n. 偏见，趋势；偏心；偏爱 [电]偏压 v. 使存偏见
forward bias [电]前向偏压
reverse bias [电]反偏压
field effect transistor circuit [计]场效应晶体管线路
principle ['prinsəpl] n. 原则；主义；原理；信条
repulsion [ri'pʌlʃn] n. 击退；拒绝；反驳；反感；憎恶
superimpose [ˌsuːpə(r)im'pəuz] v. 重叠上去；叠印；加上去
superimposed [ˌsuːpə(r)im'pəuzd] adj. 叠加的；双重的

Notes

[1] Passive elements never supply more energy than they absorb; active elements can supply more energy than they absorb.

此句可译为：无源元件提供的能量少于它们自身吸收的能量；有源元件提供的能量大于它们自身吸收的能量。

此句中两个分句均采用了比较级，注意前一分句中否定词 never 的用法，翻译时把原文的 never … more … than "不多于"转化为更加清楚的"少于"，以便和后一分句的 more … than "大于"相匹配。

[2] The cathode—a small metal tube heated by filament-frees electrons, which migrate

to the anode—a metal cylinder around the cathode (also called the plate).

此句可译为:阴极是一个小金属管,由灯丝加热而释放电子;阴极释放的电子向阳极移动,阳极也称作板极,是一个围绕阴极的金属圆筒。

句中破折号引导同位语,起补充说明作用。

[3] By inserting a grid, consisting of a spiral of metal wire, between the cathode and the anode and applying a negative voltage to the grid, the flow of electrons can be controlled.

此句可译为:在阴极阳极之间插入一个栅格,此栅格由螺旋的金属线组成,施加一个负电压给栅格,从而可以控制真空管的电流。

句中 By 引导方式状语,为保持句子平衡,句子的附加成分置于主句之前。

[4] These are materials, such as silicon or germanium, that are "doped"(have minute amounts of foreign elements added) so that either an abundance or a lack of free electrons exists.

此句可译为:半导体是硅和锗这样的材料,经过掺杂,即加入微量的外部元素,使内部的自由电子过剩或者不足。

minute 微小的,"minute amounts of foreign elements"译为"微量的外部元素"。

[5] Field-effect transistors operate more efficiently than bipolar types, because a large signal can be controlled by a very small amount of energy.

此句可译为:由于非常小能量的信号可以控制大能量信号,因此场效应管具有比三极管更高的工作效率。

此句为一典型的被动句。field-effect transistors:场效应晶体管。

Exercises

1. Put the following phrases into English.

(1) 半周期

(2) 整流管

(3) 前向偏压

(4) 反偏压

(5) 场效应晶体管

(6) 有源元件

(7) 微量的外部元素

(8) 双重电场

(9) 螺旋的金属线

(10) 自由电子不足

2. Put the following phrases into Chinese.

(1) electronic components

(2) passive elements

(3) an air-evacuated glass envelope

(4) positive half-cycle

(5) a fraction of the electrons emitted by the cathode

(6) small variations in voltage at the grid

(7) the flow of electrons

(8) negative battery

(9) the bipolar transistor

(10) an abundance of free electrons

3. Translate the following sentences into Chinese.

(1) Electronic circuits consist of interconnections of electronic components.

(2) A vacuum tube consists of an air-evacuated glass envelope that contains several metal electrodes.

(3) Transistors are made from semiconductors.

(4) By combining N-type and P-type materials, a diode can be produced.

(5) The bipolar transistor was invented in 1948 as a replacement for the triode vacuum tube.

(6) Components are classified into two categories—active and passive.

(7) If an alternating voltage is applied to the anode, electrons will only flow to the anode during the positive half-cycle.

(8) Amplification of current is accomplished in a manner similar to the grid control of a vacuum tube.

(9) Field-effect transistors operate more efficiently than bipolar types.

(10) During the negative cycle of the alternating voltage, the anode repels the electrons.

4. Translate the following paragraphs into Chinese.

(1) Electronic circuits consist of interconnections of electronic components. Components are classified into two categories—active and passive. Passive elements never supply more energy than they absorb; active elements can supply more energy than they absorb.

(2) Another type of transistor is the field-effect transistor (FET). Such a transistor operates on the principle of repulsion or attraction of charges due to a superimposed electric field. Amplification of current is accomplished in a manner similar to the grid control of a vacuum tube. Field-effect transistors operate more efficiently than bipolar types, because a large signal can be controlled by a very small amount of energy.

Text B

Semiconductor Diode

A semiconductor diode is a two-terminal device containing a single P-N junction. The general circuit symbol for a semiconductor diode is shown in Fig. 3-1 along with its relationship to the P-N structure.

Generally, diode applications can be classified according to which of the three regions of diode operation (Fig. 3-2) are used. Switching and rectifying applications involve transitions between the reverse-bias and forward-bias region.[1] In such applications care must be taken to choose a diode with a reverse breakdown voltage sufficiently large to prevent undesired reverse breakdown. The reverse breakdown region is employed primarily in voltage reference applications. There, the diode is chosen for the specific value of reverse voltage as reverse breakdown occurs.

The v-i characteristic of a typical semiconductor is shown in Fig. 3-2.

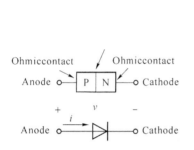

Fig. 3-1 Circuit Symbol for Semiconductor Diode   Fig. 3-2 Typical Diode Characteristic Illustrating Three Regions of Operation

The diode is the first network element we encounter that is strikingly non-linear in the middle of its normal operating range.[2] Both KVL and KCL can be used, since their validity dose not depend on the linearity or non-linearity of the network elements. However, we must exercise caution in the use of superposition, Thevenin equivalents, and Norton equivalents, because these methods are explicitly restricted to linear networks.

One generally useful approach is to separate the linear network from the non-linear elements and carry out a graphical solution for the voltage current in the non-linear elements. To illustrate the method of graphical solution, let us consider the network shown in Fig. 3-3. A single non-linear element, a diode, is connected to a network of arbitrary complexity, but containing only linear resistive elements and sources.[3] The linear portion of the network may be its Thevenin equivalent network as shown in Fig. 3-4.

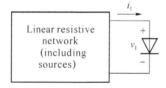   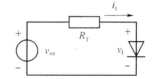

Fig. 3-3 General Non-linear Network   Fig. 3-4 Linear Network Replaced by Thevenin Equivalent Circuit

The first step in the solution is to separate the linear network from the non-linear element, as shown in Fig. 3-5. Next, we determine the relationship between v_D and i_D, the v-i characteristic of the non-linear element, by experimental measurement or from another source such as a manufacturer's data sheet, and plot this relationship as shown in Fig. 3-6. The third step in the solution is to find the relationship between v_L and i_L, the v-i characteristic for the linear network. From Fig. 3-5, we have

$$v_L = v_{oc} - i_L R_T \qquad (3-1)$$

Where v_{oc} and R_T are the Thevenin equivalent voltage and resistance of the linear network, Eq. (3-1) is then plotted on the graph containing the v-i characteristic of the non-linear element. Since Eq. (3-1) is a linear relationship between v_L and i_L, the equation plots as a straight line, and only two points on the line need to be calculated to determine the entire line. Two convenient points are the intercepts at $v_L = 0$ and $i_L = 0$ corresponding respectively to a short circuit and an open circuit at the linear network terminals. For $v_L = 0$, Eq. (3-1) yields

$$i_L = v_{oc}/R_T \quad v_L = 0 \qquad (3-2)$$

Whereas for $i_L = 0$, we obtain

$$v_L = v_{oc} \quad i_L = 0 \qquad (3-3)$$

These points, which are the x-axis and y-axis intercepts of the line in question, are indicated in Fig. 3-6 along with the resulting line. The slope of the line is seen to be $1/R_T$, so that for small value of R_T the line approaches the vertical and for large values of R_T the line becomes horizontal. [4]

If the non-linear element is connected to the linear network, as shown in Fig. 3-4, then we have the following circuit constraints imposed by the connection

$$v_L = v_D = v_1 \quad i_L = i_D = i_1 \qquad (3-4)$$

From Fig. 3-6 there is only one point where V_L equals V_D and i_L equals i_D: the intersection of the two v-i characteristic curves. Thus the required values of v_L and i_L must be the values of voltage and current at this intersection point, and can be read directly off the graph.

The linear v-i characteristic plotted in Fig. 3-6 is known as a load line, since it represents the locus of all possible loads the linear network can present to the non-linear element. [5] Also, the intersection v_L-i_L is often called the operating point or Q-point of the non-linear element.

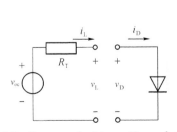

Fig. 3-5 Separate the Linear Network from the Non-Linear Element

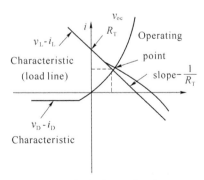

Fig. 3-6 Determine the Relationship between v_D and i_D

Words and Expressions

diode ['daiəud] *n.* 二极管
junction ['dʒʌŋkʃn] *n.* 结，连接；交叉点，会合处
symbol ['simbl] *n.* 符号，象征，记号
structure ['strʌktʃə(r)] *n.* 结构；建筑物；构造 *v.* 建筑；组织；构成
classify ['klæsifai] *v.* 分类，归类；分等
switching ['switʃiŋ] *v.* 交换；转换
switch [switʃ] *n.* 开关，转换；电闸 *v.* 转换，转变；变换
rectify ['rektifai] *v.* 矫正，调整
breakdown ['breikdaun] *n.* 崩溃；故障
undesired [ʌndi'zaiəd] *adj.* 不希望得到的，非所要求的，不需要的
reference ['refrəns] *n.* 提及，涉及；参考；参考文献 *v.* 给……加上参考书目
value ['vælju:] *n.* 价值；价格；重要性 *v.* 评价；重视；估价
characteristic [kærəktə'ristik] *n.* 特性，特色，特征 *adj.* 特有的；典型的
network ['netwɜːk] *n.* 网络，网状系统；网状物；广播网
element ['elimənt] *n.* 成分；要素；分子
strikingly ['straikiŋli] *adv.* 显著地；突出地
non-linear ['nɔn 'li:niə(r)] *adj.* 非线性的
validity [və'lidəti] *n.* 有效性；正确性；合法性
linearity [ˌlini'ærəti] *n.* 线性，成直线的状态
non-linearity [ˌnɔnlini'ærəti] *n.* [电] 非线性
caution ['kɔ:ʃn] *n.* 小心，警告；谨慎 *v.* 警告
superposition [ˌsu:pəpə'ziʃn] *n.* 重叠；叠合；重合
equivalent [i'kwivələnt] *n.* 同等物，相等物，等价物 *adj.* 相等的；相当的
Thevenin's equivalent [电] 戴维南等效原理
explicitly [ik'splisit] *adv.* 明白地；明确地
restrict [ri'strikt] *v.* 限制；限定；约束
arbitrary ['ɑ:bitrəri] *adj.* 专制的；任意的
complexity [kəm'pleksiti] *n.* 复杂；复杂性
resistive [ri'zistiv] *adj.* 有抵抗力的
portion ['pɔ:ʃn] *n.* 部分；一份 *v.* 把……分成多份；分配
data sheet 数据表
plot [plɔt] *n.* 小块土地；图；地区图 *v.* 划分；绘图；策划
solution [sə'lu:ʃn] *n.* 解决；溶液；解答
convenient [kən'vi:niənt] *adj.* 方便的；合宜的
intercept [ˌintə(r)'sept] *v.* 拦截；截击；截住；截断
corresponding [ˌkɔrə'spɔndiŋ] *adj.* 符合的；相同的；一致的；对应的
respectively [ri'spektivli] *adv.* 分别地，各自地

yield [ji:ld] n. 生产量；投资收益 v. 生产，同意，给予；出产
whereas [weər'æz] conj. 然而；鉴于；反之
slope [sləup] n. 斜率，斜坡，倾斜，斜面
vertical ['və:tikl] n. 垂直线，竖向，垂直面 adj. 垂直的；直立的；顶点的
horizontal [hɔri'zɔntl] n. 水平线，水平面 adj. 地平线的；水平的
intersection [intə(r)'sekʃn] n. 交集；交叉点
locus ['ləukəs] n. 场所，所在地；轨迹

Notes

[1] Switching and rectifying applications involve transitions between the reverse-bias and forward-bias region.

此句可译为：作为开关和整流应用时，它涉及了反向偏置和正向偏置区域的转换。

reverse-bias and forward-bias region：反向偏置和正向偏置区域。

[2] The diode is the first network element we encounter that is strikingly non-linear in the middle of its normal operating range.

此句可译为：二极管是我们所遇到的正常工作区域的中间部分为明显非线性的第一个网络元件。

该句为复合句，表语 the first network element 后接省略引导词的定语从句。

normal operating range：正常工作区域。

[3] A single non-linear element, a diode, is connected to a network of arbitrary complexity, but containing only linear resistive elements and sources.

此句可译为：一个非线性元件，二极管，连接到一个任意复杂的网络上。这个网络仅含线性电阻元件和电源。

此句谓语动词使用了被动语态，a diode 用作同位语，containing only linear resistive elements and sources 为现在分词短语做状语。

[4] The slope of the line is seen to be $1/R_T$, so that for small value of R_T the line approaches the vertical and for large values of R_T the line becomes horizontal.

此句可译为：可以看出直线的斜率为 $1/R_T$，因此当 R_T 的值很小时，这条直线接近于垂直；而 R_T 值很大时，这条直线变为水平。

slope of the line：直线的斜率。

[5] The linear *v-i* characteristic plotted in Fig. 3-6 is known as a load line, since it represents the locus of all possible loads the linear network can present to the non-linear element.

此句可译为：画在图 3-6 中的线性的 *v-i* 特性是负载线，因为它代表线性网络对非线性元件呈现出的所有可能的负载的轨迹。

plotted in Fig. 3-6 为过去分词短语做后置定语修饰 characteristic；since 引导原因状语从句。

Exercises

Mark the following statements with T (true) or F (false) according to the text.

(1) A semiconductor diode is a two-terminal device containing a double P-N junction. ( )

(2) Switching and rectifying applications involve transitions between the reverse-bias and forward-bias region. ( )

(3) The diode is not the first network element we encounter that is strikingly non-linear in the middle of its normal operating range. ( )

(4) One generally useful approach is to separate the linear network from the non-linear elements and carry out a graphical solution for the voltage current in the non-linear elements. ( )

(5) The first step in the solution is to separate the linear network from the non-linear element. ( )

(6) The general circuit symbol for a semiconductor diode is shown in Fig. 3-1 along with its relationship to the P-N structure. ( )

(7) In such applications care must be taken to choose a diode with a reverse breakdown voltage sufficiently large to prevent undesired reverse breakdown. ( )

(8) The reverse breakdown region is not employed primarily in voltage reference applications. ( )

(9) No need for us to exercise caution in the use of superposition, Thevenin equivalents, and Norton equivalents, because these methods are not explicitly restricted to linear networks. ( )

(10) The linear portion of the network may be its Thevenin equivalent network. ( )

Translating Skill 3

Tele-和-Phone 的译法

拉丁词缀或希腊词缀所派生的词,如 Unit 2 翻译技巧所述,可根据其原意翻译。但在电子信息业飞速发展的信息社会,翻译时原意往往不被使用,许多情况下需要对原意稍加转变(但又不违背原意)才能得到较为妥贴而准确的译文(词),其中前缀 tele-和后缀-phone 这两个电子信息英语中出现最频繁的词缀表现最为明显。

Tele-源于希腊语,原意为 in a distance 或 far away,即"远距离"之意,在通信中以 tele-为前缀的词常译作"电……",例如:

    telecommunication   电信

telephone	电话
telegraph	电报
television	电视
teleprinter	电传打字机

随着通信技术的飞速发展,出现了大量以 tele-为词头的词,在许多情况下翻译为"电……"已不足以表示这些词的内涵,不得不启用其原意"远距离",例如:

teleconferencing	电信会议
teleprocessing	远程信息处理
teletraffic	长途业务
telephoto-lens	远摄镜头

有时用"遥……"来表示,例如:

telemetry	遥测
teletypesetter	遥控排字机,电传排字机
telesynd	遥控装置
teleradio	无线电遥控

在翻译 tele-为词头的词时还有一种重要现象需要引起注意。有些 tele-词中的 tele-并非前缀,而是 television, telephone 等常见 tele-词的缩写形式,其翻译时要注意其原意,例如:

teleset＝television set	电视机
telesat＝telecommunication satellite	通信卫星
telecast＝television broadcast	电视广播
telelecture＝telephone lecture	电话讲课

-phone 作为后缀,源于希腊语,原意为 sound,常用于乐器和传输声音的装置,翻译为"……器","……机",例如:

xylophone	木琴
gramophone	留声机
cardiophone	心音听诊器
microphone	传声器(话筒,麦克风)
ionophone	离子扬声器

但在通信中出现的-phone 词通常都是 telephone 的缩略语,仍翻译为"……电话",这类词语在通信中出现较多,例如:

interphone ＝ inter ＋ telephone	内线自动电话
letterphone ＝ letter ＋ telephone	书写电话
picture-phone ＝ picture ＋ telephone	电视电话
babyphone ＝ baby ＋ telephone	小型电话
answerphone ＝ answer＋ telephone	应答电话

除 tele-,-phone 外,其他电子信息常用词缀的翻译均可遵循以上规律。

Exercises to Translating Skill

Translate the following words into Chinese.

(1) telegraphone

(2) teletext

(3) teletypewriter

(4) teletypist

(5) telephonist

(6) telesoftware

(7) teleguide

(8) telephoto-lens

(9) telecobalt

(10) telecommute

(11) telemicroscope

(12) bitelephone

(13) dataphone

(14) earphone

(15) geophone

(16) telecopter

(17) teletron

(18) videophone

(19) videoplayer

(20) cellphone

Unit 4　Integrated Circuits

In electronics, an integrated circuit (also known as IC, microcircuit, microchip, silicon chip, or chip) is a miniaturized electronic circuit (consisting mainly of semiconductor devices, as well as passive components) that has been manufactured in the surface of a thin substrate of semiconductor material. Integrated circuits are used in almost all electronic equipment in use today and have revolutionized the world of electronics.

在电子学中,集成电路(简称为 IC 或微电路、微芯片、硅片,或者芯片)是制作在半导体材料薄基片上的微型电子电路,它主要由半导体器件以及无源部件组成。当今集成电路几乎被用在所有电子设备上,它给电子世界带来了一场革命。

Text A

Integrated Circuits

Modern solid-state electronics has produced the integrated circuit, or IC. With the coming of the semiconductor age, it became feasible to build an entirely electronic circuit, including resistors, capacitors, inductors, diodes, and transistors onto a single chip of silicon or germanium. Other substances, notably metal oxides, are used in fabricating integrated circuits.[1] The result is a package that may be smaller than a pencil eraser, yet it can contain the complexity of a system that would have taken up an entire room just a few decades ago.[2]

Integrated circuits are classified in a variety of ways. Analog, or linear, ICs operate over a continuous range, and include such devices as operational amplifiers. Digital ICs are employed mostly in computers, electronic counters, frequency synthesizers, and digital instruments. Bipolar integrated circuits employ bipolar transistor technology. Complementary-metal-oxide-semiconductor (COMS) ICs are becoming increasingly common because of their extremely low current demand. Monolithic integrated circuits are entirely fabricated on one piece of semiconductor material; other devices may use two or more individual chips in a single package.

Integrated circuits come in various kinds of packages.[3] The most common is probably the dual in-line type. Other housing methods are the single in-line package, with pins along one edge, and the flat pack, with pins along two, three or four edges.[4]

The 8-pin 555 timer IC (Fig. 4-1) is used in many projects, a popular version is the NE555. Most circuits will just specify "555 timer IC" and the NE555 is suitable for these.

The 555 output (pin 3) can sink and source up to 200 mA. This is more than most ICs and it is sufficient to supply LEDs, relay coils and low current lamps. To switch larger currents you can connect a transistor.

The 556 (Fig. 4-2) is a dual version of the 555 housed in a 14-pin package. The two timers (A and B) share the same power supply pins.

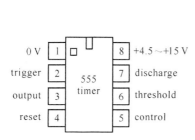

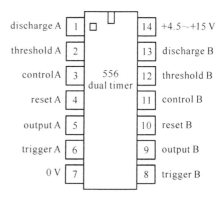

Fig. 4-1　The 555 Timer Chips

Fig. 4-2　The 556 Timer Chips

A PIC is a programmable integrated circuit (PIC) microcontroller, a "computer-on-a-chip". They have a processor and memory to run a program responding to inputs and controlling outputs, so they can easily achieve complex functions which would require several conventional ICs (Fig. 4-3).

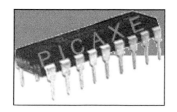

Fig. 4-3　PIC Microcontrollers

A theoretical limit probably exists for the degree of miniaturization that can be achieved. Some experts believe that limit has nearly been reached today; others think much further miniaturization is still possible.

The IC units are fast replacing discrete components in all electronic equipment except for high-power applications.[5] Digital IC packages are usually rated for 1 W or less. Linear IC units have power ratings up to 10 W. The IC packages will probably continue to grow in use because of their small size and weight, low cost, low power consumption, high reliability, and improved performance.

Words and Expressions

solid-state electronics　[电] 固态电子学；[物] 固体电子学
integrated circuit　[计] 集成电路
feasible ['fi:zəbl] adj. 能实行的，可行的；适宜的
chip [tʃip] n. 碎片；芯片；集成电路片 v. 削，铲，凿；把……切成薄片
oxide ['ɔksaid] n. 氧化物
fabricate ['fæbrikeit] v. 制造；伪造；组装

package ['pækidʒ] n. 组件；包裹，包，套装软件 v. 包装，打包
decade ['dekeid] n. 十年；十
variety [və'raiəti] n. 变化；种种；多样性
a variety of 各种各样的……，种种……
linear ['liniə(r)] adj. 线的，线状的；直线的
operational amplifier [计] 运算放大器
employ [im'plɔi] v. 使从事于；使用
synthesizer (Amer.) ['sinθəsaizə(r)] n. 合成者；合成器
CMOS(Complementary Metal Oxide Semiconductor) 互补金属氧化半导体；[计]存储计算机表面配置定义的记忆芯片
monolithic [ˌmɔnə'liθik] adj. 庞大的；整体的
dual in-line type [电] 双列直插式
house [haus] v. 封装；覆盖
single in-line package [电] 单行排齐封装
pin [pin] n. 芯片上或电插销上的金属叉状物，管脚，引线，插头 v. 钉住；阻止；别住
edge [edʒ] n. 边缘；刀刃；尖锐
theoretical [ˌθiə'retikl] adj. 理论上的；空谈的
miniaturization (Amer.) ['minətʃərai'zeiʃn /-'tjur-] n. 小型化；微型化
achieve [ə'tʃi:v] v. 实现，完成；赢得，达到；达到目的
discrete [di'skri:t] adj. 不连续的；离散的
equipment [i'kwipmənt] n. 装备，设备品
high-power adj. 大功率的，高功率的；强力的
application [ˌæpli'keiʃn] n. 申请；要求；完成；运用；适用
rate [reit] n. 比例，率 v. 认为；对……评价；列为；被列入等级
consumption [kən'sʌmpʃn] n. 消费；消耗
reliability [riˌlaiə'biləti] n. 可靠；可靠程度；可信赖性

Notes

[1] Other substances, notably metal oxides, are used in fabricating integrated circuits.

此句可译为：其他物质，特别是金属氧化物，用于制造集成电路。

句中 notably metal oxides 做 Other substances 的同位语。

[2] The result is a package that may be smaller than a pencil eraser, yet it can contain the complexity of a system that would have taken up an entire room just a few decades ago.

此句可译为：结果是小于橡皮擦大小的组件能容纳整个系统，但就在几十年前它会占据一整间房子。

that would have taken up an entire room just a few decades ago 用作定语从句，修饰先行词 system。

[3] Integrated circuits come in various kinds of packages.

此句可译为:集成电路有各种组件。

句中 come 相当于 have as its place,可译为"有"。

[4] The most common is probably the dual in-line type. Other housing methods are the single in-line package, with pins along one edge, and the flat pack, with pins along two, three or four edges.

此句可译为:最常见的可能是双列直插式。其他封装方法有管脚在一边的单列直插式组件和管脚分布在两边、三边和四边的扁平组件。

with pins along one edge 为介词短语用作定语修饰 package。

[5] The IC units are fast replacing discrete components in all electronic equipment except for high-power applications.

此句可译为:除大功率应用外,集成电路部件正迅速取代所有电子装备中的分立元件。

except for 除……以外; high-power application 表示大功率应用。

Exercises

1. Put the following phrases into English.

(1) 现代固体电子学

(2) 仅需极弱电流

(3) 单片集成电路

(4) 其他封装方法

(5) 单列直插式组件

(6) 一个理论限度

(7) 进一步微型化

(8) 分立元件

(9) 功率应用

(10) 耗能小

2. Put the following phrases into Chinese.

(1) integrated circuit

(2) semiconductor age

(3) build an entirely electronic circuit onto a single chip of silicon

(4) metal oxides

(5) low current lamps

(6) operate over a continuous range

(7) operational amplifiers

(8) frequency synthesizers

(9) bipolar integrated circuits

(10) programmable integrated circuit microcontroller

3. Translate the following sentences into Chinese.

(1) Modern solid-state electronics has produced the integrated circuit.

(2) Other substances, notably metal oxides, are used in fabricating integrated circuits.

(3) Integrated circuits are classified in a variety of ways.

(4) Digital ICs are employed mostly in computers, electronic counters, frequency synthesizers, and digital instruments.

(5) Bipolar integrated circuits employ bipolar transistor technology.

(6) Integrated circuits come in various kinds of packages.

(7) A theoretical limit probably exists for the degree of miniaturization that can be achieved.

(8) The IC units are fast replacing discrete components in all electronic equipment except for high-power applications.

(9) The IC packages will probably continue to grow in use.

(10) The two timers (A and B) share the same power supply pins.

4. Translate the following paragraphs into Chinese.

(1) The IC units are fast replacing discrete components in all electronic equipment except for high-power applications. Digital IC packages are usually rated for 1 W or less. Linear IC units have power ratings up to 10 W. The IC packages will probably continue to grow in use because of their small size and weight, low cost, low power consumption, high reliability, and improved performance.

(2) In electronics, an integrated circuit (also known as IC, microcircuit, microchip, silicon chip, or chip) is a miniaturized electronic circuit (consisting mainly of semiconductor devices, as well as passive components) that has been manufactured in the surface of a thin substrate of semiconductor material. Integrated circuits are used in almost all electronic equipment in use today and has revolutionized the world of electronics.

Text B

Application of Chips

Integrated circuits are usually called ICs or chips. They are complex circuits which have been etched onto tiny chips of semiconductor (silicon). The chip is packaged in a plastic holder with pins spaced on a 0.1 inch (2.54 mm) grid which will fit the holes on stripboard and breadboards.[1] Very fine wires inside the package link the chip to the pins.

Pin numbers (Fig. 4-4)

The pins are numbered anti-clockwise around the IC (chip) starting near the notch or dot. Fig. 4-4 shows the numbering for 8-pin and 14-pin ICs, but the principle is the same for all sizes.[2]

IC holders (DIL sockets) (Fig. 4-5)

ICs (chips) are easily damaged by heat when soldering and their short pins cannot be

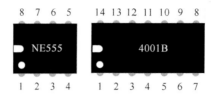

Fig. 4-4　Pin Numbers

protected with a heat sink. Instead we use an IC holder (Fig. 4-5), strictly called a DIL socket (DIL = Dual In-Line), which can be safely soldered onto the circuit board. The IC is pushed into the holder when all soldering is complete. IC holders are only needed when soldering so they are not used on breadboards.

Fig. 4-5　IC Holder

Commercially produced circuit boards often have ICs soldered directly to the board without an IC holder, usually this is done by a machine which is able to work very quickly. Please don't attempt to do this yourself because you are likely to destroy the IC and it will be difficult to remove without damage by de-soldering.

Removing a chip from its holder

If you need to remove a chip, it can be gently prised out of the holder with a small flat-blade screwdriver. Carefully lever up each end by inserting the screwdriver blade between the chip and its holder and gently twisting the screwdriver.[3] Take care to start lifting at both ends before you attempt to remove the chip, otherwise you will bend and possibly break the pins.

Datasheets

Datasheets are available for most chips giving detailed information about their ratings and functions. In some cases example circuits are shown. The large amount of information with symbols and abbreviations can make datasheets seem overwhelming to a beginner, but they are worth reading as you become more confident because they contain a great deal of useful information for more experienced users designing and testing circuits.[4]

PIC microcontrollers programming

Programming a PIC microcontroller may seem daunting to a beginner but there are a number of systems designed to make this easy. The PICAXE system is an excellent example because it uses a standard computer to program (and re-program) the PICs; no specialist equipment is required other than a low-cost download lead. Programs can be written in a simple version of BASIC or using a flowchart. The PICAXE programming software and extensive documentation is available to download free of charge, making the system ideal for education and users at home.

If you think PICs are not for you because you have never written a computer program, please look at the PICAXE system. It is very easy to get started using a few simple BASIC commands and there are a number of projects available as kits which are ideal for beginners.[5]

Words and Expressions

complex ['kɔmpleks] n. 复合物，综合体；综合设施 adj. 复杂的；合成的
etch [etʃ] v. 蚀刻，蚀镂
silicon ['silikən] n. 硅；硅元素
plastic ['plæstik] n. 塑胶；塑胶制品 adj. 塑胶的；有可塑性的；塑料的
holder ['həuldə(r)] n. 插座；持有者
breadboard ['bredbɔ:d] n. 电路试验板
link [liŋk] n. 链路；纽带；环节；联系 v. 连接，结合；联系
pin number 引脚数
notch [nɔtʃ] n. 刻痕；等级 v. 刻凹痕，用刻痕计算
dot [dɔt] n. 点，小圆点；微小的东西；点状物；少量 v. 在……上打点；用点构成；打点
socket ['sɔ:kit /'sɔk-] n. 插座
DIL sockets [计]双列直插式插座
solder ['səuldə(r) /'sɔl-] n. 焊接剂；接合物 v. 焊接；使联接在一起
sink [siŋk] n. 水槽，水池 v. 下沉；使陷入；灌
circuit board [计]电路板，焊接电路的塑料板
commercially [kə'mə:ʃəli] adv. 商业上；通商上
remove [ri'mu:v] n. 距离，间隔；搬家 v. 移动，搬开；脱掉；去掉，消除
de-soldering v. 通过电焊移除，去掉
prise [praiz] v 撬，撬开，撬动
flat-blade screwdriver 平口螺丝刀
lever ['levə(r) /'li:v-] n. 杠杆；似杠杆之工具 v. 撬起，移动；用控制杆操纵
insert [in'sə:t /-'sə:t] v. 插入；嵌入；放入，加入
twist [twist] n. 扭；搓；绞；缠 v. 扭转；旋转，绞；缠绕，扭曲
bend [bend] n. 弯，曲 v. 使弯曲，弯曲
precaution [pri'kɔ:ʃn] n. 预防；谨慎；警惕；预防措施
antistatic [ˌænti'stætik] [医] 对抗的
label ['leibl] n. 票；标签 v. 贴标签于；分类
adequate ['ædikwət] adj. 足够的，能满足需要的；胜任的
earth [ə:θ] n. 地球，世界；泥土 v. 埋入土中
earthed [ə:θt] adj. 接地的
aluminium [ˌælju'minjəm] n. 铝，一种金属（又拼作 aluminum）
foil [fɔil] n. 箔，金属薄片 v. 在……上贴箔；给……铺箔
abbreviation [əˌbri:vi'eiʃn] n. 缩写；缩写词
overwhelming [ˌəuvə'hwelmiŋ /ˌəuvə'wel-] adj. 压倒性的；无法抵抗的
specify ['spesifai] v. 具体指定；明确说明；详细指明
logic gate 逻辑门

flip-flop ['flip-fləp] *n.* 触发器
shift register 移位寄存器
counter ['kauntə] *n.* 计数器 *v.* 反对；反驳 *adv.* 反方向地，相反地
daunt [dɔːnt] *v.* 吓倒；使气馁，使畏缩
daunting ['dɔːntiŋ] *adj.* 使人畏缩的
specialist ['speʃəlist] *n.* 专科医师，专家
flowchart ['fləuˌtʃɑːt] *n.* 流程图；作业图
download ['daunləud] *v.* 下载
free of charge 免费
ideal [aiˈdiəl] *adj.* 理想的，完美的；空想的 *n.* 理想；典范
kit [kit] *n.* 成套工具；用品；工具箱

Notes

[1] The chip is packaged in a plastic holder with pins spaced on a 0.1 inch (2.54 mm) grid which will fit the holes on stripboard and breadboards.

此句可译为：该芯片用塑料封装且两侧带有引脚，每个引脚间隔0.1英寸（2.54毫米），可插在电路试验板上。

with 结构表示"用……作工具"；pins 后接定语，which 引导定语从句修饰 grid。

[2] Fig. 4-4 shows the numbering for 8-pin and 14-pin ICs, but the principle is the same for all sizes.

此句可译为：图 4.4 显示了一个 8 脚和 14 脚的集成电路芯片，但对所有尺寸的芯片引脚命名的规则都是一样的。

the principle 意指 numbering principle，命名规则。

[3] Carefully lever up each end by inserting the screwdriver blade between the chip and its holder and gently twisting the screwdriver.

此句可译为：将螺丝刀的叶片插入芯片和插座，然后轻轻地转动螺丝刀从而将芯片的两端小心地水平地起翘。

此句中祈使句用于指令描述，简洁清楚。

[4] The large amount of information with symbols and abbreviations can make datasheets seem overwhelming to a beginner, but they are worth reading as you become more confident because they contain a great deal of useful information for more experienced users designing and testing circuits.

此句可译为：大量带有符号和缩写的信息会使初学者感到资料手册难以理解。但对于有经验的使用者来说资料手册是很值得一看的，因为它包含了大量的有用信息和测试电路。

前一分句为主谓宾结构，主语部分 The large amount of information with symbols and abbreviation 的核心词为 information。后一分句中 as 引导原因状语从句。

[5] It is very easy to get started using a few simple BASIC commands and there are a number of projects available as kits which are ideal for beginners.

此句可译为：它可以通过使用一些简单的 BASIC 命令来开始，并且还有许多对初学者

非常理想的方案可作为工具。
available as kits which are ideal for beginners 为形容词短语做后置定语限定 projects。

Exercises

Mark the following statements with T (true) or F (false) according to the text.

(1) The pins are numbered anti-clockwise around the IC (chip) starting near the notch or dot.   （   ）

(2) ICs (chips) are easily damaged by heat when soldering.   （   ）

(3) Commercially produced circuit boards often have ICs soldered directly to the board without an IC holder.   （   ）

(4) It is easy to remove a chip without damage by de-soldering.   （   ）

(5) If you need to remove a chip, it can be gently prised out of the holder with a small flat-blade screwdriver.   （   ）

(6) Datasheets are not available for most chips giving detailed information about their ratings and functions.   （   ）

(7) A PIC is a programmable integrated circuit microcontroller, a "computer-on-a-chip".   （   ）

(8) The PICAXE system uses a standard computer to program the PICs.   （   ）

(9) The PICAXE programming software and extensive documentation is available to download free of charge.   （   ）

(10) It is very easy to get started using a few simple BASIC commands and there are a number of projects available as kits which are ideal for beginners in PICAXE system.
                                                                                （   ）

Translating Skill 4

广告的翻译

在国外电子信息类报纸和杂志中充斥着广告。广告形成较为独立的一种文本,我们需要熟悉这种文体并在翻译中体现其风格和特点。

1. 突出原广告的重点

例如:

FINALLY dBase you have been waiting IV.

Get the new dBase IV. *Now for just $449.*

这是一份计算机软件广告,通过变换字体可使人一目了然其重点所在。

译文:dBase IV 终于问世,人们盼望已久的 dBase 新版,目前售价仅 449 美元。

2. 注意广告中的修辞手段

例如:

Are you getting fat or lazy waiting for your plotter?
Don't wait—Get PLUMP.

这是一则推销 PLUMP 电脑的广告,采用了极为夸张的语言。

译文:用绘图仪速度太慢,使人等得又懒又胖,不如去买台 PLUMP。

3. 反映原广告的通俗性

不少广告使用口语、俚语、俗语或谚语以及其他非正式文体,翻译文要尽可能与其贴近。

例如:

Here's proof that something small can be powerful.

这是一则微机广告。

译文:别看体积小,功能不得了。或:外形虽小,功能惊人。

A whole year without a single bug!

这是一个电子公司的产品广告。

译文:全年无故障! 或:万无一失!

4. 体现原广告神韵

许多广告语言生动、传神、深刻、耐人寻味,译文要尽可能不失原味。

例如:

I feel like a donkey! For not buying the "Access" portable computer.

译文:不买"Access"便携式计算机使我劳累得像头笨驴。

5. 用汉语四字字组翻译常用广告语

有许多产品广告语看似简单,要转化为相应汉语却颇费斟酌,如果采用汉语中常用的四字字组,难题往往迎刃而解。

例如:

A wide selection of styles	品种多样
Beautiful range of colours	花式齐全
Bright colours	色彩鲜艳
In up-to-date style	款式入时
Compact	结构合理

以上翻译要点均指广告的主题部分,其实一份完整的产品广告一般都有4个内容。

(1) 标题

(2) 产品图

(3) 正文(常与图配合)

(4) 其他(商标,名称,经销地,地址等)。

Exercises to Translating Skill

Translate the following expressions into Chinese.

(1) Twice the performance at half the cost.
The New Ultra Graphics Accelerator from Metheus.

(2) Take one and your headaches are gone.

(3) Let Kelly work for you.

(4) Let the Company That Transmits Data Across The Universe.

(5) Let us help you extend yourself.

(6) Here's an offer only the most analytical minds in America can appreciate—Buy 1, Get 1 free.

(7) Spend dime, save you time.

(8) "We like the codex 2,382 high-speed modem for its brains, its brawn and its underdeveloped price."

(9) Durable

(10) Secure

(11) Handy

(12) Delicious

(13) Nourishing

(14) Catalogues and samples sent upon request

(15) Orders with customers' materials

(16) Good quality

(17) Choice materials

(18) Reliable performance

(19) Sleek design

(20) Luxuriant finish

Unit 5　Digital Signal Processor

A digital signal processor (DSP) is a specialized microprocessor with an architecture optimized for the fast operational needs of digital signal processing.

数字信号处理器(DSP)是一种专门的微处理器,它拥有最优化的结构,用于满足数字信号处理快速运行的需求。

Text A

Digital Signal Processor (DSP)[1]

A digital signal processor is a special-purpose CPU (central processing unit) that provides ultra-fast instruction sequences, such as shift and add, and multiply and add, which are commonly used in math-intensive signal processing applications.[2]

DSPs are not the same as typical microprocessors[3] though. Microprocessors are typically general purpose devices that run large blocks of software. They are not often called upon for real-time computation and they work at a slower pace, choosing a course of action, then waiting to finish the present job before responding to the next user command. A DSP, on the other hand, is often used as a type of embedded controller or processor that is built into another piece of equipment and is dedicated to a single group of tasks.[4] In this environment, the DSP assists the general purpose host microprocessor.

Digital signal processing algorithms typically require a large number of mathematical operations to be performed quickly and repeatedly on a set of data. Signals (perhaps from audio or video sensors) are constantly converted from analog to digital, manipulated digitally, and then converted back to analog form. Many DSP applications have constraints on latency; that is, for the system to work, the DSP operation must be completed within some fixed time, and deferred (or batch) processing is not viable.[5]

Most general-purpose microprocessors and operating systems can execute DSP algorithms successfully, but are not suitable for use in portable devices such as mobile phones and PDAs[6] because of power supply and space constraints. A specialized digital signal processor, however, will tend to provide a lower-cost solution, with better performance, lower latency, and no requirements for specialized cooling or large batteries.

The architecture of a digital signal processor is optimized specifically for digital signal processing. Most also support some of the features as an application processor or microcontroller, since signal processing is rarely the only task of a system.[7]

Digital signal processing

Digital signal processing is a technique that converts signals from real world sources (usually in analog form) into digital data that can then be analyzed. Analysis is performed in digital form because once a signal has been reduced to numbers, its components can be isolated, analyzed and rearranged more easily than in analog form.

Eventually, when the DSP has finished its work, the digital data can be turned back into an analog signal, with improved quality. For example, a DSP can filter noise from a signal, remove interference, amplify frequencies and suppress others, encrypt information, or analyze a complex wave form into its spectral components. This process must be handled in real-time—which is often very quickly. For instance, stereo equipment handles sound signals of up to 20 kHz (20,000 cycles per second), requiring a DSP to perform hundreds of millions of operations per second.

Types of DSPs

Because different applications have varying ranges of frequencies, different DSPs are required. DSPs are classified by their dynamic range, the spread of numbers that must be processed in the course of an application. This number is a function of the processor's data width (the number of bits it manipulates) and the type of arithmetic it performs (fixed or floating point[8]). For example, a 32 bit processor has a wider dynamic range than a 24 bit processor, which has a wider range than 16 bit processor.[9] Floating-point chips have wider ranges than fixed-point devices.

Each type of processor is suited for a particular range of applications. 16 bit fixed-point DSPs are used for voice-grade systems such as phones, since they work with a relatively narrow range of sound frequencies[10]. Hi-fidelity stereo sound[11] has a wider range, calling for a 16 bit ADC (analog/digital converter), and a 24 bit fixed point DSP. Image processing, 3D graphics and scientific simulations have a much wider dynamic range and require a 32 bit floating-point processor.

Use

DSP chips are used in sound cards, fax machines, modems, cellular phones, high-capacity hard disks and digital TVs. According to Texas Instruments, DSPs are used as the engine in 70% of the world's digital cellular phones, and with the increase in wireless applications, this number will only increase. Digital signal processing is used in many fields including biomedicine, sonar, radar, seismology, speech and music processing, imaging and communications.

Words and Expressions

optimize [ˈɔptimaiz] v. 使完善，使优化

sequence [ˈsiːkwəns] n. 顺序，次序；连续；一系列 v. 按顺序排好

multiply [ˈmʌltiplai] v. 乘；增加 v. 做乘法；繁衍

intensive [in'tensiv] adj. 密集的；彻底的；精细的；强调的 n. 强调成分
embedded [im'bedid] adj. 植入的，嵌入的
dedicated ['dedi,keitid] adj. 专注的；献身的；专用的
assists [ə'sists] n. 助攻
algorithm ['ælgə,riðəm] n. 算法
manipulate [mə'nipjuleit] v. 操纵，操作；控制；利用；（巧妙地）处理；篡改
analog ['ænəlɔ:g] adj. 模拟的，类比的 n.（=analogue）类似（模拟量）
digital ['didʒitəl] adj. 数字的，数码的；手指的；计数的
constraint [kən'streint] n. 强制；被约束，拘束
latency ['leitnsi] n. 潜伏，潜伏期；延迟
deferred [di'fə:d] adj. 延期的，延迟的
isolate ['aisəleit] vt. 使孤立，隔离 adj. 孤立的，单独的 n. 隔离种群
rearrange ['ri:ə'reindʒ] v. 重新安排，重新排序，重新布置
interference [,intə'fiərəns] n. 干扰；妨碍
amplify ['æmplifai] v. 扩大，增强；详述
frequency ['fri:kwənsi] n. 频繁；频率
encrypt [en'kript] v. 加密，将……译成密码
spectral ['spektrəl] adj. 光谱的；幽灵的
fidelity [fi'deliti] n. 准确性，保真度；忠实，忠诚
graphics ['græfiks] n. 制图法，绘图学
simulation [,simju'leiʃən] n. 模拟，仿真；赝品
dynamic [dai'næmik] adj. 动态的；动力的；有活力的

Notes

[1] 文章来源于 http://www.wave-report.com/blog/? p=55，波报告，作者不详。

[2] A digital signal processor is a special-purpose CPU (central processing unit) that provides ultra-fast instruction sequences, such as shift and add, and multiply and add, which are commonly used in math-intensive signal processing applications.

此句可译为：数字信号处理器是一种特殊用途的 CPU（中央处理器），它提供超快速的指令序列，例如移位叠加、乘法和加法，这些指令序列常用在数学密集型信号处理应用软件中。

that provides ultra-fast instruction sequences 做定语从句，修饰先行词 CPU。

which are commonly used in math-intensive signal processing applications 做定语从句，修饰先行词 instruction sequences。

[3] typical microprocessor 典型的微处理器，这里指用一片或少数几片大规模集成电路组成的中央处理器。与传统的中央处理器相比，具有体积小、重量轻和容易模块化等优点。微处理器的基本组成部分有寄存器堆、运算器、时序控制电路以及数据和地址总线。微处理器能完成取指令、执行指令以及与外界存储器和逻辑部件交换信息等操作，是微型计算机的运算控制部分。

[4] A DSP, on the other hand, is often used as a type of embedded controller or processor that is built into another piece of equipment and is dedicated to a single group of tasks.

此句可译为：另一方面，DSP 经常被用来作为一种建立在另一块设备中的嵌入式控制器或处理器，并致力于单组任务的实现。

that is built into another piece of equipment 做定语从句修饰先行词 embedded controller or processor。

嵌入式系统将在本书 Unit 9 中介绍。

[5] that is, for the system to work, the DSP operation must be completed within some fixed time, and deferred (or batch) processing is not viable.

此句可译为：也就是说想要系统工作，DSP 操作必须在一定时间内完成，延迟（或批量）处理是不可行的。

for the system to work, 表示目的状语。

[6] PDA，即 Personal Digital Assistant，掌上电脑，就是个人数字助理的意思。顾名思义就是辅助个人工作的数字工具，主要提供记事、通讯录、名片交换及行程安排等功能。

[7] Most also support some of the features as an application processor or microcontroller, since signal processing is rarely the only task of a system.

此句可译为：由于信号处理很少是一个系统的唯一任务，大多数数字信号处理器也支持一些作为应用处理器或微控制器的功能。

since 引导原因状语从句。

as an application processor or microcontroller 介词短语补充说明 the features。

[8] fixed or floating point, 定点和浮点。机器有两种办法表示实数，一种是定点，就是小数点位置是固定的；一种是浮点，就是小数点位置不固定，计算方法也比较麻烦，通常会比整数运算代价大很多。

[9] For example, a 32 bit processor has a wider dynamic range than a 24 bit processor, which has a wider range than 16 bit processor.

此句可译为：例如，32 位处理器比 24 位处理器具有更宽的动态范围，24 位处理器又比 16 位处理器具有更宽的范围。

which has a wider range than 16 bit processor 为 which 引导的定语从句，which 修饰先行词 a 24 bit processor。

[10] range of sound frequencies, 声音频率范围，人耳可以听到 20 Hz～20 kHz 的音频信号，人说话声音频率范围是 300 Hz～3.4 kHz。

[11] Hi-fidelity stereo sound 高保真立体声，高保真的定义是：与原来的声音高度相似的重放声音。高保真立体声级为 20 Hz～20 kHz。

Exercises

1. Put the following phrases into English.

(1) 中央处理器

(2) 指令序列

(3) 响应时间

(4) 模-数转换器

(5) 实时

(6) 动态范围

(7) 频率范围

(8) 蜂窝电话

(9) 调制解调器

(10) 信号处理与分析

2. Put the following phrases into Chinese.

(1) single-cycle

(2) parallel operation

(3) digital to analog conversion

(4) image processing

(5) voice recognition

(6) digital signal processing

(7) signal encryption

(8) high-fidelity signal

(9) the frequency bandwidth

(10) filter noise

3. Translate the following sentences into Chinese.

(1) Microprocessors are typically general purpose devices that run large blocks of software.

(2) Digital signal processing algorithms typically require a large number of mathematical operations to be performed quickly and repeatedly on a set of data.

(3) Signals (perhaps from audio or video sensors) are constantly converted from analog to digital, manipulated digitally, and then converted back to analog form.

(4) Most general-purpose microprocessors and operating systems can execute DSP algorithms successfully.

(5) The architecture of a digital signal processor is optimized specifically for digital signal processing.

(6) Digital signal processing is a technique that converts signals from real world sources (usually in analog form) into digital data that can then be analyzed.

(7) Eventually, when the DSP has finished its work, the digital data can be turned back into an analog signal, with improved quality.

(8) This process must be handled in real-time—which is often very quickly.

(9) Because different applications have varying ranges of frequencies, different DSPs are required.

(10) DSPs are classified by their dynamic range, the spread of numbers that must be processed in the course of an application.

4. Translate the following paragraphs into Chinese.

(1) First, let's look at how the instruction cache improves the performance of the Harvard architecture. A handicap of the basic Harvard design is that the data memory bus is busier than the program memory bus. When two numbers are multiplied, two binary values (the numbers) must be passed over the data memory bus, while only one binary value (the program instruction) is passed over the program memory bus. To improve upon this situation, we start by relocating part of the "data" to program memory.

(2) For instance, we might place the filter coefficients in program memory, while keeping the input signal in data memory. (This relocated data is called "secondary data" in the illustration). At first glance, this doesn't seem to help the situation; now we must transfer one value over the data memory bus (the input signal sample), but two values over the program memory bus (the program instruction and the coefficient). In fact, if we were executing random instructions, this situation would be no better at all.

Text B

Architecture of the Digital Signal Processor[1]

DSP algorithms generally spend most of their execution time in loops. This means that the same set of program instructions will continually pass from program memory to the CPU. The super Harvard architecture [2] takes advantage of this situation by including an instruction cache in the CPU. This is a small memory that contains about 32 of the most recent program instructions. The first time through a loop, the program instructions must be passed over the program memory bus[3]. This results in slower operation because of the conflict with the coefficients that must also be fetched along this path. However, on additional execution of the loop, the program instructions can be pulled from the instruction cache. This means that all of the memory to CPU information transfers can be accomplished in a single cycle: the sample from the input signal comes over the data memory bus, the coefficient comes over the program memory bus, and the program instruction comes from the instruction cache. In the jargon of the field, this efficient transfer of data is called a high memory-access bandwidth.

Fig. 5-1 presents a more detailed view of the SHARC architecture, showing the I/O controller connected to data memory. This is how the signals enter and exit the system. For instance, the SHARC DSPs provide both serial and parallel communications ports. These are extremely high speed connections. For example, at a 40 MHz clock speed, there are two serial ports that operate at 40 Mbit/s each, while six parallel ports each provides a

40 Mbyte/s data transfer. When all six parallel ports are used together, the data transfer rate is an incredible 240 Mbyte/s.

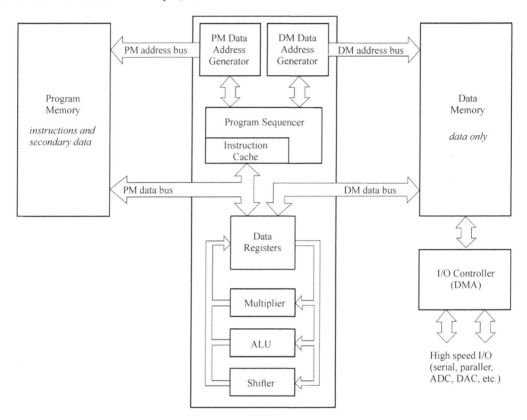

Fig. 5-1　Typical DSP Architecture

This type of high speed I/O is a key characteristic of DSPs. The overriding goal is to move the data in, perform the math, and move the data out before the next sample is available. Everything else is secondary. Some DSPs have on-board analog-to-digital and digital-to-analog converters, a feature called mixed signal. However, all DSPs can interface with external converters through serial or parallel ports.

Now let's look inside the CPU. At the top of the diagram are two blocks labeled data address generator (DAG), one for each of the two memories.[4] These control the addresses sent to the program and data memories, specifying where the information is to be read from or written to. In simpler microprocessors, this task is handled as an inherent part of the program sequencer, and is quite transparent to the programmer. However, DSPs are designed to operate with circular buffers, and benefit from the extra hardware to manage them efficiently. This avoids needing to use precious CPU clock cycles to keep track of how the data are stored. For instance, in the SHARC DSPs, each of the two DAGs can control eight circular buffers. This means that each DAG holds 32 variables (4 per buffer), plus the required logic.

The math processing is broken into three sections, a multiplier, an arithmetic logic unit (ALU), and a barrel shifter. The multiplier takes the values from two registers, multiplies them, and places the result into another register. The ALU performs addition, subtraction, absolute value, logical operations (AND, OR, XOR, NOT[5]), conversion between fixed and floating point formats, and similar functions. Elementary binary operations are carried out by the barrel shifter, such as shifting, rotating, extracting, depositing segments, and so on. A powerful feature of the SHARC family is that the multiplier and the ALU can be accessed in parallel. In a single clock cycle, data from registers 0~7 can be passed to the multiplier, data from registers 8~15 can be passed to the ALU, and the two results returned to any of the 16 registers.

Words and Expressions

cache [kæʃ] n. 隐藏所，藏身处 [计]高速缓冲存储器 v. 隐藏，贮藏；缓存
conflict ['kɔnflikt] n. 冲突，矛盾；战斗，斗争 v. 冲突；抵触；争执
coefficient [ˌkəui'fiʃənt] n. 系数
fetch [fetʃ] v. 取来；卖得 n. 取得 v. 到达；绕道；转航
transfer [træns'fə:] v. 转移；调任；转乘 n. 迁移，移动；换车；汇兑
jargon ['dʒɑ:gən] n. 行话 v. 说行话
bandwidth ['bændwidθ] n. 频带宽度，通带宽度
overriding [ˌəuvə'raidiŋ] adj. 最主要的
sample ['sæmpl] v. 采样，取样 adj. 样例的 n. 样品，样本
serial ['siəriəl] n. 连载小说，连续剧；序列；串行接口 adj. 连续的，一系列的
parallel ['pærəlel] n. 并行接口；平行线(面) adj. 平行的；并联的 v. 相比；与……平行
generator ['dʒenəreitə] n. 发电机；发生器
specify ['spesifai] v. 详细说明，指定，阐述
transparent [træns'perənt] adj. 透明的；明显的；清晰的
variable ['veəriəbl] adj. 可变的，易变的 n. 变量；易变的东西
register ['redʒistə] n. 暂存器；登记簿；记录 v. 登记，记录；注册，挂号
elementary [ˌelə'mentəri] adj. 基本的，初级的；元素的
shifter [ʃiftə] n. 移动装置，移相器，变速拨叉，印字换行器；搬移者
deposit [di'pɔzit] v. 放置；(使)沉淀；存储；付(订金等)；寄存
segment ['segmənt] n. 部分；弓形；瓣；段，节 v. 分割

Notes

[1] 文章来源 *The Scientist and Engineer's Guide to Digital Signal Processing* By Steven W. Smith, Ph.D. Chapter 28—"Digital Signal Processors / Architecture of the Digital Signal Processor"。

[2] The super Harvard architecture 超级哈佛结构，缩写为 SHARC，它在哈佛结构上增加了指令 cache（缓存）和专用的 I/O 控制器。

[3] Bus,总线,是计算机各种功能部件之间传送信息的公共通信干线,它是由导线组成的传输线束的按照计算机所传输的信息种类,计算机的总线可以划分为数据总线、地址总线和控制总线,分别用来传输数据、数据地址和控制信号。

[4] At the top of the diagram are two blocks labeled data address generator (DAG), one for each of the two memories.

此句可译为:在图的上方是两个标记为数据地址发生器(DAG)的方块,一个(方块)代表两个存储器之一。

One 指的是 two blocks 中的一个,for 这里翻译为"代表",做介词。

[5] AND, OR, XOR, NOT 译为"与、或、异或、非",属于逻辑运算,又称布尔运算,20世纪30年代,逻辑代数在电路系统上获得应用。随后,由于电子技术与计算机的发展,出现各种复杂的大系统,它们的变换规律也遵守布尔所揭示的规律。

Exercises

Mark the following statements with T (true) or F (false) according to the text.

(1) The instruction cache contains about 32 of the most recent program instructions. ( )

(2) In the SHARC architecture, all the program instructions must be passed over the program memory bus. ( )

(3) The super Harvard architecture includs the I/O controller connected to data memory. ( )

(4) Serial and parallel communications ports are extremely high speed connections. ( )

(5) Analog-to-digital and digital-to-analog converters are the fixed feature of all DSPs. ( )

(6) Some DSPs have only one of two data address generators. ( )

(7) The CPU clock cycles are saved by the circular buffers of DSPs. ( )

(8) In DSPs multiplication is performed by using three different registers. ( )

(9) Logical operations is performed by barrel shifter. ( )

(10) The multiplier and the ALU can be accessed in parallel in the SHARC architecture. ( )

Translating Skill 5

专业术语翻译

电子信息类术语专业性很强,有些词看上去很长,其词意却往往只限定于电子信息专业或其中一种业务,词意单一。例如:

flip-flop   触发器

superheterodyne	超外差式
hexadecimal	十六进制
quadraphonics	四声道立体声

这类词使用面窄,出现频率不高,其翻译一般可采用以下 4 种方法。

1. 意译

这是电信术语的主要翻译方法,可使翻译词的词义一目了然,读者不必再做解释便能理解其确切含义,例如:

loudspeaker	扬声器
payload	有效负载
dataplex	数据多路复用
waveguide	波导

掌握词缀意义对术语翻译很有帮助,例如:

underwater	水下
transconductance	跨导
superconductor	超导体
microelectronics	微电子学

2. 音译

不便意译时可采用音译或音意结合的翻译方法。

以下一些情况可音译。

(1) 计量单位

ohm	欧姆(电阻单位)
hertz	赫兹(频率单位)
bit	比特(二进制信息单位)
baud	波特(发报速率)
maxwell	麦克斯韦(磁通量单位)

(2) 新发明或新材料

quark	夸克(基本粒子)
darlington	达林顿(复合晶体管)
mavar	脉伐(可变电抗混频放大器)

(3) 原文较长的首字母或主要音节缩写词

radar	雷达
sonar	声纳
nylon	尼龙

(4) 人名,地名

音意结合的方法,例如:

Zener diode	齐纳二级管
Kelvin bridge	开耳芬电桥
logic circuit	逻辑电路

有些电子信息术语兼有音、意两种翻译方法,例如:

maser	脉测、量子放大器
laser	莱塞、激光
engine	引擎、发动机

3. 形(象)译

英语字母表示事物外形时多用此方法,例如:

T-quadripole	T 形四端网络
Q band	Q 波段
P-N-P junction	P-N-P 结
impatt diode	impatt 二极管

也有不必翻译出来的,例如:

IBMPC/XT	(一种 16 位微机)
Z80 PIO	(一种并行接口芯片)

Exercises to Translating Skill

Translate the following words into Chinese

(1) acoustooptic modulator (11) software
(2) bandwidth compression (12) hardware
(3) backfire antenna (13) flexitime
(4) blockwiring cable (14) framework ground
(5) broadcasting-satellite (15) halfwave
(6) changeback code (16) hookswitch communication
(7) crosspoint (17) keyboard transmitter
(8) datafile (18) lightwave communication
(9) echoplex (19) manhole form
(10) feedback oscillator (20) network architecture

Unit 6　Power Supply

Power supply is a reference to a source of electrical power. A device or system that supplies electrical or other types of energy to an output load or group of loads is called a power supply unit or PSU. The term is most commonly applied to electrical energy supplies, less often to mechanical ones, and rarely to others.

供电系统是指提供电能的电源。向一个或一组负载提供电力或其他能源的设备或系统称为能源供给单元或 PSU。这个术语最常用在供电领域,较少用在机械领域,很少用在其他领域。

Text A

Power Supply

A power supply is a device that produces electricity for use by electronic equipment, or that converts the electricity from the utility mains to a form suitable for use by electronic equipment.[1] Power supplies generally consist either of batteries or of transformer/rectifier/filter circuits. A generator or set of photovoltaic cells may also be used as a power supply.

A direct-current power supply is rated according to its voltage output, its current-delivering capacity, and its ability to maintain a constant voltage under varying load conditions. All of these parameters must be considered when choosing a power supply for use with a given piece of electronic apparatus.[2] The voltage must be correct; the supply must be able to deliver the necessary current; the voltage must remain within a certain range as the load impedance or resistance changes. There is no need, however, to use a supply of much greater precision than required.[3] It would be inefficient, for example, to use a 20 A power supply with a circuit that draws only 10 mA.

Power supply voltage can be as small as 1 V or less, or as large as hundreds of thousands of volts. The current delivering capacity may be just a few milliamperes, or it might be hundreds of amperes. The ability of a power supply to maintain a nearly constant voltage is called the regulation, while in other situations the regulation need not be precise.

Some electronic devices have built-in power supplies. Most receivers, tape recorders, hi-fi amplifiers, and other consumer apparatus have built-in power supplies tailored to the requirements of the current.[4] Some equipment, however, requires an external power supply. A wide variety of commercially manufactured power supplies are available for different specialized uses.

A power supply designed to produce direct current, with alternating current input, must incorporate a transformer, a rectifier, a filter, and perhaps a regulator circuit. The transformer converts the utility voltage to the proper voltage for the equipment in use. The rectifier converts the alternating current to pulsating direct current. The filter converts the pulsating direct current to more or less pure direct current.[5]

Words and Expressions

source [sɔ:s] n. 来源；根源；[计]原始码
rarely ['reəli] adv. 很少，难得
produce [prə'dju:s] n. 产品；农产品 v. 生产，制造；产生
convert [kən'və:t] v. 倒置；兑换；转变
utility [ju:'tiləti] n. 公用程序；实用，实用品
main [mein] n. [pl.]（电力等的）干线；电力网；电源
consist [kən'sist] v. 组成，构成；存在于
transformer [træns'fɔ:mə] n. 变压器
rectifier ['rektifaiə(r)] n. 整流器；矫正器
generator ['dʒenəreitə(r)] n. 生产者；发电机
according to 根据，按照；取决于
output ['autput] n. 输出；生产
maintain [mein'tein] v. 维持，保持；维修，保养
apparatus [ˌæpə'reitəs] n. 仪器，器械；设备，装置
deliver [di'livə] v. 递送；投递；传送；送货
impedance [im'pi:dəns] n. 阻抗
precision [pri'siʒn] n. 精密；精确度，精确
inefficient [ˌini'fiʃnt] adj. 无效率的，无能的
regulation [ˌregju'leiʃn] n. 规章，条例；规则
built-in 嵌入的；嵌装的；固定的
hi-fi amplifier [电]高保真度放大器
consumer [kən'sju:mə] n. 消费者
tailor ['teilə(r)] v. 裁制；使合适；匹配
manufacture [ˌmænju'fæktʃə] n. 制造；产品；制造业 v. 制造，加工
specialized ['speʃəlaizd] adj. 专门的，特别的，专用的
incorporate [in'kɔ:pəreit] v. 包含,合并 adj. 合并的，一体化的
regulator ['regjəleitə(r) /-jul-] n. 调整者；调节器；管理者；调节阀
regulator circuit 调整电路
pulsating direct current [电]脉动直流电

Notes

[1] A power supply is a device that produces electricity for use by electronic equipment, or that converts the electricity from the utility mains to a form suitable for use by electronic equipment.

此句可译为:电源是一种生产电供电子装备使用的装置,或者是一种将公用电源转换成适用于电子装备形式的装置。

or 后面省略了 a device,that 引导其定语从句;

suitable for use by electronic equipment 为形容词短语做后置定语修饰 form。

[2] All of these parameters must be considered when choosing a power supply for use with a given piece of electronic apparatus.

此句可译为:在选择一种电源用于一件特定的电子仪器时这些参数都必须考虑到。

"when choosing a power supply for use"做时间状语,相当于"when we choose a power supply for use";"a given piece of electronic apparatus" 中 given 意指"指定",在句中做定语。

[3] There is no need, however, to use a supply of much greater precision than required.

此句可译为:然而无需使用比需要精确得多的电源。

of much greater precision than required 比需要精确得多的。

[4] Most receivers, tape recorders, hi-fi amplifiers, and other consumer apparatus have built-in power supplies tailored to the requirements of the current.

此句可译为:大部分无线电接收机、磁带录音机、高保真度放大器及其他用户电器都有适合于电流要求的内装电源。

tailored to the requirements of the current 过去分词短语做后置定语修饰 power supplies,可译为使适合于电流的要求。

[5] The filter converts the pulsating direct current to more or less pure direct current.

此句可译为:滤波器把脉动直流电转换成几乎是纯直流电。

convert…to… 把……转换成……;more or less 多多少少,几乎。

Exercises

1. Put the following phrases into English.

(1) 公用电源
(2) 供电量
(3) 不定负载条件下保持稳压
(4) 特定的电子仪器
(5) 使用比需要精确得多的电源
(6) 保持在一定范围内
(7) 内装电源

(8) 适合于电流要求

(9) 商用电源

(10) 脉动直流电

2. Put the following phrases into Chinese.

(1) more or less pure direct current

(2) regulator circuit

(3) alternating current input

(4) hi-fi amplifier

(5) other consumer apparatus

(6) voltage output

(7) external power supply

(8) different specialized uses

(9) maintain a nearly constant voltage

(10) power supply

3. Translate the following sentences into Chinese.

(1) A power supply is a device that produces electricity for use by electronic equipment.

(2) Power supplies generally consist either of batteries or of transformer/rectifier/filter circuits.

(3) A generator or set of photovoltaic cells may also be used as a power supply.

(4) All of these parameters must be considered when choosing a power supply for use with a given piece of electronic apparatus.

(5) There is no need, however, to use a supply of much greater precision than required.

(6) Power supply voltage can be as small as 1 V or less, or as large as hundreds of thousands of volts.

(7) The ability of a power supply to maintain a nearly constant voltage is called the regulation.

(8) Some electronic devices have built-in power supplies.

(9) Some equipment, however, requires an external power supply.

(10) The filter converts the pulsating direct current to more or less pure direct current.

4. Translate the following paragraphs into Chinese.

(1) Some electronic devices have built-in power supplies. Most receivers, tape recorders, hi-fi amplifiers, and other consumer apparatus have built-in power supplies tailored to the requirements of the current. Some equipment, however, requires an external power supply. A wide variety of commercially manufactured power supplies are available for different specialized uses.

(2) A power supply designed to produce direct current, with alternating current input, must incorporate a transformer, a rectifier, a filter, and perhaps a regulator circuit. The transformer converts the utility voltage to the proper voltage for the equipment in use. The rectifier converts the alternating current to pulsating direct current. The filter converts the pulsating direct current to more or less pure direct current.

Text B

Types of Power Supply

There are many types of power supply. Most are designed to convert high voltage AC mains electricity to a suitable low voltage supply for electronics circuits and other devices. A power supply can be broken down into a series of blocks, each of which performs a particular function.[1]

For example, a 5 V regulated supply is shown in Fig. 6-1.

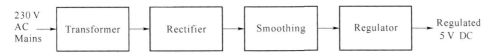

Fig. 6-1 Block Diagram of a Regulated Power Supply System

Each of the blocks is described in more detail below:

(1) Transformer—steps down high voltage AC mains to low voltage AC.

(2) Rectifier—converts AC to DC, but the DC output is varying.

(3) Smoothing—smoothes the DC from varying greatly to a small ripple.

(4) Regulator—eliminates ripple by setting DC output to a fixed voltage.

Dual supplies

Some electronic circuits require a power supply with positive and negative outputs as well as zero volt (0 V).[2] This is called a "dual supply" because it is like two ordinary supplies connected together.

Dual supplies have three outputs. For example, a ± 9 V supply has + 9 V, 0 V and − 9 V outputs.

Rectifier

There are several ways of connecting diodes to make a rectifier to convert AC to DC.[3] The bridge rectifier is the most important and it produces full-wave varying DC. A single diode can be used as a rectifier but it only uses the positive (+) parts of the AC wave to produce half-wave varying DC.

Smoothing

Smoothing is performed by a large value electrolytic capacitor connected across the DC supply to act as a reservoir, supplying current to the output when the varying DC voltage from the rectifier is falling.[4] The Fig. 6-2 shows the unsmoothed varying DC (dotted line) and the smoothed DC (solid line). The capacitor charges quickly near the peak of the varying DC, and then discharges as it supplies current to the output.

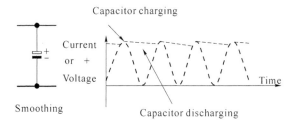

Fig. 6-2 The Unsmoothed Varying DC (dotted line) and the smoothed DC (solid line)

Note that smoothing significantly increases the average DC voltage to almost the peak value. Smoothing is not perfect due to the capacitor voltage falling a little as it discharges, giving a small ripple voltage.

Regulator

Voltage regulator ICs are available with fixed (typically 5 V, 12 V and 15 V) or variable output voltages (Fig. 6-3). They are also rated by the maximum current they can pass. Negative voltage regulators are available, mainly for use in dual supplies. Most regulators include some automatic protection from excessive current ("overload protection") and overheating ("thermal protection").[5]

Fig. 6-3 Voltage Regulator

Words and Expressions

type [taip] *n.* 类型；模范；典型

suitable ['su:təbl] *adj.* 适当的，适宜的，合适的

block [blɔk] n. 街区；石块，木块；厚块；障碍物 v. 阻塞，使成块状；封锁
regulated [科] 已调整的
step down 辞职；退休；降低（电流的）电压
eliminate [i'limineit] v. 除去，剔除；排除
ripple ['ripl] n. 细浪；波浪式；波纹 v. 呈波状；梳
dual supply 双电源
bridge rectifier [电] 桥式整流器
full-wave [电] 全波放大器
half-wave [电] 半波
electrolytic [iˌlektrə'litik] adj. 电解的；电解液的
reservoir ['rezəvwɑː] n. 蓄水库；贮存器；储藏所，仓库
unsmoothed [科] 不光滑的
dotted line 点线，虚线
solid line 实线
peak [piːk] n. 山峰；高峰，最高点 v. 使成峰状；达到高峰
due to 因为，由于
voltage regulator [电] 稳压器，调压器
variable ['veəriəbl] n. 变数；可变物 adj. 可变的，易变的；不定的
automatic protection [安] 自动保护
excessive current [电] 过量电流
overload protection [电] 过载保护
thermal protection [电] 热保护

Notes

[1] A power supply can be broken down into a series of blocks, each of which performs a particular function.

此句可译为：电源由一系列的部件组成，每个执行一种特定的功能。

句中 each of which 引导非限制性定语从句。

[2] Some electronic circuits require a power supply with positive and negative outputs as well as zero volt (0 V).

此句可译为：一些电子电路需要带有正、负和零输出电源电压。

as well as 起连接作用；positive and negative outputs 译为正、负输出电源电压。

[3] There are several ways of connecting diodes to make a rectifier to convert AC to DC.

此句可译为：有几种连接二极管组成整流器把交流电变为直流电的方法。

句中两个不定式短语 to make a rectifier 和 to convert AC to DC 分别用作定语和目的状语。

[4] Smoothing is performed by a large value electrolytic capacitor connected across the DC supply to act as a reservoir, supplying current to the output when the varying DC

voltage from the rectifier is falling.

此句可译为:滤波由并联在直流电源端的大电解电容执行,大电解电容可作为储存器。当从整流器输出的变化的直流电压下降时,电容给输出端供电。

句中 connected across the DC supply 为过去分词短语,用作定语,修饰 electrolytic capacitor;to act as a reservoir 在句中做目的状语;when 引导时间状语从句。

[5] Most regulators include some automatic protection from excessive current ("overload protection") and overheating ("thermal protection").

此句可译为:绝大多数的稳压器含有过流("过载")、过热自动保护。

此句为主谓宾结构的简单句,automatic protection 译为自动保护。

Exercises

Mark the following statements with T (true) or F (false) according to the text.

(1) Most types of power supply are designed to convert high voltage AC mains electricity to a suitable low voltage supply for electronics circuits and other devices. ( )

(2) A power supply can be broken down into a series of blocks, each of which performs a particular function. ( )

(3) A regulator steps down high voltage AC mains to low voltage AC. ( )

(4) The transformer eliminates ripple by setting DC output to a fixed voltage. ( )

(5) Some electronic circuits require a power supply with positive and negative outputs as well as zero volt (0 V). ( )

(6) Dual supplies have two outputs. ( )

(7) The bridge rectifier produces full-wave varying DC. ( )

(8) A single diode cannot be used as a rectifier and it only uses the negative (−) parts of the AC wave to produce half-wave varying DC. ( )

(9) Smoothing is performed by a large value electrolytic capacitor connected across the DC supply to act as a reservoir. ( )

(10) Most regulators include some automatic protection from excessive current ("overload protection") and overheating ("thermal protection"). ( )

Translating Skill 6

新词的翻译

在阅读和翻译新近出版的电子信息刊物上的文章或新技术资料时,常会碰到一些工具书上也难以查到的一些词语,往往使阅读和翻译中断。这些词语就可能是新词语。

所谓新词语,仅相对而言,指近期出现在英美出版物上而尚未收入工具书的词语。由于电信技术发展迅速,使新词语产生的机会增加。如一种新技术或新产品研制成功后,就可能随之出现一个新词语来代表。新词语自然是文章作者或编者根据技术需要而编造出来的,但其中绝大部分并非凭空想象,而是建立在原有语言的基础上,经加工提炼而成。摸清新词语的来龙去脉对确切的翻译有很大的帮助。电信新词语大概有以下几种来源。

1. 老词新义

把普通英语词汇用于电信业务并赋予其特定技术意义。新、老词意之间既有关系,又有很大的区别。如 20 世纪 80 年代以来兴起的移动通信技术就出现了若干常用的普通英语词汇。这些原本不常用的词语一旦有了新意,就会频频出现。

如 cellular 一词,查"Webster's Dictionary,是 cell 的形容词,有"蜂窝状"、"分格式"之意,但现在由于蜂窝式移动电话成为移动电话的主要形式,因此在电信业务中几乎成为"移动电话"的代名词,有时 cellular 即可翻译为移动电话,其所组成的短语也可照此翻译,例如:

cellular industry	移动电话工业
cellular service	移动电话业务
cellular system	移动电话系统
cellular equipment	移动电话装备

2. 从专有名词转化而来

有些词语原本是一个商标名、产品名、公司名或新技术名称,属专有名词,经一段时间的使用后脱离原依附物而成为新词语,其转化标志是大写或首字母大写变成小写。如 wordprocessing 原是国际商用机器公司 60 年代末的一个技术商标,到 80 年代初逐步与原商标脱离而成为一个独立的新词语,翻译为"字码处理"。又如 view data,原是英国可视数据的商标,现在还是商标,但也可作为新词语使用,翻译为"用户电视数据"。

3. 合成

合成新词语最为常见,可细分为 3 类。

（1）原词合成

voiceband	话音带
datatelephone	数据电话
audioteleconference	音频电视电话会议

（2）部分缩略

datacomm (data communication)	数据通信
carphone (car telephone)	汽车电话
teletraffic (telecommunication traffic)	电信业务

（3）全缩略（类似缩略词,但作为词使用）

infor (information)	信息
datel (data telex)	数据用户电报
domsat (domestic satellite)	国内卫星

新词语的翻译可从以下几条线索着手。

（1）从新词语出现的上下文猜测其词意范围。

（2）从新词语的出处及其原意推测其新的技术意义。

(3) 综合分析组成新词语的各部分而得出新意。

Exercises to Translating Skill

Translate the following expressions into Chinese.

(1) active relay station
(2) assignment selector
(3) called subscriber release
(4) dial exchange area
(5) duplex voice channel
(6) engaged signal
(7) exchange trunk carrier
(8) free line signal
(9) full period service
(10) group calling
(11) hand set
(12) head phone
(13) heavy traffic period
(14) idle frequency
(15) incoming unit
(16) line busy
(17) loop transmission
(18) multiple line
(19) overhead earth wire
(20) packet-switched network

Unit 7 Synchronous Digital Hierarchy

SDH is a standard technology for synchronous data transmission on fiber optic cables. It is the international equivalent of synchronous optical network. Both technologies provide faster and less expensive network interconnection than traditional PDH (plesiochronous digital hierarchy) equipment.

同步数字序列(SDH)是一种通过光缆进行同步数据传输的标准技术,相当于国际标准的同步光网络(SONET)。与传统的准同步数字序列(PDH)设备相比,SDH 与 SONET 可以提供速度更快、成本更低的网络互连。

Text A

Synchronous Digital Hierarchy

Since their emergence from standards bodies around 1990, synchronous digital hierarchy (SDH) and its variant, synchronous optical network (SONET), have helped revolutionize the performance and cost of telecommunications networks based on optical fibers.

SDH has provided transmission networks with a vendor-independent and sophisticated signal structure that has a rich feature set. This has resulted in new network application, the deployment of new equipment in new network topologies, and management by operations system of much greater power than previously seen in transmission network.[1]

The multiplexing technique allowed for the combining of slightly nonsynchronous rates, referred to as plesiochronous, which lead to the term plesiochronous digital hierarchy (PDH).[2]

The definition of SDH and SONET refer to a group of fiber-optic transmission rates that can transport digital signals with different capacities. It was widely accepted that the new multiplexing method should be synchronous and based not on bit interleaving as was the PDH, but on byte interleaving, as are the multiplexing structures from 64 kbit/s to the primary rates of 1,544 kbit/s (1.5 Mbit/s) and 2,048 kbit/s (2 Mbit/s).[3]

The new standard appeared first as SONET, drafted by Bellcore in the United States, and then went through revisions before it emerged in a new form compatible with the international SDH[4]. Both SDH and SONET emerged between 1988 and 1992.

SONET is an ANSI standard; it can carry as payloads the North American PDH hierarchy of bit rates: 1.5/6/45 Mbit/s, plus 2 Mbit/s (known in the United States as

E-1). SDH embraces most of SONET and is an international standard.

SDH is (a) a network node interface (NNI) defined by CCITT/ITU-TS for worldwide use and partly compatible with SONET; and (b) one of two options for the user-network interface (UNI) (i.e., the customer connection), and formally the U reference-point for support of BISDN.

The original SDH standard defined the transport of 1.5/2/6/34/45/140 Mbit/s within a transmission rate of 155.52 Mbit/s and is being developed to carry other types of traffic, such as asynchronous transfer mode (ATM) and Internet protocol (IP), with rates that are integer multiples of 155.52 Mbit/s. The basic unit of transmission in SONET is at 51.84 Mbit/s, but in order to carry 140 Mbit/s, SDH is based on three times as this, i.e., 155.52 Mbit/s (155 Mbit/s).

Through an appropriate choice of options, a subset of SDH is compatible with a subset of SONET, and therefore, traffic interworking is possible. Interworking for alarms and performance management is generally not possible between SDH and SONET systems. It is only possible in a few cases for some features between vendors of SDH and slightly more between vendors of SONET.

Although SONET and SDH were conceived originally for optical fiber transmission, SDH radio system exist at rates compatible with both SONET and SDH.

Almost all new fiber-transmission systems now being installed in public networks use SDH or SONET. They are expected to dominate transmission for decades to come, just as their predecessor PDH has dominated transmission for more than 20 years. Bit rates in long-haul systems are expected to rise to 40 Gbit/s soon after the year of 2005, at the same time as systems of 155 Mbit/s and below penetrate more deeply into access network.

Words and Expressions

synchronous ['siŋkrənəs] *adj.* 同时发生的, 同步的
hierarchy ['haiərɑːki] *n.* 等级制度; 统治集团, 领导层
variant ['veəriənt] *n.* 变种 *adj.* 不同的
revolutionize [ˌrevə'luːʃənaiz] *v.* 宣传革命; 大事改革
fiber ['faibə] *n.* 纤维(物质)
sophisticated [sə'fistikeitid] *adj.* 老练的; 精密的, 尖端的
topology [tə'pɔlədʒi] *n.* 拓扑, 布局; 拓扑结构
plesiochronous *adj.* 准同步的
interleave [ˌintə(ː)'liːv] *v.* 交错, 间隔
draft [drɑːft] *v.* 起草; 征募
compatible [kəm'pætəbəl] *adj.* 兼容的; 能和睦相处, 合得来的
payload ['peiˌləud] *n.* 有效负载
embrace [im'breis] *v.* 拥抱; 包括; 包围, 环绕
interface ['intə(ː)feis] *n.* 接口; 界面; 交接处

asynchronous [ei'siŋkrənəs] adj. 异步的
integer ['intidʒə] n. 完整的事物；整体；整数
subset ['sʌbset] n. 子集，子系统
interworking ['intə'wə:kiŋ] n. 交互工作
conceive [kən'si:v] v. 构想出，设想
install [in'stɔ:l] v. 安装，安置
dominate ['dɔmineit] v. 占首要地位；支配；俯视；拥有优势
predecessor ['pri:disesə] n. 前任，前辈；原有事物，前身
long-haul [lɔŋ'hɔ:l] adj. 长途的
penetrate ['penitreit] v. 透（渗）入；刺入，刺穿；洞察，了解

Notes

[1] This has resulted in new network application, the deployment of new equipment in new network topologies, and management by operations system of much greater power than previously seen in transmission network.

此句可译为：结果产生了新的网络应用，在新的网络拓扑结构中使用了新的设备，运营系统管理比以前我们在传输网络中看到的更加强大。

本句中 network application, the deployment 与 management by operations system 是并列宾语。

[2] The multiplexing technique allowed for the combining of slightly nonsynchronous rates, referred to as plesiochronous, which lead to the term plesiochronous digital hierarchy (PDH).

此句可译为：多路复用技术允许综合稍不同步的速率，被称为准同步，由此产生了准同步数字序列（PDH）。

本句中 referred to as plesiochronous 做后置定语，修饰前面的 slightly nonsynchronous rates。which 引导一个非限定性定语从句，which 指代整个主句。因这个非限定性定语从句和主句存在着因果关系，因此可以将其翻译成一个表示结果的句子。

[3] It was widely accepted that the new multiplexing method should be synchronous and based not on bit interleaving as was the PDH, but on byte interleaving, as are the multiplexing structures from 64 kbit/s to the primary rates of 1,544 kbit/s (1.5 Mbit/s) and 2,048 kbit/s (2 Mbit/s).

此句可译为：这种新的复用方法应该是同步的，并非像 PDH 那样基于位间隔，而是基于字间隔，如同由 64 kbit/s 到主速率 1,544 kbit/s (1.5 Mbit/s) 和 2,048 kbit/s (2 Mbit/s) 的复用结构那样。这一点已被人们广泛接受。

本句是一个多重主从复合句。that 至句末为主语从句，做主句的主语。在主语从句中，be synchronous 与 (be) based not on… but on… 为并列成分做从句谓语的一部分。主语从句中的两个 as 引导的从句都做状语，表示方式。

[4] The new standard appeared first as SONET, drafted by Bellcore in the United States, and then went through revisions before it emerged in a new form compatible with

the international SDH.

此句可译为:SDH 新标准起初出现在 SONET 系统,由美国的 Bellcore 起草,随后经历了多次修改,才以新的面貌出现,并与国际 SDH 兼容。

本句是个主从复合句。主句的主语是 the new standard,谓语是被 drafted by Bellcore in the United States 割裂开的两个并列成分:appeared 和 went through。

Exercises

1. Put the following phrases into English.

(1) 网络拓扑结构

(2) 位间隔

(3) 主速率

(4) 位速率

(5) 互联网协议

(6) 长途电话系统

(7) 网络节点接口

(8) 用户网络接口

(9) U 参考点接口

(10) 业务交互工作

2. Put the following phrases into Chinese.

(1) synchronous digital hierarchy

(2) synchronous optical network

(3) the sophisticated signal structure

(4) management by operations system

(5) multiplexing technique

(6) the combining of slightly nonsynchronous rates

(7) plesiochronous digital hierarchy

(8) asynchronous transfer mode

(9) the basic unit of transmission

(10) fiber-optic transmission rate

3. Translate the following sentences into Chinese.

(1) SDH has provided transmission networks with a vendor-independent and sophisticated signal structure that has a rich feature set.

(2) The definition of SDH and SONET refer to a group of fiber-optic transmission rates that can transport digital signals with different capacities.

(3) SDH embraces most of SONET and is an international standard.

(4) The basic unit of transmission in SONET is at 51.84 Mbit/s, but in order to carry 140 Mbit/s, SDH is based on three times as this, i.e., 155.52 Mbit/s(155 Mbit/s).

(5) Through an appropriate choice of options, a subset of SDH is compatible with a

subset of SONET, and therefore, traffic interworking is possible.

(6) Interworking for alarms and performance management is generally not possible between SDH and SONET systems.

(7) Although SONET and SDH were conceived originally for optical fiber transmission, SDH radio system exist at rates compatible with both SONET and SDH.

(8) Almost all new fiber-transmission systems now being installed in public networks use SDH or SONET.

(9) They are expected to dominate transmission for decades to come, just as their predecessor PDH has dominated transmission for more than 20 years.

(10) Bit rates in long-haul systems are expected to rise to 40 Gbit/s soon after the year of 2005.

4. Translate the following paragraphs into Chinese.

(1) SDH defines traffic interface that are independent of vendors. At 155 Mbit/s they are defined for both optical and copper interfaces and at higher rates for optical ones only. These higher rates are defined as integer multiples of 155.52 Mbit/s in an $n \times 4$ sequence, for example, 622.08 Mbit/s and 2,488.32 Mbit/s (2.5 Gbit/s). To support network growth and the demand for broadband services, multiplexing to even higher rates such as 10 Gbit/s continues in the same way, with upper limits set by technology rather than by lack of standards as was the case with PDH.

(2) Each interface rate contains overheads to support a range of facilities and a payload capacity for traffic. Both the overhead and payload areas can be fully or partially filled. Rates below 155 Mbit/s can be supported by using a 155 Mbit/s interface with only a partially filled payload area. An example of this is a radio system whose spectrum allocation limits it to a capacity less than the full SDH payload, but whose terminal traffic ports are to be connected to 155 Mbit/s ports on a cross-connect. Interfaces are sometimes available at a lower synchronous rate for access application.

Text B

The Architecture of SDH

SDH can be used in all traditional telecommunications application areas. SDH therefore makes it possible for a unified telecommunications network infrastructure to evolve. The fact that SDH provides a single common standard for this telecommunications network, which means that equipment supplied by different manufacturers may be interconnected directly. [1]

Now, let's take a look at the network "building blocks" and how they are configured. These network elements are now all defined in CCITT standards and provide multiplexing or switching functions.

Line terminal multiplexer (LTM): LTM can accept a number of tributary signals and multiplex them to the appropriate optical SDH rate carrier, i.e. STM-1, STM-4 or STM-16. The input tributaries can either be the existing PDH signals such as 2, 34 and 140 Mbit/s or lower rate SDH signals. LTM forms the main gateway from the PDH to the SDH.

Add-drop multiplexer (ADM): a particular type of terminal multiplexer designed to operate in a through mode fashion. Within the ADM it is possible to add channels to, or drop channels from the "through" signal. ADM is generally available at the STM-1 and STM-4 interface rates and may add/drop a variety of tributary signals, i.e. 2, 34 or 140 Mbit/s.

The ADM function is one of the major advantages resulting from the SDH since the similar function within a PDH network, required banks of hardwired back-back terminals.[2]

Synchronous DXC: these devices will form the cornerstone of the new synchronous digital hierarchy. They can function as semi-permanent switches for transmission channels and can switch at any level from 64 kbit/s up to STM-1. Generally such devices have interfaces at STM-1 or STM-4. The DXC can be rapidly reconfigured, under software control, to provide digital leased lines and other services of varying bandwidth.[3]

For clarity, a single frame in the STM-1 can be represented by a 2-dimensional map (Fig. 7-1). The 2-dimensional map comprises 9 rows and 270 columns of boxes. Each box represents a single 8 bit byte within the synchronous signal. Six framing bytes appear in the top left corner of the 2-dimensional map. These framing bytes act as a marker, allowing any byte in the frame to be easily located.[4]

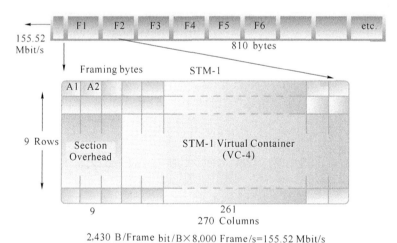

Fig. 7-1 Synchronous Transport Frame for STM-1

The signal bits are transmitted in a sequence starting with those in the first row. The order of transmission is from left to right. After transmission of the last byte in the frame (the byte located in row 9, column 270), the whole sequence repeats starting with the 6 framing bytes of the following frame.

A synchronous transport frame comprises two distinct and readily accessible parts within the frame structure—a virtual container part and a section overhead part. Virtual container (VC) is arranged mainly for user's information to be transmitted through the network, but the section overhead (SOH) provides the facilities required to support and maintain the transportation of a VC between nodes in a synchronous network, such as alarming monitoring, bit-error monitoring and data communication channels.

Words and Expressions

infrastructure ['infrəˌstrʌktʃə] n. 结构，基础设施
interconnect [ˌintə(:)kə'nekt] v. 使互相连接
configure [kən'figə] v. 配置，构成
element ['elimənt] n. 元素；成分[pl.]基础；纲要；原理
define [di'fain] v. 给……下定义，解释；限定，规定
multiplexing ['mʌltiˌpleksiŋ] n. 多路复用
multiplexer ['mʌltiˌpleksə] n. 多路复用器
tributary ['tribjutəri] adj. 支流的 n. 支流
input ['input] n. 输入；投入；输入物（数据）
gateway ['geitˌwei] n. 入口；通道；途径
bank [bæŋk] n. 堆，一堆；一团
cornerstone ['kɔːnəstəun] n. 基石
permanent ['pəːmənənt] adj. 永久(性)的，固定的
clarity ['klæriti] n. 清楚，明晰
frame [freim] n. 镜框；构架 v. 镶框；陷害；制定
dimensional [di'menʃənəl] adj. 空间的
comprise [kəm'praiz] v. 包含，包括，由……组成
column ['kɔləm] n. 柱；纵队；栏
virtual ['vəːtʃuəl] adj. 虚拟的；实质的
facility [fə'siliti] n. [pl.] 设备，设施；便利，容易，方便

Notes

[1] The fact that SDH provides a single common standard for this telecommunications network, which means that equipment supplied by different manufacturers may be interconnected directly.

此句可译为：SDH 为这个网络提供了单一的、通用的标准，这就意味着由不同厂家供应的设备可以直接互连起来。

本句是一个主从复合句。主句的主语为 the fact，其后是引导的同位语从句对其进行修

饰,谓语为 means,宾语为 that 引导的宾语从句。

[2] The ADM function is one of the major advantages resulting from the SDH since the similar function within a PDH network, required banks of hardwired back-back terminals.

此句可译为:ADM 的功能是 SDH 的主要优势之一,因为在 PDH 网络中,完成类似功能需要一套硬布线的背对背的终端设备。

本句中现在分词短语 resulting from the SDH 做后置定语修饰前面的 advantages。

[3] The DXC can be rapidly reconfigured, under software control, to provide digital leased lines and other services of varying bandwidth.

此句可译为:DXC 可以在软件控制下迅速地重构电路,以提供数字租用线路或变带宽的其他业务。

本句中 under software control 可以看成是一个插入成分,做状语说明情况、条件。

[4] These framing bytes act as a marker, allowing any byte in the frame to be easily located.

此句可译为:这些成帧字节起着标志作用,它使帧中的任何字节极易被确定位置。

本句中 allowing any byte in the frame to be easily located 为现在分词短语做状语,表示目的或结果。

Exercises

Mark the following statements with T (true) or F (false) according to the text.

(1) ADM is designed to accept a number of tributary signals and multiplex them to the appropriate optical SDH rate carrier.   (   )

(2) The ADM function doesn't require banks of hardwired back-back terminals.   (   )

(3) Synchronous DXC will form the cornerstone of the new synchronous digital hierarchy.   (   )

(4) The DXC can be rapidly reconfigured under software control.   (   )

(5) ADM forms the main gateway from the PDH to the SDH.   (   )

(6) The input tributaries are exclusively the existing PDH signals such as 2, 34 and 140 Mbit/s or lower rate SDH signals.   (   )

(7) Virtual container part and section overhead part within a synchronous transport frame are readily accessible.   (   )

(8) LTM is designed to operate in a through mode fashion.   (   )

(9) Virtual container (VC) is arranged mainly to transmit user's information through the network.   (   )

(10) The section overhead (SOH) provides the facilities required to support and maintain the transportation of a VC between nodes in a synchronous network.   (   )

Translating Skill 7

缩略词的翻译(一)

翻译电子信息类原文时会碰到许多缩略词语,其中一部分以括弧附以全文解释,翻译不甚费力,例如:

SONET (synchronous optical network)	同步光通信网
STM (synchronous transport module)	同步传送模块
O or M (operation and maintenance)	操作与维护
AM-PM (amplitude modulation-phase modulation)	调幅-调相

但也有相当多的缩略词语在原文中不附解释。在通常情况下,大凡不常用或新缩略词语在一篇材料中首先出现要以括弧附以原文解释,但所谓"不常用"或"新"乃相对于文章的编者或本国读者而言。有些电信文献为节约篇幅,大量使用缩略词语而不附解释。电信产品装备说明书、操作手册及广告册中,缩略词语比比皆是,但几乎无一附全文解释,这给翻译带来诸多不便。有时为了查找印证一个缩略词语要耗费许多时间,结果还不一定如愿。因而,熟悉、掌握破解缩略语的技巧,对提高翻译速度及译文的准确性有很大帮助。

翻译缩略语的关键在于使其恢复全文。全文一经显露,汉译即迎刃而解。掌握缩略词语的缩略规律有助于我们找出其所代表的全文。英语词汇、短语缩略大致有3种方式。

1. 节略(Clopped Words)

lab. (laboratory)	实验室
kilo. (kilogram)	千克
ad. (advertisement)	广告
dir. (directory)	号码簿

2. 缩略(Acronyms)

ROM (read only memory)	只读存储器
Radar (radio detecting and ranging)	雷达
RAM (random access memory)	随机存取存储器
UNESCO (United Nations Educational Scientific and Cultural Organization)	联合国教科文组织

先看一下使用较多的缩略(Acronyms),其构成方式有如下几种。

(1) 首字母缩略

取组成短语各词的第一个字母构成。这种方式最常见。

AC(analog computer)	模拟计算机
EDC(electronic digital computer)	电子数字计算机
PSCE(peripheral storage control element)	外存控制部件
RCDTL(resistor-capacitor diode transistor logic)	阻容二极管晶体管逻辑

(2) 首音节缩略

TABSIM(table simulation)　　　　　　　表模拟
TAPAC(tape-pack)　　　　　　　　　　磁带组
TELCO(telephone company)　　　　　　电话公司
TYPOUT(typewriter output)　　　　　　打字输出
VODACOM（voice data communication）　话音数据通信
MOBULA(model building language)　　　模块构造语言

(3) 首字母音节混合缩略

UNIPOL（universal procedure-oriented language）　面向过程的通用语言
PERCOS（performance coding system）　性能编码系统
MUX-AEEC(multipex-automatic error correction)　多路转换自动差错校正
DEFT(definite time)　　　　　　　　　定义时间

(4) 其他混合

TELEX(teleprinter exchange)　　　　　　电传打字交换机
DATACOMM(data communications)　　　数据通信
TEXFAX(text facsimile)　　　　　　　　电文传真

3. 缩写（Abbreviations）

Fig.（figure）　　　　　　　　　　　　图
Amp.（amplifier）　　　　　　　　　　放大器
O. A.（operational Amplifier）　　　　　运算放大器
MSG.（message）　　　　　　　　　　消息，信息

Exercises to Translating Skill

Translate the following words into Chinese.

(1) AF（audio frequency）

(2) BDD（binary digital data）

(3) CARD（channel allocation and routing data）

(4) DASD（direct access storage device）

(5) LBS（local battery switchboard）

(6) IC（initial circuit）

(7) PAM（pulse amplitude modulation）

(8) ALAMCABCO（all American cable company）

(9) BUTEL（bureau of telecommunications）

(10) INTADIO（inland radiotelegram）

(11) INSAT（international satellite）

(12) PARACHAN（parallel channel）

(13) TELECON（telephone conversation）

(14) CODES (communication detecting system)
(15) DATAC (data analog computer)
(16) INTIP (integrated information processing)
(17) NAVST (navigational satellite)
(18) NUSUM (numerical summary message)
(19) TOPER (toll operator)
(20) VOBANC (voice band compressor)

Unit 8　DWDM

This unit introduces you the concept of DWDM and several main components in a basic DWDM system. You can also find out the important functions of wavelength converting transponders, muxponder and reconfigurable optical add-drop multiplexer.

本单元我们要介绍 DWDM 的概念和一个基本的 DWDM 系统所包含的几个主要部分。你也可以了解波长转换器，复用转发器和可重构光分插复用器的主要功能。

Text A

DWDM[1]

Dense wavelength division multiplexing, or DWDM for short, refers originally to optical signals multiplexed within the 1,550 nm band so as to leverage the capabilities (and cost) of erbium doped fiber amplifiers (EDFAs), which are effective for wavelengths between approximately 1,525~1,565 nm (C band), or 1,570~1,610 nm (L band).[2] EDFAs were originally developed to replace SONET/SDH optical-electrical-optical (OEO) regenerators, which they have made practically obsolete. EDFAs can amplify any optical signal in their operating range, regardless of the modulated bit rate. In terms of multi-wavelength signals, so long as the EDFA has enough pump energy available to it, it can amplify as many optical signals as can be multiplexed into its amplification band[3] (though signal densities are limited by choice of modulation format). EDFAs therefore allow a single-channel optical link to be upgraded in bit rate by replacing only equipment at the ends of the link, while retaining the existing EDFA or series of EDFAs through a long haul route. Furthermore, single-wavelength links using EDFAs can similarly be upgraded to WDM links at reasonable cost.[4] The EDFAs cost is thus leveraged across as many channels as can be multiplexed into the 1,550 nm band.

At this stage, a basic DWDM system contains several main components.

1. A DWDM terminal multiplexer

The terminal multiplexer actually contains one wavelength converting transponder for each wavelength signal it will carry. The wavelength converting transponders receive the input optical signal (i.e., from a client-layer SONET/SDH or other signal), convert that signal into the electrical domain, and retransmit the signal using a 1,550 nm band laser.

2. An intermediate optical terminal, or optical add-drop multiplexer

This is a remote amplification site that amplifies the multi-wavelength signal that may have traversed up to 140 km or more before reaching the remote site. [5]

3. A DWDM terminal demultiplexer

The terminal demultiplexer breaks the multi-wavelength signal back into individual signals and outputs them on separate fibers for client-layer systems (such as SONET/SDH) to detect. [6]

4. Optical supervisory channel (OSC)

This is an additional wavelength usually outside the EDFA amplification band (at 1,510 nm, 1,620 nm, 1,310 nm or another proprietary wavelength). The OSC carries information about the multi-wavelength optical signal as well as remote conditions at the optical terminal or EDFA site. [7] It is also normally used for remote software upgrades and user (ie., network operator) network management information.

DWDM systems have to maintain more stable wavelength or frequency than those needed for CWDM because of the closer spacing of the wavelengths. Precision temperature control of laser transmitter is required in DWDM systems to prevent "drift" off a very narrow frequency window of the order of a few GHz. [8] In addition, since DWDM provides greater maximum capacity it tends to be used at a higher level in the communications hierarchy than CWDM, for example on the Internet backbone and is therefore associated with higher modulation rates, thus creating a smaller market for DWDM devices with very high performance levels. These factors of smaller volume and higher performance result in DWDM systems typically being more expensive than CWDM.

Recent innovations in DWDM transport systems include pluggable and software-tunable transceiver modules capable of operating on 40 or 80 channels. [9] This dramatically reduces the need for discrete spare pluggable modules, when a handful of pluggable devices can handle the full range of wavelengths.

Words and Expressions

optical ['ɔptikəl] *adj.* 眼睛的，视觉的；光学的
multiplex ['mʌltipleks] *adj.* 许多的，多样的；多路通信的 *v.* 多路传输
band [bænd] *n.* 波段；带子；乐队 *v.* 联合，结合
leverage ['li:vəridʒ] *n.* 杠杆作用
erbium ['ə:biəm] *n.* [化]铒(68号元素，符号 Er)
doped [dəupt] *adj.* 掺杂质的
approximately [ə'prɔksimətli] *adv.* 近似地，大约
regenerator [ri'dʒenəreitə] *n.* 更新者；蓄热器；改革者；再生器
obsolete ['ɔbsəli:t] *adj.* 已废弃的，过时的
modulated ['mɔdjuleitid] 已调整(制)的，被调的
pump [pʌmp] *n.* 抽水机，泵；打气筒 *v.* 抽水；打气；抽吸
amplification [,æmplifi'keiʃən] *n.* 增幅；放大(率)，放大倍数(系数)

format ['fɔːmæt] n. 格式，形式，版式；设计 v. 格式化；安排……的格局，安排
upgrade [ˌʌp'greid] v. 使升级，提升；改良品种
retain [ri'tein] v. 保持；保留
terminal ['təːminl] n. 终端机；终点，末端 adj. 终点的；按期的
multiplexer ['mʌltiˌpleksə] n. 多路器，多路传输装置
converting [kən'vəːtiŋ] n. 转换
transponder [træn'spɔndə(r)] n. 异频雷达收发机
client ['klaiənt] n. 顾客，委托人；客户（端）
layer ['leiə] n. 层，分层
domain [dəu'mein] n. 领域；[计] 域
intermediate [ˌintə'miːdjət] adj. 中级的；中间的
traverse ['trævə(ː)s] v. 横过；铭刻
demultiplexer [diː'mʌltipleksə] n. 多路解调器
supervisory [ˌsjuːpə'vaizəri] adj. 管理的，监控的
proprietary [prə'praiətəri] adj. 专利的(所有的) n. 所有权（所有人）
transmitter [trænz'mitə] n. 转送器；传达人
drift [drift] n. 漂移，漂流 v. 漂移，漂流
maximum ['mæksiməm] n. 极点，最大量，极大 adj. 最高的，最大极限的
hierarchy ['haiərɑːki] n. 等级制度；[计] 层级
backbone ['bækbəun] n. 志气；脊椎；网络的骨干，通常要求具有更高的带宽和更高的可靠性
associated [ə'səuʃiˌeitid] adj. 联合的
performance [pə'fɔːməns] n. 表演，表现；性能
innovation [ˌinəu'veiʃən] n. 创新，革新
tunable ['tjuːnəbl] adj. 可合调的，可调音的，音调美的
transceiver [træn'siːvə] n. 收发器，无线电收发机
module ['mɔdjuːl] n. [计] 模块，组件
dramatically [drə'mætikəli] adv. 戏剧地，从戏剧角度；引人注目地，显著地
discrete [dis'kriːt] adj. 不连续的，离散的；[计] 分立元件
spare [speə] n. 剩余；备用零件，备用轮胎 adj. 多余的，备用的；简陋的

Notes

[1] 本文涉及光纤通信领域，题目可译为密集型波分复用（DWDM，dense wavelength division multiplexing）。

[2] Dense wavelength division multiplexing, or DWDM for short, refers originally to optical signals multiplexed within the 1,550 nm band so as to leverage the capabilities (and cost) of erbium doped fiber amplifiers (EDFAs), which are effective for wavelengths between approximately 1,525~1,565 nm (C band), or 1,570~1,610 nm (L band).

此句可译为：密集型波分复用，或缩写为 DWDM，最初是指在 1,550 纳米波段内复用的

光信号,以便能够控制掺铒光纤放大器(缩写为 EDFAs)的容量(和成本),这对于波长约 1,525~1,565 纳米(C 波段)的波,或 1,570~1,610 纳米(L 波段)的波是有效的。

refers to 提及,指;multiplexed within the 1,550 nm band 是过去分词短语做后置定语,修饰 optical signals;which 引导非限定性定语从句。

[3] In terms of multi-wavelength signals, so long as the EDFA has enough pump energy available to it, it can amplify as many optical signals as can be multiplexed into its amplification band.

此句可译为:就多波长信号而言,只要掺铒光纤放大器有足够的泵能量提供给它,它能放大可以复用进其放大带的许多光信号。

In terms of 依照,就……而言;so long as 引导条件状语从句,意为只要。

[4] Furthermore, single-wavelength links using EDFAs can similarly be upgraded to WDM links at reasonable cost.

此句可译为:此外,使用掺铒光纤放大器的单波长连接同样可以以合理的费用升级到 WDM 连接。

using EDFAs 是现在分词短语做后置定语,修饰 single-wavelength links;be upgraded to 是被动语态,意为被升级到。

[5] This is a remote amplification site that amplifies the multi-wavelength signal that may have traversed up to 140 km or more before reaching the remote site.

此句可译为:这是一个远程放大站点,它能放大也许要跨过长达 140 千米或更长距离才能到达远程站点的多波信号。

第一个 that 引导定语从句,修饰先行词 a remote amplification site;第二个 that 也引导定语从句,修饰先行词 the multi-wavelength signal。

[6] The terminal demultiplexer breaks the multi-wavelength signal back into individual signals and outputs them on separate fibers for client-layer systems (such as SONET/SDH) to detect.

此句可译为:该终端多路解调器把多波信号转换成单波信号并在客户层系统(如 SONET/SDH)的独立光纤上输出他们来进行检测。

SONET:同步光纤网络。

SDH:同步数字系列。

[7] The OSC carries information about the multi-wavelength optical signal as well as remote conditions at the optical terminal or EDFA site.

此句可译为:该光监控信道传输多波长光信号信息以及在光终端或掺铒光纤放大器站点上的远程条件。

as well as 也,还有,以及。

[8] Precision temperature control of laser transmitter is required in DWDM systems to prevent "drift" off a very narrow frequency window of the order of a few GHz.

此句可译为:DWDM 系统需要光传送器的高精密温度控制来防止只有几个千兆赫的非常狭窄的频率带发生漂移。

[9] Recent innovations in DWDM transport systems include pluggable and software-

tunable transceiver modules capable of operating on 40 or 80 channels.

此句可译为:DWDM 传输系统最近的革新包括热插拔和软件可调的收发器模块,能操作 40 频道或 80 频道。

software-tunable 意为软件可调的;capable of operating……是形容词短语做后置定语,修饰 transceiver modules。

Exercises

1. Put the following phrases into English.

(1) 密集型波分复用

(2) 掺铒光纤放大器

(3) 放大带

(4) 调制格式

(5) 终端复用器

(6) 终端多路解调器

(7) 客户层系统

(8) 光监控通道

(9) 激光发射器

(10) 收发器模块

2. Put the following phrases into Chinese.

(1) dense wavelength division multiplexing

(2) optical signal

(3) operating range

(4) modulated bit rate

(5) electrical domain

(6) software upgrade

(7) stable wavelength or frequency

(8) maximum capacity

(9) pluggable module

(10) transport system

3. Translate the following sentences into Chinese.

(1) EDFAs can amplify any optical signal in their operating range, regardless of the modulated bit rate.

(2) Furthermore, single-wavelength links using EDFAs can similarly be upgraded to WDM links at reasonable cost.

(3) The terminal multiplexer actually contains one wavelength converting transponder for each wavelength signal it will carry.

(4) This is a remote amplification site that amplifies the multi-wavelength signal that may have traversed up to 140 km or more before reaching the remote site.

(5) The terminal demultiplexer breaks the multi-wavelength signal back into individual signals and outputs them on separate fibers for client-layer systems to detect.

(6) This is an additional wavelength usually outside the EDFA amplification band.

(7) The OSC carries information about the multi-wavelength optical signal as well as remote conditions at the optical terminal or EDFA site.

(8) It is also normally used for remote software upgrades and user (ie., network operator) network management information.

(9) DWDM systems have to maintain more stable wavelength or frequency than those needed for CWDM because of the closer spacing of the wavelengths.

(10) Recent innovations in DWDM transport systems include pluggable and software-tunable transceiver modules capable of operating on 40 or 80 channels.

4. Translate the following paragraphs into Chinese.

(1) Dense wavelength division multiplexing, or DWDM for short, refers originally to optical signals multiplexed within the 1,550 nm band so as to leverage the capabilities (and cost) of erbium doped fiber amplifiers (EDFAs), which are effective for wavelengths between approximately 1,525~1,565 nm (C band), or 1,570~1,610 nm (L band). EDFAs were originally developed to replace SONET/SDH optical-electrical-optical (OEO) regenerators, which they have made practically obsolete. EDFAs can amplify any optical signal in their operating range, regardless of the modulated bit rate. In terms of multi-wavelength signals, so long as the EDFA has enough pump energy available to it, it can amplify as many optical signals as can be multiplexed into its amplification band (though signal densities are limited by choice of modulation format). EDFAs therefore allow a single-channel optical link to be upgraded in bit rate by replacing only equipment at the ends of the link, while retaining the existing EDFA or series of EDFAs through a long haul route. Furthermore, single-wavelength links using EDFAs can similarly be upgraded to WDM links at reasonable cost. The EDFAs cost is thus leveraged across as many channels as can be multiplexed into the 1,550 nm band.

(2) DWDM systems have to maintain more stable wavelength or frequency than those needed for CWDM because of the closer spacing of the wavelengths. Precision temperature control of laser transmitter is required in DWDM systems to prevent "drift" off a very narrow frequency window of the order of a few GHz. In addition, since DWDM provides greater maximum capacity it tends to be used at a higher level in the communications hierarchy than CWDM, for example on the Internet backbone and is therefore associated with higher modulation rates, thus creating a smaller market for DWDM devices with very high performance levels. These factors of smaller volume and higher performance result in DWDM systems typically being more expensive than CWDM.

Text B

DWDM—Wavelength Converting Transponders, Muxponder and the Reconfigurable Optical Add-Drop Multiplexer

Wavelength converting transponder

At this stage, some details concerning wavelength converting transponders should be discussed, as this will clarify the role played by current DWDM technology as an additional optical transport layer. [1] It will also serve to outline the evolution of such systems over the last 10 or so years.

As stated above, wavelength converting transponders served originally to translate the transmit wavelength of a client-layer signal into one of the DWDM system's internal wavelengths in the 1,550 nm band (note that even external wavelengths in the 1,550 nm will most likely need to be translated, as they will almost certainly not have the required frequency stability tolerances nor will it have the optical power necessary for the system's EDFA). [2]

In the mid 1990s, however, wavelength converting transponders rapidly took on the additional function of signal regeneration. Signal regeneration in transponders quickly evolved through 1R to 2R to 3R and into overhead-monitoring multi-bit rate 3R regenerators. [3] These differences are outlined below:

1R retransmission

Basically, early transponders were "garbage in garbage out" in that their output was nearly an analogue "copy" of the received optical signal, with little signal clean-up occurring. [4] This limited the reach of early DWDM systems because the signal had to be handed off to a client-layer receiver (likely from a different vendor) before the signal deteriorated too far. Signal monitoring was basically confined to optical domain parameters such as received power.

2R re-time and re-transmit

Transponders of this type were not very common and utilized a quasi-digital Schmidt-triggering method for signal clean-up. Some rudimentary signal quality monitoring was done by such transmitters that basically looked at analogue parameters. [5]

3R re-time, re-transmit, re-shape

3R transponders were fully digital and normally able to view SONET/SDH section layer overhead bytes such as A1 and A2 to determine signal quality health. [6] Many systems will offer 2.5 Gb transponders, which will normally mean the transponder is able to perform 3R regeneration on OC-3/12/48 signals, and possibly gigabit Ethernet, and reporting on signal health by monitoring SONET/SDH section layer overhead bytes. Many transponders will be able to perform full multi-rate 3R in both directions. Some vendors offer 10 giga transponders, which will perform section layer overhead monitoring to all rates up to and including OC-192. [7]

Muxponder

The muxponder (from multiplexed transponder) has different names depending on vendor. It essentially performs some relatively simple time division multiplexing of lower rate signals into a higher rate carrier within the system (a common example is the ability to accept 4 OC-48s and then output a single OC-192 in the 1,550 nm band). More recent muxponder designs have absorbed more and more TDM (time division multiplex and multiplexer) functionality, in some cases obviating the need for traditional SONET/SDH transport equipment. [8]

The reconfigurable optical add-drop multiplexer

As mentioned above, intermediate optical amplification sites in DWDM systems may allow for the dropping and adding of certain wavelength channels. In most systems deployed as of August 2006, this is done infrequently, because adding or dropping wavelengths requires manually inserting or replacing wavelength-selective cards. [9] This is costly, and in some systems requires that all active traffic be removed from the DWDM system, because inserting or removing the wavelength-specific cards interrupts the multi-wavelength optical signal.

With a reconfigurable optical add-drop multiplexer (ROADM), network operators can remotely reconfigure the multiplexer by sending soft commands. The architecture of the ROADM is such that dropping or adding wavelengths does not interrupt the "pass-through" channels. Numerous technological approaches are utilized for various commercial ROADMs, the trade off being among cost, optical power and flexibility.

Words and Expressions

transponder [trænˈspɔndə(r)] n. 异频雷达收发机
clarify [ˈklærifai] v. 澄清,阐明,使……明晰
evolution [ˌiːvəˈluːʃən] n. 进化;发展,进展
transmit [trænzˈmit] v. 传输;转送,传达
internal [inˈtəːnl] adj. 国内的;内部的
tolerance [ˈtɔlərəns] n. 公差
regeneration [riˌdʒenəˈreiʃən] n. 再生;重建
monitor [ˈmɔnitə] n. 监督器;级长,监听员 v. 监视,监听,监督
garbage [ˈgɑːbidʒ] n. 垃圾
analogue [ˈænəlɔg] n. 类似物;模拟
receiver [riˈsiːvə] n. 接收器;收款员,接待者

deteriorate [di'tiəriəreit] v. 恶化
confine ['kənfain] v. 限制
utilize [ju:'tilaiz] v. 利用
quasi ['kwɑ:zi(:), 'kweisai] adj. 类似的；外表的；准的
triggering ['trigəriŋ] n. 起动；触发；控制
rudimentary [ru:di'mentəri] adj. 基本的
transmitter [trænz'mitə] n. 转送者，传达人；传导物
gigabit ['dʒigəbit] n. 吉(咖)比特(10^9 比特)
Ethernet ['i:θənet] n. 以太网
vendor ['vendɔ:] n. 厂商；小贩；卖主
division [di'viʒən] n. 区分；分开；除法
obviate ['ɔbvieit] v. 除去；排除；回避
deploy [di'plɔi] v. 展开；配置；部署
inserting [in'sə:tiŋ] n. 插入
selective [si'lektiv] adj. 选择的，选择性的
traffic ['træfik] adj. 交通的 n. 交通
reconfigure [,ri:kən'figə(r)] v. 重新装配，改装
architecture ['ɑ:kitektʃə] n. 建筑学；建筑业
approach [ə'prəutʃ] n. 途径；方法
flexibility [,fleksə'biliti] n. 灵活性；柔韧性

Notes

[1] At this stage, some details concerning wavelength converting transponders should be discussed, as this will clarify the role played by current DWDM technology as an additional optical transport layer.

此句可译为：在这一阶段，应该讨论有关波长转换器的一些细节，因为这将澄清目前 DWDM 技术作为一项额外的光传输层所发挥的作用。

concerning wavelength converting transponders 是现在分词短语做后置定语，修饰 some details。

as 引导原因状语从句。

played by current DWDM technology 是过去分词短语做后置定语，修饰 the role。

[2] as they will almost certainly not have the required frequency stability tolerances nor will it have the optical power necessary for the system's EDFA.

此句可译为：因为它们几乎肯定会没有所需的频率稳定度公差，也不会有系统的掺铒光纤放大器所必需的光功率。

as 引导原因状语从句。

necessary for the system's EDFA 是形容词短语做后置定语，修饰 the optical power。

[3] Signal regeneration in transponders quickly evolved through 1R to 2R to 3R and into overhead-monitoring multi-bit rate 3R regenerators.

此句可译为：转换器中的信号再生迅速从 1R,2R,3R 演变为间接/高架监测多比特率 3R 再生器。

evolved…into… 演变为……

[4] Basically, early transponders were "garbage in garbage out" in that their output was nearly an analogue "copy" of the received optical signal, with little signal clean-up occurring.

此句可译为：基本上，早期的转换器是"无用输入和无用输出"，因为它们所输出的信号几乎是收到的光信号的一个模拟"复制"，基本上没有信号清理。

in that 既然，因为。

with little signal clean-up occurring 是介词短语的复合结构做伴随状语。

[5] Some rudimentary signal quality monitoring was done by such transmitters that basically looked at analogue parameters.

此句可译为：一些最基本的信号质量监测工作由传送器来完成，这些传送器基本上要考虑模拟参数。

that 引导定语从句，修饰先行词 transmitters；looked at 考虑。

[6] 3R transponders were fully digital and normally able to view SONET/SDH section layer overhead bytes such as A1 and A2 to determine signal quality health.

此句可译为：3R 转换器是全数字化的，通常可以查看 SONET/SDH 层架空部分，如字节 A1 和 A2，以确定信号质量的好坏。

to determine 这里的 to 表目的。

[7] Some vendors offer 10 giga transponders, which will perform section layer overhead monitoring to all rates up to and including OC-192.

此句可译为：一些厂商提供 10 个千兆转发器，这将执行速率等于和超过 OC-192 的层架空监测。

which 引导非限定性定语从句，修饰 transponders。

[8] More recent muxponder designs have absorbed more and more TDM (time division multiplex and multiplexer) functionality, in some cases obviating the need for traditional SONET/SDH transport equipment

此句可译为：最近的 muxponder 设计吸收了更多的 TDM 功能，在某些情况下，无需传统的 SONET/SDH 传输设备。

TDM (time division multiplex and multiplexer)：时分复用和复用器。

in some cases 在某些情况下。

[9] In most systems deployed as of August 2006, this is done infrequently, because adding or dropping wavelengths requires manually inserting or replacing wavelength-selective cards.

此句可译为：2006 年 8 月所配置的大多数系统是很少这样做的，因为增加或降低波长需要手动插入或更换波长选择卡。

deployed as of August 2006 是过去分词短语做后置定语，修饰 systems。

adding or dropping wavelengths 是动名词短语做主语。

inserting or replacing wavelength-selective cards 是动名词短语做宾语。

Exercises

Mark the following statements with T (true) or F (false) according to the text.

(1) At this stage, all details concerning wavelength converting transponders should be discussed. ( )

(2) Wavelength converting transponders served originally to translate the transmit wavelength of a client-layer signal into one of the DWDM system's internal wavelengths in the 1,550 nm band.

( )

(3) In the mid 1980s, however, wavelength converting transponders rapidly took on the additional function of signal regeneration. ( )

(4) Basically, early transponders were "garbage in garbage out" in that their output was nearly an analogue "copy" of the received optical signal, with much signal clean-up occurring. ( )

(5) Signal monitoring was basically confined to optical domain parameters such as received power. ( )

(6) Transponders of this type were very common and utilized a quasi-digital Schmidt-triggering method for signal clean-up. ( )

(7) 2R transponders were fully digital and normally able to view SONET/SDH section layer overhead bytes such as A1 and A2 to determine signal quality health. ( )

(8) Some vendors offer 10 giga transponders, which will perform section layer overhead monitoring to all rates up to and including OC-192. ( )

(9) More recent muxponder designs have absorbed more and more TDM functionality, in some cases obviating the need for traditional SONET/SDH transport equipment.

( )

(10) The architecture of the ROADM is such that dropping or adding wavelengths interrupt the "pass-through" channels. ( )

Translating Skill 8

缩略词的翻译(二)

这里主要指由一个单词(也有两个或两个以上的)缩略而成的词,大多均以一个句号结束(节略词无句号),电信英语中缩写和节略词数量很大,有的长达近10个字母。例如:

Appx. (Appendix)　　　　　　　　　　　附录
Fig. (Figure)　　　　　　　　　　　　图
cf. (confer＜拉＞意为 compare)　　　　比较

vs.（versus）	与……比较
Ltd.（limited）	有限的
ff.（following）	下列
etc.（et cetera＜拉＞意为 and so forth）	等等
e.g.（exempli gratia＜拉＞意为 for example）	例如
I.O.（Input Output）	输入 输出

4. 缩写和节略较为灵活，以小写字母为主，也有大写和大、小写混合的。缩写和节略有如下几种缩略方式。

（1）取首音节

lab.（laboratory）	实验室
freq.（frequency）	频率
ent.（entry）	入口
dyn.（dynamometer）	功率计
sig.（signal）	信号

也有取前两个或几个音节的。

navig.（navigation）	导航
telecom.（teleconference）	远程电视电话会议

（2）取主要字母（以辅音字母为主）

txt.（text）	电文
tty.（teletype）	电传打字
st.（subsequent）	随后的
ss.（supersensitive）	超灵敏度
gr.（ground）	接地
chg.（charge）	电荷

如过去分词常连带取词尾。

DISCONTD（discontinued）	中止
DLVD（delivered）	已投送的

（3）取读音

fax（facsimile）	传真
ur（your）	你的，你们的
BOZ（both）	双方
WIZ（with）	和……一起
Ky（key）	开关

（4）取主要字母和音节（尾字母居多）

apx（appendix）	附录
assy（assembly）	装备
desr（designer）	设计员
mbar（millibar）	毫巴

msec (millisecond)　　　　　　　　　　　　　　毫秒

5. 缩略词语汉译的一般顺序和技巧要点

(1) 根据原文所给全文(大都附在该缩略词语后的括号内)解释汉译。

(2) 根据缩略词语构成规律写出全文,然后汉译。

(3) 部分单词缩略可先尝试读出,再汉译。例如:

　　FXD—fixed
　　RMX—remarks
　　WUD—would

(4) 查阅相关工具书。

6. 在上述诸法都无效的情况下,可尝试若干模糊技巧

(1) 确定该缩略词语所在文章所属的专业范围,范围缩得越小越好。在许多缩略词语工具书上,同一缩略语往往有几个解释,缩小专业范围有助于正确选择。例如:

PCM　　plug-compatible mainframe　　　插接兼容主机
　　　　process control monitor　　　　过程控制监视器
　　　　pulse code modulation　　　　　脉冲编码调制
　　　　punched card machine　　　　　穿孔卡片机

究竟选哪一个,要根据专业内容决定。

(2) 利用缩略词语出现的上下文猜破,从上下文有时可以找到缩略词语的全文。通过文章内容的提示也可对缩略词语作出较准确的推测。

(3) 分解拼凑。有些缩略词语可能由两个或很多缩略词语组成。先对其施加分割,得意译后再合在一起。例如:

DVTLC=DIG+LC (direct-coupling transistor+logic circuit) 直接耦合晶体管逻辑电路
DIG-MOD=DIG+MOD (digital+modulation) 数字调制器
FACTS=FAC+TS (facsimile+transmission system) 传真传输系统
FAXAMMODE=FAX+AM+MO+DE (facsimile+amplitude+modulation+mode) 传真调幅方式
TELECOMM=TELE+COMM (telephone+communication) 电话通信

Exercises to Translating Skill

Translate the following words into Chinese.

(1) VOL　　　　　　　　　　　　　(11) workg. pr
(2) term　　　　　　　　　　　　　(12) revs
(3) EMER　　　　　　　　　　　　(13) recr
(4) WDG　　　　　　　　　　　　 (14) Priv. X
(5) UG　　　　　　　　　　　　　 (15) nsec
(6) OVLD　　　　　　　　　　　　(16) exp.

(7) lgth
(8) fdrs
(9) DWG
(10) Db

(17) equip
(18) tgm
(19) equiv
(20) X-MITTR

Unit 9 Embedded System

In today's world, embedded systems are everywhere—homes, offices, cars, factories, hospitals, plans and consumer electronics.

在今天的世界里,到处都是嵌入式系统——家庭、办公室、汽车、工厂、医院、计划和消费电子产品。

Text A

Overview of an Embedded System[1]

Computer systems are everywhere. They fall into essentially two separate categories.[2] The first and most obvious is that of the desktop computer. This is the machine that first comes in our mind when we talk about computers. Desktop computers are designed to be flexible and to meet a wide range of user needs. The end users can change the functionality of a desktop computer by simply changing the application program. One moment you may be using it as a word processor, the next you as an MP3 player or a game station.[3]

The second type of computer is the embedded computer (or embedded system), a computer that is embedded into a bigger electronics system and repeatedly carrying out a particular function, often going completely unrecognized by the system's user.[4] If you ask somebody how many computers he has got in his home, he would probably count his desktop computer and his laptop. However, computers have always been embedded into all sorts of everyday items. In fact, he may have over 20 computers, hidden or embedded inside washing machines, TVs, digital cameras, cell phones, ovens, air conditioners, DVD players, etc. Unlike desktop computers, an embedded computer is normally dedicated to a specific task.

An embedded system is a computer system that is built to control one or a few dedicated functions, and is not designed to be programmed by the end user in the same way that a desktop computer is.[5]

A user can make choices concerning the functionality but cannot change the system functionality by adding or replacing software. For example, a programmable digital thermostat has an embedded system that has a dedicated function of monitoring and controlling the surrounding temperature. You may have choices for setting the desired low and high temperatures but you cannot just change its functionality as a temperature controller. The software for an embedded system is often referred to as firmware, and is contained in the system's non-volatile memory.[6]

In most cases, an embedded system is used to replace an application-specific electronics in the consumer products. By doing so, most of the system's functionality is encapsulated in the firmware that runs the system, and it is possible to change and upgrade the system by changing the firmware, while keeping the hardware same.[7] This reduces the cost of production even lower because many different systems can share the same hardware base and the functionality is determined by the firmware loaded into them.

Another advantage of using an embedded computer to replace a dedicated electronics circuit is the protection of intellectual property. If your design is completely hardware based, it is easier to steal the design. All you need is to identify the circuit components and trace the tracks on the circuit board. With an embedded system, the hardware can be identified but the software, which really supplies the system's functionality, can be hidden and more difficult to crack.

Let's now discuss about the embedded system inside a digital thermostat. The functional block diagram is shown in Fig. 9-1.

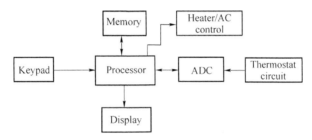

Fig. 9-1 A Digital Thermostat as an Example of Embedded System

The surrounding temperature is sensed by the thermostat (a temperature sensor) and is converted to a proportional analog voltage. The processor cannot manipulate this signal directly, so it is converted to an equivalent digital number through a process called analog-to-digital conversion (ADC). The processor then compares this temperature reading with the high and low temperatures settings defined by the user, and turns the heater/AC on or off if required. The user uses keypad to enter the temperature settings, which are saved into the memory. The processor displays the temperature settings and the current temperature on the LCD screen. The software to perform the entire function of monitoring and controlling the temperature is stored in the memory. The processor reads instructions from the memory and executes them.

Words and Expressions

essentially [iˈsenʃəli] *adv.* 本质上；本来

separate [ˈsepəreit] *adj.* 分开的 *v.* 分开，隔开 *n.* 分开；抽印本

laptop ['læptɔp] n. 便携式电脑，笔记本电脑
sort [sɔːt] n. 种类；某一种人
conditioner [kən'diʃənə] n. 调节器，调节装置；护发素
concerning [kən'səːniŋ] prep. 关于
programmable ['prəugræməbəl] adj. 可编程的
thermostat ['θəːməstæt] n. 恒温器，温度调节器
desire [di'zaiə] n. 渴望，愿望，欲望 v. 渴望，向往，要求
firmware ['fəːmweə] n. [计] 固件
volatile ['vɔlətail] adj. 不稳定的；反复无常的；易挥发的 n. 挥发物
encapsulate [in'kæpsjuˌleit] v. 装入胶囊；封进内部；压缩；概括
intellectual [ˌintə'lektʃuəl] n. 凭理智做事者；知识分子 adj. 智力的，聪明的
trace [treis] n. 痕迹；微量；踪迹 v. 追踪；描绘；找出根源
crack [kræk] v. 破裂；砸开 n. 裂缝，裂痕，爆裂 adj. 训练有素的
sense [sens] v. 感觉；意识到；理解；检测
sensor ['sensə] n. 传感器，探测器
proportional [prə'pɔːʃənəl] adj. 成比例的，相称的 n. [数] 比例项
voltage ['vəultidʒ] n. 电压
manipulate [mə'nipjuleit] vt. 操纵，操作，控制；利用，（巧妙地）处理；篡改
equivalent [i'kwivələnt] adj. 等价的；相等的 n. 相等物
reading ['riːdiŋ] n. 阅读，读物；读数；理解
entire [in'taiə] adj. 全部的，完整的，全面的

Notes

[1] 本文摘自 http://embedded-lab.com，嵌入式实验室网站。

[2] They fall into essentially two separate categories.

此句可译为：它们从本质上分成两个不同的类别。

fall into 译为"分成"，they 指的是前句中提到的 computer systems。

[3] One moment you may be using it as a word processor, the next you as an MP3 player or a game station.

此句可译为：一会儿你可以将它作为一个文字处理器来使用，一会儿你可以将它作为一个 MP3 播放器或游戏机来使用。

one moment … the next … 译为"时而……时而……"、"一会儿……一会儿……"。

后半句中省略了谓语和宾语，完整的句子应为"the next you may be using it as an MP3 player or a game station"。

[4] The second type of computer is the embedded computer (or embedded system), a computer that is embedded into a bigger electronics system and repeatedly carrying out a particular function, often going completely unrecognized by the system's user.

此句可译为：第二类计算机是嵌入式计算机（或嵌入式系统），一个被嵌入到更大的电子系统，并重复实现特定功能，系统用户往往完全无法识别的计算机。

[5] An embedded system is a computer system that is built to control one or a few dedicated functions, and is not designed to be programmed by the end user in the same way that a desktop computer is.

此句可译为：嵌入式系统是一个被开发来控制一个或几个专用功能的计算机系统，并且终端用户不能以在台式电脑上编程的方式来对该系统进行编程。

that is built to control one or a few dedicated functions, and is not designed to be programmed by the end user in the same way 是 that 引导限制性定语从句，修饰先行词 computer system；that a desktop computer is 也是 that 引导限制性定语从句，修饰先行词 way。

[6] non-volatile memory 非易失性内存，缩写为 NVRAM，是指当电流关掉后，所储存的资料不会消失的电脑内存，已大量用于电子产品，尤其可携带性产品之中（如移动电话、数码相机、MP3 等），依内存内的资料是否能在使用电脑时随时改写为标准，可分为二大类产品，即 ROM(Read-only memory，只读存储器)和 Flash memory(闪存)，非易失性内存。

[7] By doing so, most of the system's functionality is encapsulated in the firmware that runs the system, and it is possible to change and upgrade the system by changing the firmware, while keeping the hardware same.

此句可译为：通过这样做，绝大多数系统功能封装在运行系统的固件中，并有可能通过改变固件来改变和升级系统，同时保持相同的硬件。

while 在这里是介词，译为"同时"。

Exercises

1. Put the following phrases into English.

(1) 终端用户
(2) 台式电脑
(3) 嵌入式计算机
(4) 可编程控制器
(5) 知识产权
(6) 模拟电压
(7) 温度传感器
(8) 专用功能
(9) 环境温度
(10) 升级系统

2. Put the following phrases into Chinese.

(1) hardware peripherals
(2) dedicated computer system
(3) embedded in electronic devices
(4) real time operating system
(5) system response time

(6) interrupt latency

(7) development cycle

(8) auxiliary systems

(9) system kernel

(10) AC signal

3. Translate the following sentences into Chinese.

(1) This is the machine that first comes in our mind when we talk about computers.

(2) The end users can change the functionality of a desktop computer by simply changing the application program.

(3) Unlike desktop computers, an embedded computer is normally dedicated to a specific task.

(4) A user can make choices concerning the functionality but cannot change the system functionality by adding or replacing software.

(5) In most cases, an embedded system is used to replace an application-specific electronics in the consumer products.

(6) Another advantage of using an embedded computer to replace a dedicated electronics circuit is the protection of intellectual property.

(7) With an embedded system, the hardware can be identified but the software, which really supplies the system's functionality, can be hidden and more difficult to crack.

(8) The surrounding temperature is sensed by the thermostat (a temperature sensor) and is converted to a proportional analog voltage.

(9) The processor cannot manipulate this signal directly, so it is converted to an equivalent digital number through a process called analog-to-digital conversion (ADC).

(10) The user uses keypad to enter the temperature settings, which are saved into the memory.

4. Translate the following paragraphs into Chinese.

(1) At the heart of the embedded system is the central processing unit or processor. It is the hardware that executes the software and brings life to the embedded system. It also controls the activities of all the other circuits. There are varieties of processors available for embedded systems, and the main criteria for selection is "Can it provide the processing power needed to perform the tasks within the system?" Besides, the system cost, power consumption, software development tools, and component availability are also important factors to be considered while selecting a processor for embedded system design.

(2) The embedded system also has memory, often several different types in one system. The memory is used to store the software that the processor will run. It also provides storage for data such as program variables, intermediate results, status information and any other data generated throughout the operation. The memory is an

important part of any embedded system because it may dictate how the software is designed, written, and developed.

Text B

Regulated Power Supply for Embedded Systems[1]

Power is an important aspect of all embedded systems. Nothing works without electric power. Depending upon the type of applications, several options for power are available. For example, if the system doesn't need to be portable, it can be powered directly from the wall source using AC adaptors.[2] AC[3] adaptors are cheap and easily available at any electronics store. They are used to power a bunch of electronics gadgets at home, like radios, answering machines, wireless routers, etc. They also come with mobile phones as chargers. They convert the high voltage AC in the wall socket to low voltage DC[4] suitable to run the appliances. They usually provide the output voltage somewhere in the range of $+3.3 \sim +12$ V DC, and supply current up to few amperes.

An embedded system consists of many different components that can operate from a wide range of power supply. But some components, such as analog-to-digital converters (ADCs), require a constant voltage supply to provide an accurate output because they need a reference voltage for converting the analog signal to digital count. A device, known as voltage regulator, is used for this purpose.[5] Its job is to convert a range of input DC voltages to a constant output voltage. Besides, a voltage regulator also minimizes the power supply noise and provides a sort of protection for the embedded system from any possible damages due to fluctuating input voltages. The bottom line is that including a voltage regulator in your design is always good.[6]

Types of voltage regulators

1. Linear regulators

Linear regulators use at least one active component (like transistor[7]) and require a higher input voltage than the output. They are small, cheap, easy to implement, provide clean output voltage with low noise, and therefore are very popular. However, they generate a lot of waste heat (note that the difference of input and output voltage is dropped across the regulator) that must be dissipated with bulky heatsinks. So, in terms of efficiency they are not a good choice, especially for battery-powered embedded system. Furthermore, they can only step a voltage down and cannot boost the input voltage.

2. Switching regulators

Unlike linear regulators, switching regulators can step up (boost), step down (buck), or invert the input voltage. A switching regulator works by transferring energy in discrete packets from the input voltage source to the output. This is accomplished with the help of an electrical switch (usually MOSFET) and a controller which regulates the rate at which energy is transferred to the output.[8] They use an inductor or a capacitor as an energy-storing element in order to transfer energy from the input to the output. Since the energy is delivered as required they waste less power, and are very efficient than linear regulators. However, their drawback are that they require more components (that makes them expensive), take up more space, and are complex circuits to design. That's why they are not popular among hobbyists. Besides, the high switching frequency in the circuit generates far more noise than linear regulators.

LM78xx voltage regulators

There are hundreds of voltage regulators available. The most commonly used are LM78xx series linear regulators manufactured by several companies like Fairchild[9], Semelab[10], and ST Microelectronics[11]. They typically come in a TO-220[12] package, and have a metallic attachment point for a heatsink. The part number designates the output voltage. For example, LM7805 provides a 5 V regulated output, while LM7809 provides a regulated 9 V output (Tab. 9-1). They can provide an output current up to 1 A, and have overload and short-circuit protection features.

Tab. 9-1 LM78xx Voltage Regulators

Part Number	Input Voltage Range(V)	Output Voltage(V)
LM7805	7~25	5
LM7806	8~25	6
LM7808	10.5~25	8
LM7809	11.5~25	9
LM7810	12.5~25	10
LM7812	14.5~30	12
LM7815	17.5~30	15
LM7818	21~33	18
LM7824	27~38	24

The Fig. 9-2 shows how to use a LM7805 to get a regulated +5 V power supply. Decoupling capacitors (nominally between 1 μF and 47 μF) are used to filter input and output voltages, and they also help in removing any momentary glitches in the power source. The input DC voltage for LM7805 is obtained by rectifying the low-voltage AC output from a step-down transformer using a diode-bridge rectifier.[13]

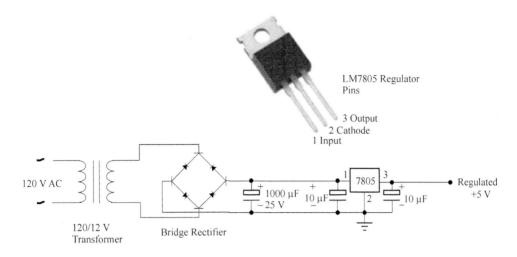

Fig. 9-2　LM7805

Words and Expressions

portable ['pɔːtəbl] *adj.* 轻便的，手提式的；[计] 可移植的 *n.* 便携的东西
gadget ['gædʒit] *n.* 小机件，小玩意儿，小巧的机械
wireless ['waiəlis] *adj.* 无线的 *n.* 无线电 *v.* 用无线电发送（通信）
router ['ruːtə] *n.* 路由器
charger ['tʃɑːdʒə] *n.* 充电器；战马；大浅盘
socket ['sɔkit] *n.* 插座，插口；窝，穴孔 *v.* 装上或插入插座
somewhere ['sʌmweə] *adv.* 在某处；到某种程度；大约 *n.* 某处
constant ['kɔnstənt] *adj.* 不变的；经常的 *n.* 常数，恒量
reference ['refrəns] *n.* 参考，参照；推荐函
regulator ['reɡjuleitə] *n.* 调整者，调整器
fluctuating ['flʌktʃueitiŋ] *adj.* 上下浮动的
linear ['liniə] *adj.* 直线的；长度的；线性的
transistor [træn'zistə] *n.* 晶体管，晶体管收音机
generate ['dʒenəreit] *v.* 产生，发生，引起
dissipate ['disipeit] *v.* 驱散，消散，散去；浪费，挥霍；放荡
bulky ['bʌlki] *adj.* 庞大的，笨重的，肥大的
heatsink 散热器
efficiency [i'fiʃənsi] *n.* 效率；功率
furthermore ['fəːðə'mɔː] *adv.* 而且，此外
invert [in'vəːt] *v.* 倒置；反转，颠倒 *adj.* 转化的 *n.* 颠倒物；[心] 同性恋者
inductor [in'dʌktə] *n.* [电] 感应器；授职者；[化] 感应物质
capacitor [kə'pæsitə] *n.* 电容器
drawback ['drɔːbæk] *n.* 缺点，不利条件；退税

hobbyist [ˈhɔbiist] n. 沉溺于某种癖好者，业余爱好者
decoupling [diˈkʌpliŋ] n. 去耦合装置，退耦
momentary [ˈməumənteri] adj. 短暂的，瞬间的，刹那间的，时时刻刻的
glitch [glitʃ] n. 小故障，小失误；［电］短时脉冲波形干扰
rectify [ˈrektifai] v. 改正；［化］精馏；［电］整流
transformer [trænsˈfɔːmə] n. 变压器
diode [ˈdaiəud] n. 二极管
rectifier [ˈrektifaiə] n. ［电］整流器；改正者

Notes

［1］本文摘自 http：//embedded-lab.com。

［2］For example, if the system doesn't need to be portable, it can be powered directly from the wall source using AC adaptors.

此句可译为：例如，如果系统不需要便携性，它可以使用交流适配器直接从墙壁电源供电。

wall source 即指墙上供电电源，国内即为 220 V 交流电。

［3］AC，alternating current 的缩写，也称"交变电流"，简称"交流"。一般指大小和方向随时间作周期性变化的电压或电流。

［4］DC，direct current 的缩写，又称恒定电流，是指方向和时间不作周期性变化的电流，但电流大小可能不固定而产生波形。

［5］A device, known as voltage regulator, is used for this purpose.

此句可译为：被称为稳压器的装置用于此目的。

known as 译为"称为"；known as voltage regulator 对 a device 进行补充说明。

［6］The bottom line is that including a voltage regulator in your design is always good.

此句可译为：底线是，包括稳压器在内的设计始终是好的。

that including a voltage regulator in your design is always good 为 that 引导的表语从句。

［7］Transistor，晶体管，是一种固体半导体器件，包括各种半导体材料制成的二极管、三极管、场效应管、可控硅等，通常多指晶体三极管，可用于检波、整流、放大、开关、稳压、信号调制和许多其他功能。

［8］This is accomplished with the help of an electrical switch (usually MOSFET) and a controller which regulates the rate at which energy is transferred to the output.

此句可译为：这是在电子开关（通常使用 MOSFET）和一个调节能量转换率的控制器的帮助下完成的。

an electrical switch 和 a controller 都作为提供帮助的对象；which regulates the rate 为限制性定语从句，修饰先行词 a controller；at which energy is transferred to the output 为"介词＋which"引导的定语从句，其中的 which 修饰先行词 the rate。

［9］Fairchild 仙童半导体公司，由美国企业家和发明家谢尔曼·费尔柴尔德

(S. Fairchild)于 1920 年创办，起初只是一家航空摄影公司。1956 年，发明了晶体管的肖克利创办了自己的公司，并吸引了大量的优秀青年科学家加盟。

［10］Semelab 是 TT 电子集团的一部分，TT 电子有限公司是一个全球领先的电子产品制造商，市场涉及汽车、航天航空、国防、电信、计算机和工业等诸多行业，可提供全方位的先进技术，应用程序特定的工程解决方案和标准产品，拥有世界一流的生产设施和应用工程团队，销售市场遍布世界各地，包括北美、欧洲、英国、墨西哥、巴巴多斯、马来西亚、日本、新加坡、印度、中国香港地区和中国大陆地区。

［11］ST Microelectronics 意法半导体（ST）成立于 1987 年，是意大利 SGS 微电子公司和法国汤姆逊（Thomson）半导体合并后的新企业。1998 年 5 月，SGS-THOMSON Microelectronics 将公司名称改为意法半导体有限公司（ST Microelectronics）。据最新的工业统计数据，意法半导体是全球第五大半导体厂商，在很多市场居世界领先水平。例如，意法半导体是世界第一大专用模拟芯片和电源转换芯片制造商，世界第一大工业半导体和机顶盒芯片供应商，而且在分立器件、手机相机模块和车用集成电路领域居世界前列。

［12］TO-220，一种电子器件的封装形式，常见的是 3 脚，是最常见的封装之一。2 脚一般为单个二极管，两个二极管封装在一起的也为 3 个脚。4 个以上引脚基本上都是集成电路。这种封装有一面会有裸露的金属片，用于直接与散热器相连，散热效果较好。

［13］The input DC voltage for LM7805 is obtained by rectifying the low-voltage AC output from a step-down transformer using a diode-bridge rectifier.

此句可译为：通过调整来自降压变压器的低压交流输出，使用一个二极管桥式整流器获得 LM7805 的输入直流电压。

by rectifying the low-voltage AC output 说明 obtain 的方式，from a step-down transformer 说明 the low-voltage AC output 的出处，using a diode-bridge rectifier 说明 LM7805 获得直流电压所用到的电路。

Exercises

Mark the following statements with T (true) or F (false) according to the text.

(1) All embedded systems need electric power to work.　　　　　　　(　)

(2) The portable system can be powered directly from the wall source using AC adaptors.
　　　　　　　　　　　　　　　　　　　　　　　　　　　　　　　(　)

(3) AC adaptors can convert DC voltages to AC voltages.　　　　　　(　)

(4) Analog-to-digital converters can operate from a wide range of power supply.　(　)

(5) A voltage regulator provides a constant voltage supply.　　　　　(　)

(6) The fluctuating input voltages possible damage the embedded system.　(　)

(7) Linear regulators need bulky heatsinks to dissipate waste heat.　　(　)

(8) For wasting less power switching regulators are cheaper than linear regulators.
　　　　　　　　　　　　　　　　　　　　　　　　　　　　　　　(　)

(9) Switching regulators are more popular because they are very efficient than linear regulators.　　　　　　　　　　　　　　　　　　　　　　　　　　　　(　)

(10) Decoupling capacitors help in removing any momentary glitches in the power source. （　）

Translating Skill 9

数量词的翻译

电子信息类英文中经常出现表示数量的词,为使文章紧缩,总是尽可能多地使用数量词,英汉在数量词表达上有不同特点,翻译时要持谨慎态度,不小心错译哪怕是一位数字,也可能酿成严重后果。译后对数字部分要反复校核,使其准确无误。

数量词翻译要点

1. 英汉数字表达差异

英语中无"万"单位,要以"千"累计。

| a ten thousand | 一万（十千） |
| a hundred thousand | 十万（百千） |

2. 百万以上数量词

百万以上的大数量词分为大陆制（thousand system——美国、法国和欧洲大部分国家采用）和英国制（million system——英国,德国采用）。汉译这种数字首先搞清不同的制,其主要区别为

数字 \ 制	英国	大陆
10^9（10亿）	a thousand million	a billion
10^{12}（兆）	a billion	a trillion
10^{15}（千兆）	a thousand billion	a quadrillion

3. 数量单位及序号

120 V	120 伏
20 ℃	20 摄氏度
550 kHz	550 千赫

但有些词并非数量单位,例如:bit, byte, digit, phase 等。

| 8-bit | 8 位字 |
| Three-phase poser | 三相电 |

以上用"-"连接的为形容词,下列为名词。例如,

4 inputs	4 输入
Page 1,321	第 1 321 页
1993 years	1993 年
1,072 Main Street	曼恩大街 1 072 号

4. 斜线和分数

5/8	八分之五
1/8 inch	八分之一英寸
3-11/16	三又十六分之十一
two-thirds voltage	三分之二伏
one-millionth of a fara	百万分之一法(拉)

5. Increase 和增加

(1) 翻译中的 $n-1$ 规则适用于以下句子。

Increase by a factor, increase…

The drain voltage has been increased by a factor of five.

漏电压增加了 4 倍。

The production of various electron tubes has been increased four times as against 1958.

各种电子管产量比 1958 年增加了 3 倍。

(2) 以下句子不适于 $n-1$ 译法。

A is five times bigger than B.

A 比 B 大 5 倍。

This year the value of our industrial output has increase by twice as compared with that of last year.

今年我国工业产值比去年增加了 2 倍。

A temperature rise of one degree centigrade raises the electric conductivity of a semiconductor by 3%～6%.

温度升 1 ℃,半导体导电度就增大 3%～6%。

(3) 另外,double, treble, quadruple… 译为"1,2,3……倍"

As the high voltage was abruptly trebled, all the valves burnt.

由于高压突然增加了 2 倍,电子管都烧坏了。

6. Reduce 和减少

Cost of radio receivers was reduced by 80%.

收音机成本降低了 80%。

The length of laser tube was reduced ten times.

激光管长度缩短了十分之九(为十分之一)。

This kind of film is twice thinner than ordinary paper.

这种薄膜的厚度只是普通纸张的一半。

The members have decreased to 50.

人员减少到 50 名。

Switching time of the new type transistor is shortened three times.

新型晶体管开关时间缩短为三分之一(可缩短三分之二)。

7. 模糊数

tens	数十

millions	千百万
dozen	几十
over two years	2年以上
under two hours	不足2小时
five to nine volts	5~9伏
nearly one tenth	接近十分之一
a thousand and one	无数的
ten to one	十之八九

Exercises to Translating Skill

Translate the following expressions into Chinese.

(1) 17 million
(2) 2.5 billion
(3) fifty-five
(4) one hundred
(5) two hundred fifty-seven
(6) five thousand four hundred twenty
(7) forty 1-volt divisions
(8) 16 two-cent stamps
(9) two-thirds of the space
(10) nine-tenths of the ICs
(11) 15 years
(12) 1.5 mA
(13) 200 meters
(14) 150 V
(15) 127.16 K(Kelvins)
(16) 0.15 V
(17) five percent rate
(18) 0~64℃
(19) －5~＋5 V
(20) 25~100,000 Hz

Unit 10   PLC

A programmable logic controller (PLC) is a digital computer used for automation of electromechanical processes, such as control of machinery on factory assembly lines, amusement rides, or light fixtures. PLCs are used in many industries and machines.

可编程逻辑控制器(PLC)是一种用于机电过程自动控制的数字化计算机,如对工厂生产线的机械控制,游乐设施,或灯光设备。PLC 被用于许多行业和机器中。

Text A

Ladder Logic

Ladder logic is the main programming method used for PLCs. As mentioned before, ladder logic has been developed to mimic relay logic. The decision to use the relay logic diagrams was a strategic one. By selecting ladder logic as the main programming method, the amount of retraining needed for engineers and tradespeople was greatly reduced.[1]

Modern control systems still include relays, but these are rarely used for logic.[2] A relay is a simple device that uses a magnetic field to control a switch, as shown in Fig. 10-1. When a voltage is applied to the input coil, the resulting current creates a magnetic field. The magnetic field pulls a metal switch (or reed) towards it and the contacts touch, closing the switch. The contact that closes when the coil is energized is called normally open[3]. The normally closed[4] contacts touch when the input coil is not energized. Relays are normally drawn in schematic form using a circle to represent the input coil. The output contacts are shown with two parallel lines. Normally open contacts are shown as two lines, and will be open (non-conducting) when the input is not energized. Normally closed contacts are shown with two lines with a diagonal line through them.[5] When the input coil is not energized, the normally closed contacts will be closed (conducting).

Relays are used to let one power source close a switch for another (often high current) power source, while keeping them isolated.[6] An example of a relay in a simple control application is shown in Fig. 10-2. In this system, the first relay on the left is used as normally closed, and will allow current to flow until a voltage is applied to the input A. The second relay is normally open and will not allow current to flow until a voltage is applied to the input B. If current is flowing through the first two relays, then current will flow through the coil in the third relay, and close the switch for output C. This circuit would normally be drawn in the ladder logic form. This can be read logically as C will be on if A is off and B is on.

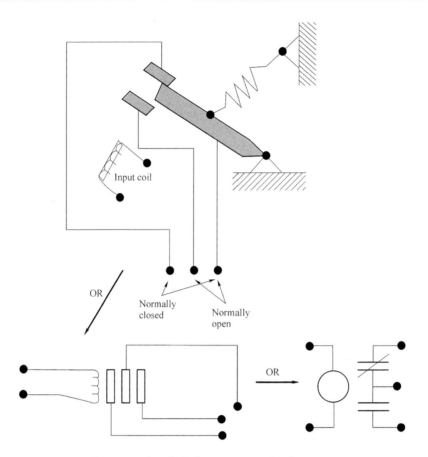

Fig. 10-1 Simple Relay Layouts and Schematics

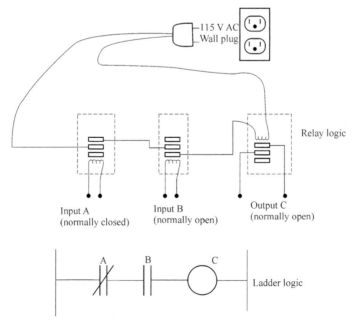

Fig. 10-2 A Simple Relay Controller

The example in Fig. 10-2 does not show the entire control system, but only the logic. [7] When we consider a PLC there are inputs, outputs, and the logic. Fig. 10-3 shows a more complete representation of the PLC. Here there are two inputs from push buttons. We can imagine the inputs as activating 24 V DC relay coils in the PLC. This in turn drives an output relay that switches 115 V AC, which will turn on a light. [8] Note, in actual PLCs inputs are never relays, but outputs are often relays. The ladder logic in the PLC is actually a computer program that the user can enter and change. Notice that both of the input push buttons are normally open, but the ladder logic inside the PLC has one normally open contact, and one normally closed contact. Do not think that the ladder logic in the PLC needs to match the inputs or outputs. Many beginners will get caught trying to make the ladder logic match the input types.

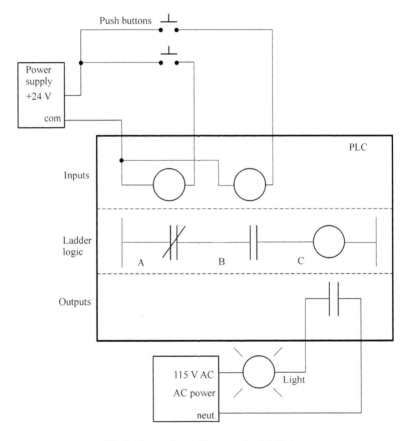

Fig. 10-3 A PLC Illustrated with Relays

Many relays also have multiple outputs (throws) and this allows an output relay to be also an input simultaneously. The circuit shown in Fig. 10-4 is an example of this, it is called a seal in circuit. In this circuit, the current can flow through any branch of the circuit through the contacts labelled A or B. The input B will only be on when the output B is on. If B is off, and A is energized, then B will turn on. If B turns on then the input B will turn on, and keep output B on even if input A goes off. After B is turned on the output B will not turn off.[9]

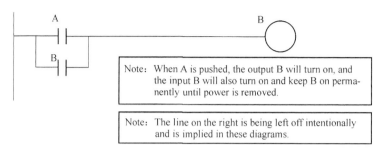

Fig. 10-4　A Seal-in Circuit

Words and Expressions

automation [ˌɔːtəˈmeiʃən] *n.* 自动化
electromechanical [iˈlektrəumiˈkænikəl] *adj.* 电装置的
machinery [məˈʃiːnəri] *n.* 机械；(总称)机器
assembly [əˈsembli] *n.* 集会，集合；议会；装配；[计] 汇编
amusement [əˈmjuːzmənt] *n.* 娱乐，消遣
fixture [ˈfikstʃə] *n.* 固定物；固定装置；固定成员；设备
mimic [ˈmimik] *v.* 模仿，模拟 *n.* 模仿者；仿制品 *adj.* 模仿的；假的
relay [riˈlei] *n.* 继电器；接力赛；替班
strategic [strəˈtiːdʒik] *adj.* 战略的；重要的；基本的
tradespeople [ˈtreidzˌpiːpl] *n.* 零售商；店主
magnetic [mægˈnetik] *adj.* 有磁性的，有吸引力的；催眠术的
reed [riːd] *n.* 芦苇，芦杆；[音] 簧舌，簧片
energize [ˈenədʒaiz] *v.* 使活跃，给予精力；加强；给予……电压
schematic [skiːˈmætik] *adj.* 图解的；扼要的
parallel [ˈpærəlel] *adj.* 平行的；并联的 *n.* 对比；平行线(面)；相似物 *v.* 相比，相应；与……平行
diagonal [daiˈægənl] *adj.* 对角线的；斜的；斜纹的 *n.* 对角线；斜线；斜列
representation [ˌreprizenˈteiʃən] *n.* 陈述；表现；表示法
simultaneously [saiməlˈteiniəsli] *adv.* 同时地

Notes

[1] By selecting ladder logic as the main programming method, the amount of retraining needed for engineers and tradespeople was greatly reduced.

此句可译为：选择梯形逻辑作为主要的编程方法，使工程师和零售商的再培训资金大大减少。

该句的主句应为 the amount of retraining was greatly reduced，其中 by selecting ladder logic as the main programming method 为介词短语做状语,对主句进行补充说明;needed for engineers and tradespeople 过去分词做后置定语,修饰 retraining。

［2］Modern control systems still include relays, but these are rarely used for logic.

此句可译为:现代控制系统仍包括继电器,但这些继电器很少用于逻辑控制。

句中 these 应指前句中的 relays。

［3］normally open 常开,在常态(不通电)的情况下处于断开状态的触点叫常开触点。通常情况下是开状态,即线圈未得电的情况下断开的。

［4］normally closed 常闭,在常态(不通电)的情况下处于闭合状态的触点叫常闭触点。通常情况下是关状态,即线圈未得电的情况下闭合的。

［5］Normally closed contacts are shown with two lines with a diagonal line through them.

此句可译为:常闭触点用两条竖线表示,且有一条对角斜线穿过这两条竖线。

with two lines 表示 contacts 的方式,with a diagonal line through them 说明 two lines 的状态,其中的 them 指的是 two lines。

［6］Relays are used to let one power source close a switch for another (often high current) power source, while keeping them isolated.

此句可译为:继电器用来让一个电源关闭另一个电源(通常高电流),同时保持它们隔离。

let sth. do sth. 让……做……,for another power source 表示这么做的目的;while 在这里翻译成"同时",them 指句中提到的两个 power sources。

［7］The example in Fig. 10-2 does not show the entire control system, but only the logic.

此句可译为:图 10-2 的例子并没有显示整个控制系统,而只显示了逻辑。

not…but… 不是……而是……当主语一样时,把两句合为一句,省略后一句的主语和谓语,改为 but 连接,有两者对比的转折意思。

［8］This in turn drives an output relay that switches 115 V AC, which will turn on a light.

此句可译为:这反过来又驱动一个输出继电器,它开关 115 V 交流电,打开一盏灯。

that switches 115 V AC 为限制性定语从句,that 修饰先行词 output relay;which will turn on a light 为非限制性定语从句,that 修饰先行词 115 V AC。

［9］If B is off, and A is energized, then B will turn on. If B turns on then the input B will turn on, and keep output B on even if input A goes off. After B is turned on the output B will not turn off.

此句可译为:如果 B 是关闭的,而 A 通电,则 B 将打开。如果 B 打开则输入点 B 将打开,并且即使输入点 A 关闭,输出点 B 仍保持打开。B 打开后,输出点 B 将不会关闭。

If B is off, and A is energized, then B will turn on. 句中第一个 B 是输入点 B,第二个 B 是输出点 B;If B turns on then the input B will turn on, and keep output B on even if input A goes off. 句中第一个 B 是输出点 B;After B is turned on the output B will not turn off.

句中第一个 B 是输入点 B。

Exercises

1. Put the following phrases into English.

(1) 常开触点

(2) 常闭触点

(3) 梯形逻辑图

(4) 工厂生产线

(5) 模拟逻辑

(6) 平行线

(7) 输入线圈

(8) 多输出

(9) 继电器控制器

(10) 自保持电路

2. Put the following phrases into Chinese.

(1) automation of electromechanical processes

(2) magnetic field

(3) drive an output relay

(4) a PLC illustrated with relay

(5) logic wiring schematics

(6) electrical control

(7) mechanical switch

(8) equivalent program

(9) switch power off

(10) programmable controller

3. Translate the following sentences into Chinese.

(1) A relay is a simple device that uses a magnetic field to control a switch.

(2) When a voltage is applied to the input coil, the resulting current creates a magnetic field.

(3) Normally open contacts are shown as two lines, and will be open (non-conducting) when the input is not energized.

(4) In this system, the first relay on the left is used as normally closed, and will allow current to flow until a voltage is applied to the input A.

(5) If current is flowing through the first two relays, then current will flow through the coil in the third relay.

(6) In actual PLCs inputs are never relays, but outputs are often relays.

(7) Many beginners will get caught trying to make the ladder logic match the input types.

(8) Many relays also have multiple outputs (throws) and this allows an output relay to be also an input simultaneously.

(9) In this circuit, the current can flow through any branch of the circuit through the contacts labelled A or B.

(10) The decision to use the relay logic diagrams was a strategic one.

4. Translate the following paragraphs into Chinese.

(1) Control engineering has evolved over time. In the past, humans were the main method for controlling a system. More recently electricity has been used for control and early electrical control was based on relays. These relays allow power to be switched on and off without a mechanical switch. It is common to use relays to make simple logical control decisions. The development of low cost computer has brought the most recent revolution, the programmable logic controller (PLC). The advent of the PLC began in the 1970s, and has become the most common choice for manufacturing controls.

(2) When a process is controlled by a PLC, it uses inputs from sensors to make decisions and update outputs to drive actuators. The process is a real process that will change over time. Actuators will drive the system to new states (or modes of operation). This means that the controller is limited by the sensors available, if an input is not available, the controller will have no way to detect a condition.

Text B

PLC Programming

The first PLCs were programmed with a technique that was based on relay logic wiring schematics. This eliminated the need to teach the electricians, technicians and engineers how to program a computer—but, this method has stuck and it is the most common technique for programming PLCs today. An example of ladder logic can be seen in Fig. 10-5. To interpret this diagram, imagine that the power is on the vertical line on the left hand side, we call this the hot rail. [1] On the right hand side is the neutral rail. In the figure there are two rungs, and on each rung there are combinations of inputs (two vertical lines) and outputs (circles). If the inputs are opened or closed in the right combination, the power[2] can flow from the hot rail, through the inputs, to power the outputs, and finally to the neutral rail. An input can come from a sensor, switch or any other type of sensor. An output will be some device outside the PLC that is switched on or off, such as lights or motors. In the top rung the contacts are normally open and normally closed, which means if input A is on and input B is off, then power will flow through the output and activate it. Any other combination of input values will result in the output X being off.

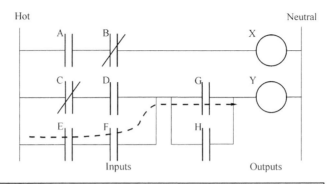

Note: Power needs to flow through some combination of the inputs (A,B,C,D,E,F,G,H) to turn on outputs(X, Y).

Fig. 10-5 A Simple Ladder Logic Diagram

The second rung of Fig. 10-5 is more complex, there are actually multiple combinations of inputs that will result in the output Y turning on. On the left most part of the rung, power could flow through the top if C is off and D is on. Power could also (and simultaneously) flow through the bottom if both E and F are true[3]. This would get power half way across the rung, and then if G or H is true the power will be delivered to output Y.

There are other methods for programming PLCs. One of the earliest techniques involved mnemonic instructions. These instructions can be derived directly from the ladder logic diagrams and entered into the PLC through a simple programming terminal. An example of mnemonics is shown in Fig. 10-6. In this example the instructions are read one line at a time from top to bottom. The first line 00000 has the instruction LDN (input load and not) for input A. This will examine the input to the PLC and if it is off it will remember a 1 (or true), if it is on it will remember a 0 (or false). The next line uses an LD (input load) statement to look at the input. If the input is off it remembers a 0, if the input is on it remembers a 1 (note: this is the reverse of the LDN). The AND statement recalls the last two numbers remembered and if they are both true the result is a 1, otherwise the result is a 0. This result now replaces the two numbers that were recalled, and there is only one number remembered. The process is repeated for lines 00003 and 00004, but when these are done there are now three numbers remembered. The oldest number is from the AND, the newer numbers are from the two LD instructions. The AND in line 00005 combines the results from the last LD instructions and now there are two numbers remembered. The OR instruction takes the two numbers now remaining and if either one is a 1 the result is a 1, otherwise the result is a 0. This result replaces the two numbers, and there is now a single number there. The last instruction is the ST (store output) that will look at the last value stored and if it is 1, the output will be turned on, if it is 0 the output will be turned off.

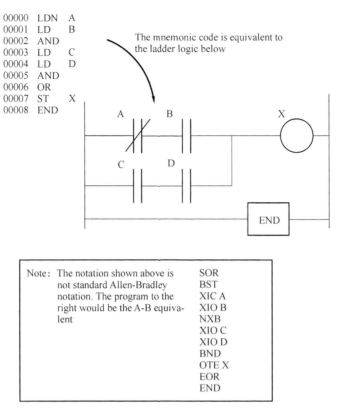

Fig. 10-6 An Example of a Mnemonic Program and Equivalent Ladder Logic[4]

The ladder logic program in Fig. 10-6 is equivalent to the mnemonic program. Even if you have programmed a PLC with ladder logic, it will be converted to mnemonic form before being used by the PLC. In the past mnemonic programming was the most common, but now it is uncommon for users to even see mnemonic programs.

Sequential function charts (SFCs) have been developed to accommodate the programming of more advanced systems. These are similar to flowcharts[5], but much more powerful. The example seen in Fig. 10-7 is doing two different things. To read the chart, start at the top where it says start. Below this there is the double horizontal line that says follow both paths. As a result the PLC will start to follow the branch on the left and right hand sides separately and simultaneously. On the left there are two functions: the first one is the power up function. This function will run until it decides it is done, and the power down function will come after. [6] On the right hand side is the flash function, this will run until it is done. These functions look unexplained, but each function, such as power up, will be a small ladder logic program. This method is much different from flowcharts because it does not have to follow a single path through the flowchart.

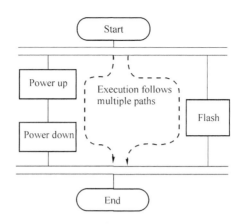

Fig. 10-7　An Example of a Sequential Function Chart

Words and Expressions

wiring ['waiəriŋ] n. 配线，布线
schematics [skiː'mætik] n. 图表
eliminate [i'limineit] v. 除去，剔除；忽略；淘汰
electrician [ilek'triʃən] n. 电工，电气技师
interpret [in'təːprit] v. 口译；解释；诠释
neutral ['njuːtrəl] adj. 中立的；中性的；素净色的 n. 中立者
rung [rʌŋ] n. 阶梯；横档；(社会、职业、组织等的)阶层
combination [ˌkɔmbi'neiʃən] n. 结合，结合到一起的事物或人；密码
power ['pauə] n. 力量；力；权力；[数]幂 v. 使有力量，给……提供动力 adj. 电力的；力量的
motor ['məutə] n. 马达，发动机；机动车 adj. 机动的，汽车的；运动神经的
mnemonic [niː'mɔnik] adj. 助记的，记忆的 n. 记忆方法，助记符号
statement ['steitmənt] n. 陈述，声明
otherwise ['ʌðəwaiz] adv. 否则；不同地；在不同方面 adj. 不同的
accommodate [ə'kɔmədeit] v. 使适应；供给住宿
flowchart ['fləuˌtʃɑːt] n. 流程图

Notes

[1] To interpret, this diagram, imagine that the power is on the vertical line on the left hand side, we call this the hot rail.

此句可译为：为了解释这个图，假想电源是在左手边垂直线一方，我们称之为母线。

that the power is on the vertical line on the left hand side 做宾语从句；hot rail 这里译为"母线"，实际 PLC 中的母线共有两条，在分析梯形图的逻辑关系时，为了借用继电器电路图的分析方法，可以想象左右两侧母线（左母线和右母线）之间有一个左正右负的直流电源电压，母线之间有"能流"从左向右流动。右母线可以不画出。

［2］power 这里译为"能流"，这是一个假想的"概念电流"，利用能流这一概念，可以帮助我们更好地理解和分析梯形图。

［3］true 逻辑代数中变量的两个取值之一，逻辑中，解释 0 为假，1 为真。

［4］Fig. 10-6 An Example of a Mnemonic Program and Equivalent Ladder Logic，图中提到的"Allen Bradley"是自动化行业全球领先的公司之一，ALLEN-BRADLEY 公司为 Rockwell 自动化的全球战略品牌，其生产的 PLC 被人们称为"A-B PLC"或"AB PLC"。

［5］Flowchart，流程图，是由一些图框和流程线组成的，其中图框表示各种操作的类型，图框中的文字和符号表示操作的内容，流程线表示操作的先后次序。

［6］This function will run until it decides it is done, and the power down function will come after.

此句可译为：此函数将运行至其判决完成，之后 power down 函数接着运行。

it is done 指的是该分句中提到 this function 被执行完。

Exercises

Mark the following statements with T (true) or F (false) according to the text.

(1) The most common technique for programming PLCs today is based on relay logic wiring schematics.　　　　　　　　　　　　　　　　　　　　　　　　　　　(　　)

(2) There have to be only two rungs in the ladder logic diagrams.　　(　　)

(3) From the Fig. 10-5 it is true that if input A and B are both on, then power will not flow through the output.　　　　　　　　　　　　　　　　　　　　　　　　(　　)

(4) In the second rung of the Fig. 10-5 the power will flow to output Y only if G and H are both true.　　　　　　　　　　　　　　　　　　　　　　　　　　　　(　　)

(5) The technique of mnemonic instruction is one of the methods for programming PLCs.　　　　　　　　　　　　　　　　　　　　　　　　　　　　　　　　　(　　)

(6) When the instructions of lines 00003 and 00004 in the Fig. 10-6 are done there are two numbers remembered.　　　　　　　　　　　　　　　　　　　　　　　(　　)

(7) The result of the OR instruction in the Fig. 10-6 brings two new numbers remembered.　　　　　　　　　　　　　　　　　　　　　　　　　　　　　　　(　　)

(8) It is uncommon for users to even see mnemonic programs.　　　(　　)

(9) Sequential function charts is equivalent to flowcharts.　　　　　　(　　)

(10) In the Fig. 10-7 the flash function will run after the power down function is done.

(　　)

Translating Skill 10

长句的翻译

电子信息类英文，文章要求合乎逻辑，句子要求结构严谨，因而长句使用较多。长句按其结构,大部分属于主从复合句和并列复合句,也有一些简单句。

翻译长句,首先要把全文看上几遍,直到弄懂大意为止。然后再把长句看上几遍,设法抓住其主要内容。如果这时仍然感到无从下笔翻译,可对句子加以分析,弄清长句各部分之间的语法关系,层次关系和前后关系,确定中心内容后根据汉语习惯表达方式加以转换。

To illustrate, the solution of the mathematical equations for the trajectory of a space rocket would require nearly two of work by one computer operating an ordinary adding machine, while an electronic computing machine can do the same job in seconds without any error.

该句可以分成三部分。

主句部分:… the solution of the mathematical equations for the trajectory of a space rocket would require nearly two of work by one computer operating an ordinary adding machine,

并列句部分:… while an electronic computing machine can do the same job in seconds without any error.

插入语部分:To illustrate.

全句译为:举例来说,一个计算工作者用一架普通加法机来解决一个宇宙火箭轨迹的数学方程式,差不多需要两年的工作时间,而一台电子计算机却可以毫无误差地在几秒钟之内完成同样工作。

The unit of p. d. like that of e. m. f. is the volt which is that p. d. existing between two points in a circuit where one unit of electrical energy has been changed to some other form of energy as a consequence of one coulomb passing between the points.

该句为复合句,也可分为三部分。

主句部分:The unit of p. d. like that of e. m. f. is the volt…

定语从句部分:which is that p. d. existing between two points in a circuit…

以上修饰主句中的 volt.

另一定语从句部分:where one unit of electrical energy has been changed to some other form of energy as a consequence of one coulomb passing between the points.

用以修饰 which 定语从句中的 circuit.

全句译为:电位差的单位同电动势的单位一样是伏特。伏特就是存在于电路两端之间的电位差。在这一电路上由于每一库仑的电荷通过两端的结果,电能的每个单位转换成了能的某种另外形式。

注意,此句译为三句,主句和两个定语从句分别成为一句。

由于英语表达方式有时在顺序上与汉语不尽相同,在翻译长句时为了调整这种顺序,常采用三种不同的方法。

1. 顺译

按英语原句表达顺序用汉语依次译出,其中,"主 + 谓 + 宾"结构的英语长句多采用此法。

In addition to malleability and ductility, some metals possess the power to conduct electric current and the ability to be magnetized, two special properties not possessed by any other class of materials.

除展性和延性外,某些金属还具有导电能力和磁化能力,这是任何其他材料所不具备的两种特性。

Lecture "Holography" was delivered by D. Gabor on the occasion of his receiving the 1971 Noble Prize for physics for his invention and development of the holographic method.

D. 盖伯由于发明和发展了全息照相术而获得1971年诺贝尔物理学奖。本文是他受奖时宣读的报告《全息照相》。

2. 倒译

倒译即改变英语原句的顺序,又称变序译法,许多长句用倒译可以比较顺利地译出,顺译反倒难度很大甚至不可能。

In the case where the waves are incident on a boundary separating two regions where their velocity is different they will in general be divided into a reflected train and a transmitted train whose relative intensities will depend on the magnitude of the velocity change at the boundary, on the abruptness of this change, and on the angle of incidence.

在波射到速度不同的两个地区的分界面上的情况下,它们一般都会分成反射波列和透射波列,这两者的相对强度取决于界面上速度变化的大小,变化的缓急度以及入射角的大小。

In this way the distinction between heavy current electrical engineering and light current electrical engineering can be said to have disappeared, but we still have the conceptual difference in that in power engineering the primary concern is to transport energy between distant points in space; while with communications system the primary objective is to convey, extract and process information, in which process considerable amounts of power may be consumed.

在这一方面,强电工程和弱电工程间的区别可以说已经消失;但我们仍然认为它们在概念上有所不同,因为电力工程的主要任务是在空间相距较远的各地之间输送能量,而通信系统的主要目的是传递、提取和处理信息,尽管在这个时候或许消耗相当大的电力。

3. 混合译

实际上完全倒译或完全顺译的句子并不多见而两者同时使用的情况居多。

The two-electrode tube consists of a tungsten filament, which gives off electrons when it is heated, and a plate toward which the electrons migrate when the field is in the right direction.

二极管由一根钨丝和一个极板组成,钨丝受热时放出电子,当电场方向为正时,电子就移向极板。

Less voltage is required to breakdown a given thickness of air than glass, and more suitable in this respect for a high voltage condenser.

击穿一定厚度的空气比击穿同等厚度的玻璃所需的电压要小,所以玻璃比空气绝缘性好,而且在这一方面对高压电容器来说玻璃较为适合。

Exercises to Translating Skill

Translate the following sentences into Chinese.

(1) The method normally employed for free electrons to be produced in electron tubes is thermionic emission, in which advantage is taken of the fact that, if a solid body is heated sufficiently, some of the electrons that it contains will escape from its surface into the surrounding space.

(2) On account of the accuracy and ease with which resistance measurements may be made and the well-known manner in which resistance varies with temperature, it is common to use this variation to indicate changes in temperature.

(3) Experiments have proved that those elements which we ordinarily class as metals, such as silver, copper and gold are good conductors are good non-conductors and therefore good insulators.

(4) An actual thermodynamic system has many characteristics, some of which are highly pertinent to the behavior under study, many of which are immaterial, and some of which may have slight or unknown influence.

(5) Manufacturing processes may be classified as unit production with small quantities of parts being made and mass production with large numbers of identical parts being produced.

(6) Radar depends on the principle that short electromagnetic wave having frequencies above 100 megacycles per second can be reflected by objects in their path somewhat as sound produces an echo.

Unit 11　3G

3G refers to the third generation of mobile communications technology. Integrating broad wireless access and Internet, 3G promises mobile multimedia services and offers the potential to keep people being connected at all times and in all places. 3G can work over wireless air interfaces such as GSM, TDMA, and CDMA.

3G 指第三代移动通信技术。它结合了宽带无线接入与国际互联网技术,使得实现移动多媒体业务以及人们在任何时间、任何地点保持通信成为可能。3G 可以工作于 GSM, TDMA 和 CDMA 等无线空中接口。

Text A

IMT-2000 Global 3G Standard

IMT-2000 is the term used by the International Telecommunications Union (ITU) for a set of globally harmonized standards for Third Generation (3G) mobile telecoms services and equipment. 3G services are designed to offer broadband wireless access at the speed of 2 Mbit/s, which will allow mobile multimedia services to become possible. In 1998, the ITU called for proposals for IMT-2000 from different interested parties and it received many different ideas based on time division multiple access (TDMA) and code division multiple access (CDMA) technology. The European Telecommunications Standards Institute (ETSI) and Global System for Mobile Communications (GSMC) companies, such as the infrastructure vendors Nokia and Ericsson, are backing wideband code division multiple access (W-CDMA), whilst the US vendors, including Qualcomm and Lucent Technologies, are backing CDMA2000.

To take account of the different vested interests, the ITU has proposed that IMT-2000 is a CDMA-based standard, which encompasses three different modes of operation, each of which should be able to work over both the GSM and IS-41 network architectures.[1] The three modes are as follows:

Direct sequence frequency division duplex (FDD). Based on the first operational node of the UMTS terrestrial radio access (UTRA) proposal, this mode is supported by the GSM network operators and vendors, plus Japan's ARIB community.

Multi-carrier FDD. Based on the CDMA2000 proposal of the US Telecommunications Industry Association, this mode is supported by the US cellular network operators and vendors.

Time division duplex. Based on the second operational node of the UTRA proposal, this unpaired band solution has been harmonized with China's TD-SCDMA proposal.

The green light for the development of these services was given at the ITU's World Radiocommunication Conference, held from May 8 to June 3 2000 in Istanbul, Turkey.[2] This decision provides for a number of frequency bands available on a global basis for countries wishing to implement IMT-2000. Making use of existing mobile and mobile-satellite frequency allocations, the agreement also provides for a high degree of flexibility, to allow operators to migrate towards IMT-2000 according to market and other national considerations.[3]

At the same time, it does not preclude the use of these bands for other types of mobile applications, or by other services to which these bands are allocated — a key factor that enabled the consensus to be reached.[4] While the decision of the conference globally provides for the licensing and manufacturing of IMT-2000 in the identified bands on a globally harmonized basis, each country will decide on the timing of availability at the national level according to their specific needs.

The frequencies for IMT-2000 were allocated in two phases, the first made in 1992 when IMT-2000 began development, and the second set at the recent conference. The bands that had initially been identified in 1992, on the basis of which licensing has already been made or is under way in many parts of the world, remained unchanged.[5] These bands are 1,885~2,025 MHz and 2,110~2,200 MHz. The additional bands identified for the terrestrial component of IMT-2000 are 806~960 MHz, 1,710~1,885 MHz and 2,500~2,690 MHz. All bands globally identified for IMT-2000 have equal status.

Words and Expressions

globally ['gləubli] *adv.* 世界上（全世界）
harmonize ['ha:mənaiz] *v.* 使……调和，使……一致
multimedia ['mʌlti'mi:djə] *n.* 多媒体
back [bæk] *v.* 支持；援助，赞助
whilst [wailst] *conj.* 当……时
take account of 考虑到，顾及；体谅
vested ['vestid] *adj.* 既得的（法律规定的）
encompass [in'kʌmpəs] *v.* 包围，包含，包括
node [nəud] *n.* 节点
terrestrial [ti'restriəl] *adj.* 地球的；陆地的
community [kə'mju:niti] *n.* 社区；团体；界
multi-carrier [ˌmʌlti'kæriə] *n.* 多载波
provide for 供给；提供；规定
implement ['implimənt] *v.* 使生效；履行；实施
make use of 利用

allocation [ˌæləˈkeiʃən] n. 拨给；分配
preclude [priˈkluːd] v. 阻止；排除；妨碍
factor [ˈfæktə] n. 因素；要素
consensus [kənˈsensəs] n. (意见等)一致，一致同意
timing [ˈtaimiŋ] n. 时间安排；时间选择；计时，定时
initially [iˈniʃəli] adv. 最初；开头
under way 在进行中
status [ˈsteitəs] n. 地位，身份；情形，状况

Notes

[1] To take account of the different vested interests, the ITU has proposed that IMT-2000 is a CDMA-based standard, which encompasses three different modes of operation, each of which should be able to work over both the GSM and IS-41 network architectures.

此句可译为：为照顾各方利益，国际电信联盟提出，IMT-2000 标准以 CDMA 为基础，包括 3 个不同的工作模式。其中每一个工作模式都应当能够工作于 GSM 和 IS-41 的网络体系。

本句中 To take account of the different vested interests 为目的状语；that 引导宾语从句做 proposed 的宾语；两个 which 引导的都是非限定性定语从句，分别限定 standard 和 modes of operation。

[2] The green light for the development of these services was given at the ITU's World Radiocommunication Conference, held from May 8 to June 3 2000 in Istanbul, Turkey.

此句可译为：国际电信联盟于 2000 年 5 月 8 日至 6 月 3 日期间在土耳其的伊斯坦布尔召开世界无线通信大会，同意开发以上业务。

本句中 green light 意为"准许、许可"，常用搭配为 give/get the green light，意为给予/获得许可。give the green light 在本句中以被动语态的形式出现。

[3] Making use of existing mobile and mobile-satellite frequency allocations, the agreement also provides for a high degree of flexibility, to allow operators to migrate towards IMT-2000 according to market and other national considerations.

此句可译为：该决议利用现有的移动通信和移动卫星通信的频率分配，为运营商们根据市场情况和国情向 IMT-2000 过渡提供了高度的灵活性。

本句中 Making use of existing mobile and mobile-satellite frequency allocations 为现在分词短语，做方式状语。

[4] At the same time, it does not preclude the use of these bands for other types of mobile applications, or by other services to which these bands are allocated — a key factor that enabled the consensus to be reached.

此句可译为：同时，该决议并未排除使用应用于其他移动通信的或分配给其他业务的频带，这是大会达成一致意见的关键因素。

本句中 which 引导的是定语从句，限定 other services；a key factor 为前面整个主句的

同位语,其后是 that 引导的定语从句,对其进行限定。

[5] The bands that had initially been identified in 1992, on the basis of which licensing has already been made or is under way in many parts of the world, remained unchanged.

此句可译为:早在 1992 年确定的频带保持不变,因为全世界许多地方已发放的或正在发放的频带使用许可证是以这些频带为基础的。

本句中 The bands 和 remained unchanged 构成主谓表结构,充当全句的主句。that 引导的定语从句与 which 引导的非限定性定语从句共同限定、修饰 the bands,但 which 引导的非限定性定语从句在此处更侧重于说明主句的原因。

Exercises

1. Put the following phrases into English.

(1) 国际电信联盟(ITU)

(2) 宽带无线接入

(3) 移动多媒体业务

(4) 宽带码分多址(W-CDMA)

(5) 时分多址(TDMA)

(6) 欧洲电信标准化协会(ETSI)

(7) 频分双工模式

(8) 美国电信工业委员会(TIA)

(9) 时分双工模式

(10) 世界无线通信大会

2. Put the following phrases into Chinese.

(1) modes of operation

(2) operational node

(3) network architecture

(4) frequency allocation

(5) a set of globally harmonized standards

(6) a CDMA-based standard

(7) a high degree of flexibility

(8) the licensing and manufacturing of IMT-2000

(9) cellular network operators and vendors

(10) UMTS terrestrial radio access (UTRA) proposal

3. Translate the following sentences into Chinese.

(1) 3G services are designed to offer broadband wireless access at the speed of 2 Mbit/s.

(2) IMT-2000 is a CDMA-based standard, which encompasses three different modes of operation.

(3) Each mode should be able to work over both the GSM and IS-41 network architectures.

(4) This decision provides for a number of frequency bands available on a global basis for countries wishing to implement IMT-2000.

(5) Each country will decide on the timing of availability at the national level according to their specific needs.

(6) The bands that had initially been identified in 1992 remained unchanged.

(7) All bands globally identified for IMT-2000 have equal status.

(8) Time division duplex has been harmonized with China's TD-SCDMA proposal.

(9) The ITU received many different proposals based on time division multiple access (TDMA) and code division multiple access (CDMA) technology.

(10) The agreement also provides for a high degree of flexibility, to allow operators to migrate towards IMT-2000 according to market and other national considerations.

4. Translate the English paragraphs into Chinese.

(1) China announced in May 2008, that the telecoms sector was re-organized and three 3G networks would be built so, that the largest mobile operator, China Mobile would retain its GSM customer base and launch 3G onto the Chinese standard, TD-SCDMA. China Unicom would retain its GSM customer base but relinquish its CDMA2000 customer base, and launch 3G on the globally leading W-CDMA (UMTS) standard. The CDMA2000 customers of China Unicom would go to China Telecom, which would then launch 3G on the CDMA 1x EV-DO standard. This means that China will have all three main cellular technology 3G standards in commercial use.

(2) Key features of 3G systems are compatibility of services, small pocket terminals, world wide roaming capability, Internet applications, better-quality voice, high-speed data and a wide range of services and terminals. Therefore, with it, you do enjoy convenience of life and work. Imagine that you have a video conference over wireless phones, check e-mails and browse the web without wires. Nowadays, as nothing can compare with 3G in respect of its powerful functions, many countries view 3G as a great chance in the development of telecommunications. Many Asian and Europian countries have increased investment in their research on 3G, hoping that the lead in 3G would bring them great benefits in the future.

Text B

Implementation and History of 3G

The first pre-commercial 3G network was launched by NTT DoCoMo in Japan branded as FOMA, in May of 2001 on a pre-release of W-CDMA technology. The first commercial launch of 3G was also by NTT DoCoMo in Japan on October 1, 2001. The second network to go commercially live was by SK Telecom in South Korea on the CDMA2000 1xEV-DO technology in January 2002.[1] By May 2002 the second South Korean 3G network was launched by KTF on EV-DO and thus the Koreans were the first to see competition among 3G operators.

The first European pre-commercial network was at the Isle of Man by Manx Telecom, the operator owned by British Telecom,[2] and the first commercial network in Europe was opened for business by Telenor in December 2001 with no commercial handsets and thus no paying customers.[3] These were both on the W-CDMA technology.

The first commercial United States 3G network was by Monet, on CDMA2000 1xEV-DO technology, but this network provider later shut down operations. The second 3G network operator in the USA was Verizon in October 2003 also on CDMA2000 1xEV-DO, and this network has grown strongly since then.

The "first pre-commercial demonstration network" in the southern hemisphere was built in Adelaide, South Australia by m.Net Corporation in February 2002 using UMTS on 2,100 MHz. This was a demonstration network for the 2002 IT World Congress. The first "commercial" 3G network was launched by Hutchison Telecommunications branded as "Three" in April 2003. Australia's largest and fastest 3G UMTS/HSDPA network was launched by Telstra branded as "NextG(tm)" on the 850 MHz band in October 2006, intended as a replacement of their cdmaOne network Australia wide.[4]

In December 2007, 190 3G networks were operating in 40 countries and 154 HSDPA networks were operating in 71 countries, according to the Global Mobile Suppliers Association. In Asia, Europe, Canada and the USA, telecommunication companies use W-CDMA technology with the support of around 100 terminal designs to operate 3G mobile networks.

In Europe, mass market commercial 3G services were introduced starting in March 2003 by "3" (Part of Hutchison Whampoa) in the UK and Italy. The European Union Council suggested that the 3G operators should cover 80% of the European national populations by the end of 2005.

Roll-out of 3G networks was delayed in some countries by the enormous costs of additional spectrum licensing fees. In many countries, 3G networks do not use the same radio frequencies as 2G, so mobile operators must build entirely new networks and license entirely new frequencies; an exception is the United States where carriers operate 3G service in the same frequencies as other services. The license fees in some European countries were particularly high, bolstered by government auctions of a limited number of licenses and sealed bid auctions, and initial excitement over 3G's potential.[5] Other delays were due to the expenses of upgrading equipment for the new systems.

By June 2007, 200 million 3G subscribers had been connected. Out of 3 billion mobile phone subscriptions worldwide this is only 6.7%. In the countries where 3G was launched first — Japan and South Korea — over half of all subscribers use 3G. In Europe the leading country is Italy with a third of its subscribers migrated to 3G. Other leading countries by

3G migration include UK, Austria, Australia and Singapore at the 20% migration level. A confusing statistic is counting CDMA2000 1xRTT customers as if they were 3G customers. If using this oft-disputed definition, then the total 3G subscriber base would be 475 million at June 2007 and 15.8% of all subscribers worldwide.

Words and Expressions

pre-commercial [pri:kə'mə:ʃəl] *n.* 试商用
launch ['lɔ:ntʃ] *v.* 发动,推出;发射 *n.* 发射;下水;投产
brand [brænd] *n.* 商标,牌子;烙印 *v.* 打烙印,铭刻
pre-release [pri:ri'li:s] *n.* 试发布
competition [ˌkɔmpə'tiʃən] *n.* 竞争;比赛
handset ['hændset] *n.* 电话听筒,手机,手持机
shut down (使)关闭,(使)停工
hemisphere ['hemisfiə] *n.* 地球的半球
demonstration [ˌdemən'streiʃən] *n.* 示范;证明;论证
congress ['kɔŋgres] *n.* 代表大会;国会,议会
replacement [ri'pleismənt] *n.* 代替,取代;更换;替代的人(或物)
supplier [sə'plaiə] *n.* 供应商
introduce ['intrə'dju:s] *v.* 推行,推销
council ['kaunsəl] *n.* 委员会,理事会
roll-out [rəul'aut] 首次展示;推出,推广
enormous [i'nɔ:məs] *adj.* 巨大的,极大的,庞大的
fee [fi:] *n.* 费用
exception [ik'sepʃən] *n.* 例外
bolster ['bəulstə] *v.* 支撑,支持;鼓励
seal [si:l] *v.* (密)封
bid [bid] *n.* 企图;投标
initial [i'niʃəl] *adj.* 开始的;最初的
subscriber [səb'skraibə] *n.* 订户;电话用户
subscription [səb'skripʃən] *n.* 预订,预约
worldwide [ˌwə:ld'waid] *adj.* 世界范围(的),全世界(的)
leading ['li:diŋ] *adj.* 最重要的;首位的,带头的
migration [mai'greiʃən] *n.* 迁移;移居
confusing [kən'fju:ziŋ] *adj.* 使人困惑的,令人费解的;容易引起混乱的
statistic [stə'tistik] *n.* 统计数值,统计资料
oft-disputed [ɔ:ftdis'pju:tid] *adj.* 经常引起争议的

Notes

[1] The second network to go commercially live was by SK Telecom in South Korea

on the CDMA2000 1xEV-DO technology in January 2002.

此句可译为：2002年1月，世界第二个3G网络由韩国SK电信投入商用。该网络以CDMA2000 1xEV-DO技术为基础。

本句中 to go commercially live 做后置定语限定 The second network。On…结构做状语，意为"以……为基础"。

[2] The first European pre-commercial network was at the Isle of Man by Manx Telecom, the operator owned by British Telecom.

此句可译为：英国电信公司下属的Manx电信公司在马恩岛推出了欧洲第一个3G试商用网络。

本句中 the operator 做 Manx Telecom 的同位语。owned by British Telecom 为过去分词短语做后置定语，限定 the operator。

[3] … and the first commercial network in Europe was opened for business by Telenor in December 2001 with no commercial handsets and thus no paying customers.

此句可译为：欧洲第一个3G商用网络由挪威的Telenor电信公司于2001年12月投入运营。因为没有商用手机可供使用，所以该网络也没有付费的客户。

本句中 with…结构做状语，表示伴随状况。

[4] Australia's largest and fastest 3G UMTS/HSDPA network was launched by Telstra branded as "NextG(tm)" on the 850 MHz band in October 2006, intended as a replacement of their cdmaOne network Australia wide.

此句可译为：2006年10月，澳大利亚电讯公司（Telstra）推出了澳大利亚规模最大、速度最快的3G网络。该网络名为"NextG(tm)"，采用UMTS/HSDPA标准，工作于850 MHz频带，用来替代澳大利亚的cdmaOne网络。

本句中 branded as…结构为过去分词短语做定语，限定主语 network。intended as…结构为过去分词短语做状语，说明主语 network 的用途。HSDPA是一种移动通信协议，为 high speed downlink packet access 的缩写，指高速下行分组接入，也称为3.5G。

[5] The license fees in some European countries were particularly high, bolstered by government auctions of a limited number of licenses and sealed bid auctions, and initial excitement over 3G's potential.

此句可译为：由于政府拍卖的频谱使用许可证数量有限和密封投标拍卖方式的影响以及大家在初期阶段热情看好3G的发展前景，这就使得频谱使用许可费在一些欧洲国家非常高。

本句中 bolstered by…结构为过去分词做状语，说明频谱使用许可费高的原因。government auctions of…和 initial excitement…为并列成分，做 by 的宾语。

Exercises

Mark the following statements with T(true) or F(false) according to the text.

(1) It was Koreans who were the first to launch the first commercial network on the CDMA2000 1xEV-DO technology. ( )

(2) The first commercial launch of 3G was by NTT DoCoMo in Japan in May of 2001.　　　　　　　　　　　　　　　　　　　　　　　　　　　　( )

(3) The 3G network built by Monet on CDMA2000 1x EV-DO technology has grown strongly.　　　　　　　　　　　　　　　　　　　　　　　　　　　( )

(4) The 3G networks deployed by Manx Telecom, Telenor and Telstra were all on the WCDMA technology.　　　　　　　　　　　　　　　　　　　　　　( )

(5) The 3G networks in Australia were based on UMTS.　　　　　( )

(6) South Korea was the first country to have different 3G networks in commercial operation.　　　　　　　　　　　　　　　　　　　　　　　　　　　　( )

(7) Britain has the largest 3G subscription in Europe.　　　　　　( )

(8) The first Australian commercial 3G network was launched by Hutchison Telecommunications.　　　　　　　　　　　　　　　　　　　　　　　　　　　( )

(9) There is no consensus as to whether CDMA 2000 1x RTT customers should be defined as 3G customers.　　　　　　　　　　　　　　　　　　　　　　( )

(10) The United States mobile network operators have to build entirely new networks and license entirely new frequencies to operate their 3G services.　　　( )

Translating Skill 11

被 动 句

比较汉语,英语中的被动语态要多一些;比较普通英语,电子信息专业英语中的被动语态更多。由于要求客观性,专业英语中即使使用主动语态句,其主语也常用事物而非人或动物。据统计,科技专业英语中的被动句占所有句子的35%~50%。被动句简单明了,使读者(或译者)一眼就能发现放在句首的最重要信息,即事实和行为,而把行为者隐去。

电子信息专业英语中被动句汉译一般有以下几种主要方法。

1. 被动译法

这是被动句最简易而又最基本的一种译法。把原文中的被动句译为汉语被动型,经常用一些能表示被动意义的汉字,如"被","由","为","给","受","遭"以及"经过","为……所"等。

例如:

Electricity itself had been known to man.

电为人类所熟知。

Telephone was invented by Alexander Graham Bell in 1875.

电话在1875年由亚历山大·格雷厄姆·贝尔发明。

Besides voltage, resistance and capacitance, an alternating current is also influenced by inductance.

除电压、电阻和电容外,交流电还受电感的影响。

2. 主动译法

由于汉语中的主动语态多于被动,故这种译法也自然成为使用最多的一种,多用汉语"是……的","加以……"等。

例如:

Resistance is measured in ohm.

电阻是以欧姆为单位计量的。

20 volts were read from the voltmeter.

电压表读数为 20 伏。

也可加"人们"、"有人"、"我们"、"大家"等主语。

例如:

The mechanical energy can be changed into electrical energy by a generator.

人们用发电机可将机械能转化为电能。

The advent of numerical control was predicted by many to be the end of copying.

许多人预言数控技术的出现将是仿形加工的终结。

3. 常见句型译法

电子信息专业英语中常用被动句型"It is ＋ past participle ＋ that…"这种句型一般译为"据说(称,信)……"、"人们认为……"、"有人……"等。

例如:

It is noticed that in addition to its high conductivity, copper is corrosion resistant and easily processed.

人们注意到铜除导电率高之外,还耐腐蚀并容易加工。

It is said that there are five generations of computers at present.

据说现在有 5 代计算机。

4. 转化译法

(1) 将被动句中的动作者转译为主语。

例如:

Many complicated problems will be solved by computers.

计算机能解决许多复杂问题。

The office will be computerized by the workers.

工人们将使办公室计算机化。

(2) 将被动句中的主语转译为宾语。

例如:

Much progress has been made in videophone in less than two decades.

不到二十年可视电话取得许多进展。

Measures have been taken to develop optical fiber technology.

已采取措施发展光纤技术。

(3) 其他转化。

例如:

Computers are used in everyday life.

日常生活中都要用计算机。

A brief account has been made about the operation of the new electronic computer.

已简单地叙述了这台新型电子计算机的操作方法。

Exercises to Translating Skill

Translate the following sentences into Chinese.

(1) Current will not flow continually, since the circuit is broken by the insulating material.

(2) When he entered the operating room, he found that all the lights had been turned on.

(3) The working plan will be examined by a special committee first.

(4) The section of the power supply is not allowed to touch with fingers.

(5) They were seen repairing these machine tools.

(6) Considerable use is made of these data.

(7) It is required that the machine should be maintained at regular intervals.

(8) Brief reference should be made to the law of the conservation of energy.

(9) It should be pointed out that this process is called oxidation.

(10) It is generally recognized that the insulation resistance of a cable is inversely proportional to its length.

Unit 12   ADSL

ADSL is a new technology that allows more data to be sent over existing copper telephone lines. ADSL supports data rates of from 1.5~9 Mbit/s when receiving data (known as the downstream rate) and from 16~640 kbit/s when sending data (known as the upstream rate). ADSL is growing in popularity as more areas around the world gain access.

非对称数字用户线(ADSL)是一种可以通过现有铜芯电话线大量传输数据的新技术。ADSL在接收数据时支持1.5~9 Mbit/s的数据率(称为下行数据率),在发送数据时支持16~640 kbit/s的数据率(称为上行数据率)。随着全世界更多的地区可以实现ADSL接入,ADSL越来越受到人们的青睐。

Text A

ADSL

Connection to the Internet can be in various ways. One might connect a computer to the Internet over a regular modem, on an integrated services digital network (ISDN) line, through a local area network in the office, through a cable modem, and through a digital subscriber line (DSL) connection. ADSL (asymmetric digital subscriber line) is a high-speed Internet access service that utilizes existing copper telephones lines to send and receive data at speeds that far exceed conventional dial-up modems.[1] The fastest dial-up modems are rated at 57 kilobits per second (kbit/s), and usually operate at about 53 kbit/s under good conditions. By comparison, ADSL allows data stream speeds from 1.5 to 8 megabits per second (Mbit/s), depending on the grade of ADSL service purchased.

ADSL uses standard telephone lines to transmit upstream and downstream data on a digital frequency, which sets these data streams apart from the analog signals telephones and fax machines use.[2] Because the ADSL signal is operating on a different frequency, the telephone can be used normally, even when surfing the Web with ADSL service. The only requirement will probably be inexpensive DSL filters on each phone or fax line, to remove any "white noise" on the line that might be generated from ADSL service.[3]

The "asymmetric" in ADSL refers to the fact that the downstream data rate, or the data coming to your computer from the Internet, is traveling faster than upstream data, or the data traveling from your computer to the Internet.[4] Upstream data rates are slower because Web page requests are fairly miniscule data strings that do not require much bandwidth to handle.[5]

ADSL will play a crucial role as telephone companies, and other service providers, enter new markets for delivering information in video and multimedia formats. New broadband cabling will take decades to reach all prospective subscribers, but success of these new services will depend upon reaching as many subscribers as possible during the first few years. By bringing movies, television, video catalogs, corporate LANs, and the Internet into homes and small businesses, ADSL will make these markets viable and profitable, for telephone companies and application suppliers alike.

An ADSL circuit connects an ADSL modem on each end of a twisted-pair telephone line, creating three information channels—a high speed downstream channel, a medium speed upstream channel, and a duplex telephone channel, depending on the implementation of the ADSL architecture. ADSL depends upon advanced digital signal processing and creative algorithms to squeeze so much information through twisted-pair telephone lines. In addition, many advances have been required in transformers, analog filters, and A/D converters. Long telephone lines may attenuate signals at one megahertz by as much as 90 dB, forcing analog sections of ADSL modems to work very hard to realize large dynamic ranges, separate channels, and maintain low noise figures. To create multiple channels, ADSL modems divide the available bandwidth of a telephone line in one of two ways: frequency division multiplexing (FDM) or echo cancellation. FDM assigns one band for upstream data and another band for downstream data. The downstream path is then divided by time division multiplexing into one or more high speed channels and one or more low speed channels. Echo cancellation assigns the upstream band to overlap the downstream, and separates the two by means of local echo cancellation, a technique well known in V. 32 and V. 34 modems.[6]

Words and Expressions

integrated ['intigreitid] *adj.* 综合的；集成的
modem ['məudem] *n.* 调制解调器
asymmetric [ˌeisi'metrik] *adj.* 不对称的
access ['ækses] *n.* 通道，入口；接近，进入 *v.* 存取
megabit ['megəbit] *n.* 兆位，兆比特
upstream ['ʌp'stri:m] *adj. & adv.* 上行(游)的
downstream [ˌdaun'stri:m] *adj. & adv.* 下行(游)的
fax [fæks] *n.* 传真(机)，传真件 *v.* 传真传输
normally ['nɔ:məli] *adv.* 通常；正常地
miniscule ['miniskju:l] *adj.* 很小的，很不重要的
string [striŋ] *n.* 弦，线；一串，一行
provider [prə'vaidə] *n.* 供应者
video ['vidiəu] *n.* 录像；视频 *adj.* 录像的；视频的

cabling ['keibliŋ] n. 成缆，布线
prospective [prə'spektiv] adj. 预期的；未来的；可能的
catalog ['kætəlɔg] n. 目录（册）
corporate ['kɔːpərit] adj. 法人团体的，公司的；全体的，共同的
viable ['vaiəbəl] adj. 可行的；能活下去的
profitable ['prɔfitəbl] adj. 有利可图的，有益的
algorithm ['ælgəriðəm] n. 算法
converter [kən'vəːtə(r)] n. 转换器
attenuate [ə'tenjueit] v. 削弱；减弱；衰减
megahertz ['megəˌhəːts] n. 兆赫
section ['sekʃən] n. 部分，段
dynamic [dai'næmik] adj. 有活力的；动力的；动态的
echo ['ekəu] n. 回音，共鸣
cancellation [ˌkænsə'leiʃən] n. 取消
assign [ə'sain] v. 指（选）派；指定；分配，布置
overlap [ˌəuvə'læp] v. （与……）重叠

Notes

[1] ADSL (asymmetric digital subscriber line) is a high-speed Internet access service that utilizes existing copper telephones lines to send and receive data at speeds that far exceed conventional dial-up modems.

此句可译为：ADSL（非对称数字用户线）是一种高速互联网接入业务，它使用现有的电话线来发送和接收数据，其速度远高于传统的拨号方式。

本句中有两个 that，分别引导各自的定语从句。定语从句 that utilizes existing copper telephones lines 修饰前面的 service，定语从句 that far exceed conventional dial-up modems 修饰前面的 speed。to send and receive data 为并列的不定式短语，表示目的。

[2] ADSL uses standard telephone lines to transmit upstream and downstream data on a digital frequency, which sets these data streams apart from the analog signals telephones and fax machines use.

此句可译为：ADSL 使用标准的电话线在数字频率上传送上行和下行数据流，数字频率将这些数据流和电话与传真机使用的模拟信号分开。

本句中 which sets these data streams apart from the analog signals telephones and fax machines use 为非限制性定语从句，修饰 digital frequency。该非限制性定语从句可采用分译的方法。to transmit upstream and downstream data 为不定式短语，做主句的目的状语。

[3] The only requirement will probably be inexpensive DSL filters on each phone or fax line, to remove any "white noise" on the line that might be generated from ADSL service.

此句可译为：唯一的需要是在每个电话线或传真线使用并不贵的 DSL 滤波器，以去除 ADSL 业务产生的线路"白噪声"。

本句中 to remove any "white noise" on the line that might be generated from ADSL service，不定式短语做主句的目的状语。on the line，介词短语做后置定语。that might be generated from ADSL service，由 that 引导的定语从句，修饰 white noise。

[4] The "asymmetric" in ADSL refers to the fact that the downstream data rate, or the data coming to your computer from the Internet, is traveling faster than upstream data, or the data traveling from your computer to the Internet.

此句可译为：ADSL 中的非对称是指下行数据流速率大于上行数据流，下行数据流是从互联网上到你计算机的数据，上行数据流是从你计算机上到互联网的数据。

本句中 that 至句末为同位语从句，修饰 the fact。or the data coming to your computer from the Internet 和 or the data traveling from your computer to the Internet，可以看成插入语，分别修饰各自前面的 data；coming to your computer from the Internet 和 traveling from your computer to the Internet 是现在分词短语，修饰各自前面的 data。

[5] Upstream data rates are slower because Web page requests are fairly miniscule data strings that do not require much bandwidth to handle.

此句可译为：上行数据速率较小是由于网络请求是相当小的数据串，为有效操作并不需要很大的带宽。

本句中 because 引出原因状语从句。that do not require much bandwidth to handle 为定语从句修饰前面的 data string。to handle 为动词不定式做主句的目的状语。

[6] Echo cancellation assigns the upstream band to overlap the downstream, and separates the two by means of local echo cancellation, a technique well known in V. 32 and V. 34 modems.

此句可译为：回声抵消技术安排上行频带与下行频带重叠，通过本地回声抵消来分开两个频带。这种技术在 V. 32 和 V. 34 调制解调器中用得较多。

本句中 and 连接两个并列谓语 assign 和 separate。a technique well known in V. 32 and V. 34 modems 做 echo cancellation 的同位语，其中的 well known in V. 32 and V. 34 modems 为过去分词短语，修饰前面的 technique，该同位语可翻译成一个与主句并列的单句。

Exercises

1. Put the following phrases into English.

(1) 综合业务数字网   (6) 模拟滤波器
(2) 传真机   (7) 数据流
(3) 局域网   (8) 回声消除
(4) 双工电话信道   (9) 白噪声
(5) 数字用户线   (10) A/D 变换器

2. Put the following phrases into Chinese.

(1) asymmetric digital subscriber line
(2) high speed Internet access service

(3) the grade of ADSL service purchased

(4) the analog signal telephones and fax machine use

(5) the data coming to your computer from the Internet

(6) twisted pair telephone lines

(7) the available bandwidth of a telephone line

(8) time division multiplexing

(9) digital signal processing

(10) frequency division multiplexing

3. Translate the following sentences into Chinese.

(1) The fastest dial-up modems are rated at 57 kilobits per second (kbit/s), and usually operate at about 53 kbit/s under good conditions.

(2) Because the ADSL signal is operating on a different frequency, the telephone can be used normally, even when surfing the Web with ADSL service.

(3) ADSL will play a crucial role as telephone companies, and other service providers, enter new markets for delivering information in video and multimedia formats.

(4) ADSL depends upon advanced digital signal processing and creative algorithms to squeeze so much information through twisted-pair telephone lines.

(5) In addition, many advances have been required in transformers, analog filters, and A/D converters.

(6) The downstream path is then divided by time division multiplexing into one or more high speed channels and one or more low speed channels.

(7) FDM assigns one band for upstream data and another band for downstream data.

(8) Success of these new services will depend upon reaching as many subscribers as possible during the first few years.

(9) ADSL will make these markets viable and profitable, for telephone companies and application suppliers alike.

(10) Analog sections of ADSL modems work very hard to realize large dynamic ranges, separate channels, and maintain low noise figures.

4. Translate the following paragraphs into Chinese.

(1) ADSL works on the principle that since voice does not use all of the bandwidth available from a standard copper twisted-pair line; it is possible to maintain a high-speed data connection at the same time. To do this, ADSL splits the 1 MHz maximum bandwidth of a copper wire connection into 4 kHz channels, only the bottom 4 kHz channel used for plain old telephone system (POTS) conversations, fax and analog modem data. The other 256 available channels are used for parallel digital communication. Being asymmetric, 192 channels of 4 kHz are used for the downlink and only 64 for the uplink. In this way ADSL can be viewed as simply taking a serial string of digital data and converting it into a parallel string, thereby increasing data throughput.

(2) The modulation technique employed in ADSL is known as discrete multi-tone (DMT), the encoding and decoding is performed at the exchange and at the user end respectively, in the same way it is by a conventional dial-up modem. An earlier system, called carrier-less amplitude phase (CAP), able to use all the bandwidth above 4 kHz as a single transmission channel, had the advantage of being closely related to the quadrature amplitudes modulation (QAM) technique used by high-speed modems at rates above 9.6 kbit/s and was also cheaper to implement. However, DMT is a more reliable, sophisticated and flexible technology, and has succeeded in becoming the universally adopted standard.

Text B

Application for ADSL

Asymmetric digital subscriber line (ADSL) is a form of DSL, a data communications technology that enables faster data transmission over copper telephone lines than a conventional voice band modem can provide.[1] The distinguishing characteristic of ADSL over other forms of DSL is that the volume of data flow is greater in one direction than the other, i.e., it is asymmetric. The bandwidth in the downstream direction from the network to the subscriber is designed to be substantially higher than that of the upstream from the subscriber to the network. This arrangement suits a number of services and applications.

The delivery of entertainment video as a video on demand (VOD) service is one of the services that drove early development of ADSL. Here, the high bandwidth in the downstream direction can support a low number of digitally compressed video channels. In addition, a much lower speed control channel in the upstream direction toward the network provides the viewer with VCR type functions such as stop, play, pause, fast-forward and rewind.

VOD is reliant on a suitable standard video compression technology for entertainment video, which determines the bandwidth of the downstream video channels.[2] The ISO Motion Picture Experts Group (MPEG) have developed such standards for the storage and broadcasting of video and audio signals. Unlike the compression for interactive video communications, the compression and decompression of a film for entertainment requires a significantly higher quality in the decompressed picture, although the compression process need not be real-time but can take place as an "off-line" conversion and storage prior to transmission.[3] The MPEG standard also includes the compression of high-quality stereo sound. Using MPEG standards, an entertainment video (together with audio soundtrack) can be compressed into a digital data stream that requires a communications channel bandwidth of 1.5 Mbit/s, while a broadcast television channel would require of the order of 6 Mbit/s.

ADSL will be used to deliver a range of services in addition to VOD according to customer demand and location. Another popular application which is suited to asymmetric communication is Internet access. The Internet protocol (IP) is a packet-based, connection-oriented protocol that relies on the use of acknowledgement packets to confirm correct receipt of transmitted data packets before more data packets are sent.[4] When a user accesses the World Wide Web (WWW) pages on the Internet, the volume of data is predominantly in the direction towards the user, and takes the form of WWW pages that frequently contain large amounts of graphical information, or file downloads. In the opposite direction towards the network, there exists mainly acknowledgment packets and control packets that, due to their smaller size, require only a smaller channel bandwidth.[5] However, the upstream bandwidth must not be as small as to cause undue queuing delays to acknowledgment packets, as this may significantly reduce the throughput of packets in the downstream direction towards the user. A ratio of upstream bandwidths of the order of 10∶1 is expected to be needed. In the future, the requirement for downstream bandwidth will undoubtedly increase as the content of Web pages increases through the use of video and sound.

Other services that are expected to be delivered on ADSL are interactive games, home shopping and education.

Words and Expressions

DSL (digital subscriber line) *abbr.* 数字用户线路
substantially [səbˈstænʃəli] *adv.* 大体上；本质上；重大地；相当大地
here [hiə] (hereupon) *adv.* 于此；随后，随即；关于这个
compress [kəmˈpres] *v.* 压紧，压缩
compression [kəmˈpreʃ(ə)n] *n.* 压缩，压榨
VCR *abbr.* 盒式录像机
rewind [riːˈwaind] *v.* & *n.* 回绕；倒带
ISO (International Standards Organization) *abbr.* 国际标准化组织
MPEG (Motion Picture Experts Group) *abbr.* 活动图片专家组
interactive [ˌintərˈæktiv] *adj.* 交互式的
decompress [ˌdiːkəmˈpres] *v.* 解压缩
decompression [ˌdiːkəmˈpreʃn] *n.* 解压缩
significantly [sigˈnifəkəntli] *adv.* 较大地（重要地）
off-line [ˈɔfˌlain] *adj.* 脱机的，离线的
conversion [kənˈvəːʃən] *n.* 转变；变换
prior to *adv.* 在前，居先
stereo [ˈsteriəu] *adj.* 立体声的 *n.* 立体声（装置）
soundtrack [ˈsaundˌtræk] *n.* 声道；音带；声迹
order [ˈɔːdə] *n.* 命令；规则；等级

a range of 在……范围；一系列的
protocol ['prəutəkɔl] *n.* 协议；外交礼节
connection-oriented *adj.* 面向连接的
acknowledgement packet 应答包
confirm [kən'fə:m] *v.* 证实，肯定；确认
WWW(World Wide Web) *abbr.* 万维网，互联网
graphical ['græfikəl] *adj.* 图解的
control packet 控制包
undue [ˌʌn'dju:] *adj.* 过度的；过分的；不适当的
queuing delay 排队时延
throughput ['θru:put] *n.* 吞吐量，总处理能力

Notes

[1] Asymmetric digital subscriber Line (ADSL) is a form of DSL, a data communications technology that enables faster data transmission over copper telephone lines than a conventional voice band modem can provide.

此句可译为：数字用户线(DSL)是一种通过铜质电话线进行数据传输的数据通信技术，其传输速率大于传统的话音频带调制解调器。

本句中 a data communications technology 做 DSL 的同位语。that 引导的定语从句修饰前面的 data communications technology。该定语从句在此处可采用分译的办法处理。

[2] VOD is reliant on a suitable standard video compression technology for entertainment video, which determines the bandwidth of the downstream video channels.

此句可译为：视频点播依靠一种适合娱乐视频的标准视频压缩技术，这种技术决定了下行视频信道的带宽大小。

本句中 which 引导的非限定性定语从句修饰前面的 video compression technology，翻译时可采用分译的办法处理。

[3] Unlike the compression for interactive video communications, the compression and decompression of a film for entertainment requires a significantly higher quality in the decompressed picture, although the compression process need not be real-time but can take place as an "off-line" conversion and storage prior to transmission.

此句可译为：与交互式视频通信不同，娱乐影片的压缩过程不要求是实时的，而且可在传输之前以"离线"转换、存储的方式进行，但其压缩与解压缩要求具有相当高的解压缩图片质量。

本句为一个主从复合句，其中 although 引导的让步状语从句包含了 but 连接的两个并列部分：need not be real-time 和 can take place as… 。

[4] The Internet protocol (IP) is a packet-based, connection-oriented protocol that relies on the use of acknowledgement packets to confirm correct receipt of transmitted data packets before more data packets are sent.

此句可译为：互联网协议(IP)是一个面向连接的包协议。它依靠使用应答包来确认在

大量数据包发出之前发出的数据包能否被正确接收。

本句为一个多重主从复合句。that 引导的定语从句修饰主句的表语 protocol；to confirm… 为定语从句的目的状语，before 引导的时间状语从句说明 to confirm… 发生的时间。that 引导的定语从句在此处采用分译处理为宜。

[5] In the opposite direction towards the network, there exists mainly acknowledgment packets and control packets that, due to their smaller size, require only a smaller channel bandwidth.

此句可译为：在相反方向上，从用户到互联网的数据则主要是应答包和控制包。这些应答包和控制包的数据相对较小，因此它们仅需要很小的信道带宽。

本句中 that 引导的定语从句修饰前面的主句主语 acknowledgment packets 和 control packets，其后的 due to their smaller size 可以看成插入语，说明 require only a smaller channel bandwidth 的原因。at 引导的定语从句在此处采用分译处理为宜。

Exercises

Mark the following statements with T (true) or F (false) according to the text.

(1) In ADSL, the downstream direction refers to the direction from the subscriber to the network. ( )

(2) In ADSL, the downstream bandwidth is higher than the upstream bandwidth. ( )

(3) All of DSL can be used to transmit data over existing copper telephone lines. ( )

(4) The delivery of entertainment video as a video on demand (VOD) service played a positive role in the early development of ADSL. ( )

(5) The downstream bandwidth of ADSL can support a lot of digitally compressed video channels. ( )

(6) The bandwidth of the downstream video channels depends on standard video compression technology for entertainment video. ( )

(7) The compression process of a film for entertainment needs be real-time. ( )

(8) ADSL is widely used in Internet access. ( )

(9) Acknowledgment packets and control packets in the opposite direction towards the network require only a high channel bandwidth. ( )

(10) Undue queuing delays to acknowledgment packets will arise if the downstream bandwidth is too small. ( )

Translating Skill 12

专有名词的翻译（一）

在电子信息类科技原文中经常出现专有名词（proper names），其中包括人名、地名、单位名、事件名和广告名。专有名词在一般《英汉词典》中甚少收录,给翻译带来困难。专有名词翻译是全文翻译的重要组成部分,正确译出专有名词有时对全文理解有很大帮助。

专有名词翻译多采用音译,少数意译或音、意结合,但都必须遵循约定俗成,名从主人的原则,所以专有名词汉译首先要依靠相关翻译资料,若自己动手译出则要顾及已有的译词。

翻译不同类专有名词时要注意许多细节,以下分别加以说明。

1. 姓名

英、美人姓名通常为:教名 + 名 + 姓,有如下译法,例如:

Alexander Graham Bell	亚历山大·格雷厄姆·贝尔
	A. G. 贝尔
	亚历山大·G. 贝尔
	A. 格雷厄姆·贝尔
Isaac. C. Smith	伊萨克·C. 史密斯
	I. C. 史密斯

父子使用同名,子名后加 Jr.(Junior),译为"小",例如:

Charles Brown, Jr.	小查尔斯·布朗或小布朗

2. 地名

地名汉译以中国地名委员会制定的有关规定为依据,力求准确和规范化,并适当顾及习惯译名。

地名以音译为主。

Hartford, Conn	康涅狄格州哈德福德
San Francisco, Cal	加州圣弗朗西斯科
Kansas City	堪萨斯城
Capitol Ave	卡皮特大街

少数意译。

Grand Canyon	大峡谷
Silicon Valley	硅谷
One Hundred and Two River	一〇二河

译名为一个汉字时酌情加字。

Bonn	波恩
Bern	伯尔尼
Leh	列城

日本、越南等国地名不用音译。

Edo-gawa	江川户(日)
Cua Cam Song	楚门河(越)

Exercises to Translating Skill

Translate the following names into Chinese.

(1) Samuel Frinley Breese Morse
(2) King Island
(3) Guglielmo Marconi
(4) Newport
(5) Thomas Edison
(6) Sahara Desert
(7) Isaac Newton
(8) Toyohashi
(9) Almon B. Strowger
(10) Van
(11) George. W. Coy
(12) Yellowstone National Park
(13) Howard Gammage, Jr.
(14) Kyoto
(15) Franklin, Benjamin
(16) Cape York
(17) John Henry Smith
(18) Yosu
(19) Washington George
(20) Michigan

Unit 13　The Wireless Web

There is considerable interest in small portable devices capable of accessing the Web via a wireless link. In fact, the first tentative steps in that direction have already been taken. No doubt there will be a great deal of change in this area in the coming years, but it is still worth examining some of the current ideas relating to the wireless Web to see where we are now and where we might be heading. We will focus on the first two wide area wireless Web systems to hit the market: WAP and i-mode[1].

人们对能够通过无线链路来访问网络的小型便携式设备有相当大的兴趣。事实上,人们在这个方向上已经采取了一些试探性的措施。毫无疑问,在接下来的几年里,这个领域将会发生许多变化,但是当前一些与无线网络相关的思想仍然值得我们去研究,这样我们就可以知道目前的状况以及可能的发展。本单元,我们将迎合当前的市场情况,重点讨论两个广域无线网络系统:WAP 和 i-mode。

Text A

Second-Generation Wireless Web

WAP 1.0, based on recognized international standards, was supposed to be a serious tool for people in business on the move. It failed.[2] I-mode was an electronic toy for Japanese teenagers using proprietary everything. It was a huge success. What happens next? Each side learned something from the first generation of wireless Web. The WAP consortium learned from contents. Not having a large number of Web sites that speak your markup language is fatal.[3] NTT DoCoMo learned that a closed, proprietary system closely tied to tiny handsets and Japanese culture is not a good export product. The conclusion that both sides drew is that to convince a large number of Web sites to put their content in your format, it is necessary to have an open, stable, markup language that is universally accepted.[4] Format wars are not good for business.

Both services are about to enter the second generation of wireless Web technology. WAP 2.0 came out first, so we will use that as our example. WAP 1.0 got some things right, and they have been continued. For one thing, WAP can be carried on a variety of different networks. The first generation used circuit-switched networks, but packet-switched networks were always an option and still are. Second-generation systems are likely to use packet switching, for example, GPRS. For another, WAP initially was aimed at supporting a wide variety of devices, from mobile phones to powerful notebook computers, and still is.[5]

WAP 2.0 also has some new features. The most significant ones are:
(1) Push model as well as pull model.
(2) Support for integrating telephony into applications.
(3) Multimedia messaging.
(4) Inclusion of 264 pictograms.
(5) Interface to a storage device.
(6) Support for plug-ins in the browser.

The pull model is well known: the client asks for a page and gets it. The push model supports data arriving without being asked for, such as a continuous feed of stock prices or traffic alerts.[6]

Voice and data are starting to merge, and WAP 2.0 supports them in a variety of ways. We saw one example of this earlier with i-mode's ability to hyperlink an icon or text on the screen to a telephone number to be called.[7] Along with e-mail and telephony, multimedia messaging is supported.

The huge popularity of i-mode's emoji stimulated the WAP consortium to invent 264 of its own emoji. The categories include animals, appliances, dress, emotion, food, human body, gender, maps, music, plants, sports, time, tools, vehicles, weapons and weather.[8] Interesting enough, the standard just names each pictogram; it does not give the actual bit map, probably out of fear that some culture's representation of "sleepy" or "hug" might be insulting to another culture.[9] I-mode did not have that problem since it was intended for a single country.

Providing for a storage interface does not mean that every WAP 2.0 phone will come with a large hard disk. Flash ROM is also a storage device. A WAP-enabled wireless camera could use the flash ROM for temporary image storage before beaming the best pictures to the Internet.

Finally, plug-ins can extend the browser's capabilities. A scripting language is also provided.[10]

Various technical differences are also present in WAP 2.0. The two biggest ones concern the protocol stack and the markup language. WAP 2.0 continues to support the old protocol, but it also supports the standard Internet stacked with TCP and HTTP/1.1 as well. However, four minor (but compatible) changes to TCP were made (to simplify the code): (1) use of a fixed 64 KB window, (2) no slow start, (3) a maximum MTU of 1,500 B, and (4) a slightly different retransmission algorithm.[11]

The other technical difference with WAP 1.0 is the markup language. WAP 2.0 supports XHTML Basic, which is intended for small wireless devices. Since NTT DoCoMo has also agreed to support this subset, Web site designers can use this format and know that their pages will work on the fixed Internet and on all wireless devices.[12] These decisions will end the markup language format wars that were impeding growth of the wireless Web industry.

Words and Expressions

WAP (wireless application protocol) *abbr.* 无线应用协议
consortium [ˈkənˈsɔːtjəm] *n.* 社团，协会，联盟
markup language 标记语言
fatal [ˈfeitl] *adj.* 致命的，灾难性的；重大的，决定性的
convince [kənˈvins] *v.* 使确信，使信服；说服
stable [ˈsteibəl] *adj.* 稳定的；沉稳的，持重的 *n.* 马厩
universally [ˌjuːniˈvəːsəli] *adv.* 普遍地
circuit-switched 电路交换
packet-switched 分组交换
option [ˈɔpʃən] *n.* 选择(权)；可选择的事物；[经]买卖的特权
significant [sigˈnifikənt] *adj.* 有意义的；重大的，重要的
pictograms [pikˈtəgræms] 象形文字
plug-in *n.* [计]插件程序
merge [məːdʒ] *v.* 合并，并入，结合，融合
hyperlink [ˈhaipəliŋk] *n.* 超链接
icon [ˈaikɔn] *n.* 图标
emoji 手机表情符号，在日文中被称作"绘文字"
stimulate [ˈstimjuleit] *v.* 刺激，激励
appliance [əˈplaiəns] *n.* 用具，器具
gender [ˈdʒendə] *n.* 性别；(语法中的)性
bit map 位图
insulting [inˈsʌltiŋ] *adj.* 侮辱的，污蔑的，无礼的，损害人体的
Flash ROM 闪存
WAP-enabled 支持 WAP 功能的
scripting [skˈriptiŋ] *n.* 脚本
TCP (transfer control protocol) *abbr.* 传输控制协议
HTTP (hypertext transfer protocol) *abbr.* 超文本传输协议
retransmission [ˈriːtrænzˈmiʃən] *n.* 转播，中继，重发
MTU (maximum translation unit) *abbr.* 最大传输单元
NTT (Nippon Telegraph and Telephone Public Corporation) *abbr.* 日本电报电话公共公司
impede [imˈpiːd] *v.* 阻止，阻碍，妨碍

Notes

[1] i-mode 技术(其中的 i 代表 information)是由日本 NTT DoCoMo 公司开发的一种

无线通信技术标准。i-mode 是基于数据信息包的传输技术,用户可以据此使用自己的手机访问互联网以及收发电子邮件和一些其他信息。这种技术使得用户能够通过蜂窝电话使用 Internet 服务。

NTT DoCoMo 不仅是日本领先的移动通信运营商,而且在推进全球移动通信技术的发展方面起着举足轻重的作用。

DoCoMo 是英文"Do Communications Over Mobile Network"的首字母缩写。

〔2〕 WAP 1.0, based on recognized international standards, was supposed to be a serious tool for people in business on the move. It failed.

此句可译为:WAP 1.0 基于一些被公认的国际标准,人们曾经期望它是未来移动商务中的重要工具,但是它失败了。

based on recognized international standards 过去分词短语做定语。WAP = wireless application protocol,无线应用协议。

〔3〕 Not having a large number of Web sites that speak your markup language is fatal.

此句可译为:没有足够多的网络站点使用你的标记语言,这将是致命的。

Not having a large number of Web sites … 是-ing 分词短语做主语;that speak your markup language 是定语从句,修饰先行词 Web sites。

〔4〕 The conclusion that both sides drew is that to convince a large number of Web sites to put their content in your format, it is necessary to have an open, stable, markup language that is universally accepted.

此句可译为:双方得出的结论是要想让大量的网络站点采用你的格式来表达它们的内容,那么,一个开放的、稳定的、可被普遍接受的标记语言是非常必要的。

that both sides drew 和 that is universally accepted 都是定语从句,分别修饰先行词 conclusion 和 language。

〔5〕 For another, WAP initially was aimed at supporting a wide variety of devices, from mobile phones to powerful notebook computers, and still is.

此句可译为:另外,WAP 最初的目标是支持各种各样的设备,从移动电话到功能强大的笔记本式计算机,现在仍然坚持这个目标。

notebook computers 笔记本式计算机。

〔6〕 The push model supports data arriving without being asked for, such as a continuous feed of stock prices or traffic alerts.

此句可译为:推模型是指无需请求就可以获得数据,例如,连续地获得股票价格或者交通路况报警信息。

〔7〕 We saw one example of this earlier with i-mode's ability to hyperlink an icon or text on the screen to a telephone number to be called.

此句可译为:我们在前面介绍中已经看到过一个例子,即 i-mode 能够把一个屏幕图标或者文本链接到一个要呼叫的电话号码上。

hyperlink(超链接)是万维网上使用最多的一种技巧,它通过事先定义好的关键字或图形,只要你用鼠标单击该段文字或图形,就可以自动连上相对应的其他文件。通过这种方式,就可以实现不同网页间的跳转问题。

[8] The categories include animals, appliances, dress, emotion, food, human body, gender, maps, music, plants, sports, time, tools, vehicles, weapons and weather.

此句可译为：其中类别包括动物、器具、衣服、情绪、食物、人体、性别、地图、音乐、植物、体育、时间、工具、汽车、武器和天气。

[9] Interesting enough, the standard just names each pictogram; it does not give the actual bit map, probably out of fear that some culture's representation of "sleepy" or "hug" might be insulting to another culture.

此句可译为：非常有意思的是，该标准只是命名了每个象形文字，而并没有给出实际的位图，可能是担心某一种文化中表达"睡觉"或者"拥抱"的图案冒犯了其他的文化。

[10] Finally, plug-ins can extend the browser's capabilities. A scripting language is also provided.

此句可译为：最后，插件能够扩展浏览器的功能。并且WAP 2.0还提供了一种脚本语言。scripting 脚本，在网页中插入的脚本有JavaScript 和 VBScript 两种，它们都是一种解释性的脚本语言，它的代码可以直接嵌入到HTML命令中。JavaScript 和 VBScript 的最大特点是可以很方便地操纵网页上的元素，并与网络浏览器交互；同时，JavaScript 和 VBScript 可以捕捉客户的操作并作出反应。

[11] However, four minor (but compatible) changes to TCP were made (to simplify the code): (1) use of a fixed 64 KB window, (2) no slow start, (3) a maximum MTU of 1,500 B, and (4) a slightly different retransmission algorithm.

此句可译为：然而，它对TCP作了4个小的（但是兼容的）修改（以便简化代码）：(1)使用固定的64 KB窗口，(2)没有慢启动，(3)最大MTU为1 500字节，(4)一直略微不同的重传算法。

[12] Since NTT DoCoMo has also agreed to support this subset, Web site designers can use this format and know that their pages will work on the fixed Internet and on all wireless devices.

此句可译为：由于NTT DoCoMo公司也同意支持这个子集，所以，网络站点设计者可以使用这种格式，并且知道他们的页面既可以在固定位置的互联网上正常工作，也可以在所有的无线设备上正常工作。

Exercises

1. Put the following phrases into English.

(1) 绘文字 (6) 闪存
(2) 象形文字 (7) 标记语言
(3) 位图 (8) 推模型
(4) 存储接口 (9) 拉模型
(5) 硬盘 (10) 多媒体信息

2. Put the following phrases into Chinese.

(1) a tiny handset

(2) the format war

(3) the circuit-switched network

(4) the packet-switched network

(5) inclusion of 264 pictograms

(6) the storage device

(7) wireless camera

(8) to simplify the code

(9) slow start

(10) retransmission algorithm

3. Translate the following sentences into Chinese.

(1) The wireless Web is an exciting new development, but it is not the only one.

(2) WAP 1.0, based on recognized international standards, was supposed to be a serious tool for people in business on the move.

(3) Each side learned something from the first generation of wireless Web.

(4) For one thing, WAP can be carried on a variety of different networks.

(5) The first generation used circuit-switched networks, but packet-switched networks were always an option and still are.

(6) The pull model is well known: the client asks for a page and gets it.

(7) The huge popularity of i-mode's emoji stimulated the WAP consortium to invent 264 of its own emoji.

(8) Providing for a storage interface does not mean that every WAP 2.0 phone will come with a large hard disk.

(9) Finally, plug-ins can extend the browser's capabilities. A scripting language is also provided.

(10) These decisions will end the markup language format wars that were impeding growth of the wireless Web industry.

4. Translate the following paragraphs into Chinese.

(1) Despite its massive success in Japan, i-mode is far from clear whether it will catch on in the U.S. and Europe. In some ways, the Japanese circumstances are different from those in the West. First, most potential customers in the West (e.g., teenagers, college students and businesspersons) already have a large-screen PC at home, almost assuredly with an Internet connection at a speed of at least 56 kbit/s, often much more. In Japan, few people have an Internet-connected PC at home, in part due to lack of space, but also due to NTT's exorbitant charges for local telephone services (something like $700 for installing a line and $1.50 per hour for local calls). For most users, i-mode is their only Internet connection.

(2) Second, people in the West are not used to paying $1 a month to access CNN's Web site, $1 a month to access Yahoo's Web site, $1 a month to access Google's Web site, and so on, not to mention a few dollars per MB downloaded. Most Internet providers in the West now charge a fixed monthly fee independent of actual usage, largely in response to customer demand.

(3) Third, for many Japanese people, prime i-mode time is while they are commuting to or from work or school on the train or subway. In Europe, fewer people commute by train than in Japan, and in the U.S. hardly anyone does. Using i-mode at home next to your computer with a 17 inch monitor, a 1 Mbit/s ADSL connection, and all the free megabytes you want does not make a lot of sense. Nevertheless, nobody predicted the immense popularity of mobile phones at all, so i-mode may yet find a niche in the West.

Text B

I-Mode

While a multi-industry consortium of telecom vendors and computer companies was busy hammering out an open standard using the most advanced version of HTML available, other developments were going on in Japan. There, a Japanese woman, Mari Matsunaga, invented a different approach to the wireless Web called i-mode (information-mode). [1] She convinced the wireless subsidiary of the former Japanese telephone monopoly that her approach was right, and in February 1999, NTT DoCoMo (literally: Japanese Telephone and Telegraph Company everywhere you go) launched the service in Japan. [2] Within three years it had over 35 million Japanese subscribers, who could access over 40,000 special i-mode Web sites. It also had most of the world's telecom companies drooling over its financial success, especially in light of the fact that WAP appeared to be going nowhere. [3] Let us now take a look at what i-mode is and how it works.

The i-mode system has three major components: a new transmission system, a new handset, and a new language for Web page design. The transmission system consists of two separate networks: the existing circuit-switched mobile phone network (somewhat comparable to D-AMPS), and a new packet-switched network constructed specifically for i-mode service. [4] Voice mode uses the circuit switched network and is billed per minute of connection time. I-mode uses the packet-switched network and is always on (like ADSL or cable), so there is no billing for connect time. Instead, there is a charge for each packet sent. It is not currently possible to use both networks at once.

The handsets look like mobile phones, with the addition of a small screen. NTT DoCoMo heavily advertises i-mode devices as better mobile phones rather than wireless Web terminals, even though that is precisely what they are. [5] In fact, probably most customers are not even aware they are on the Internet. They think of their i-mode devices as mobile phones with enhanced services. In keeping with this model of i-mode being a service, the handsets are not user programmable, although they contain the equivalent of a 1995 PC and could probably run Windows 95 or UNIX. [6]

When the i-mode handset is switched on, the user is presented with a list of categories of the officially-approved services. There are well over 1,000 services divided into about 20 categories. Each service, which is actually a small i-mode Web site, is run by an independent company. The major categories on the official menu include e-mail, news, weather, sports, games, shopping, maps, horoscopes, entertainment, travel, regional guides, ringing tones, recipes, gambling, home banking and stock prices.[7] The service is somewhat targeted at teenagers and people in their 20s, who tend to love electronic gadgets, especially if they come in fashionable colors.[8] The mere fact that over 40 companies are selling ringing tones says something. The most popular application is e-mail, which allows up to 500 B messages, and thus is seen as a big improvement over SMS (short message service) with its 160 B messages. Games are also popular.

Current handsets have CPUs that run at about 100 MHz, several megabytes of Flash ROM, perhaps 1 MB of RAM, and a small built-in screen.[9] I-mode requires the screen to be at least 72 pixels×94 pixels, but some high-end devices have as many as 120 pixels×160 pixels. Screens usually have 8 bit color, which allows 256 colors. This is not enough for photographs but is adequate for line drawings and simple cartoons. Since there is no mouse, on-screen navigation is done with the arrow keys.

Words and Expressions

multi-industry consortium 多产业联盟
hammer out 打造
subsidiary [səbˈsidiəri] adj. 辅助的，补充的
monopoly [məˈnɔpəli] n. 垄断；专利权
drool [druːl] v. 流口水；说昏话
comparable [ˈkɔmpərəbəl] adj. 可比较的，比得上的
precisely [priˈsaisli] adv. 正好
enhance [inˈhaːns] v. 提高，增加，加强
programmable [ˈprəugræməbl] adj. 可设计的，可编程的
UNIX n. UNIX 操作系统（一种多用户的计算机操作系统）
officially-approved adj. 官方批准的
recipe [ˈresipi] n. 处方
SMS (short message service) abbr. 短消息服务

Notes

[1] There, a Japanese woman, Mari Matsunaga, invented a different approach to the wireless Web called i-mode (information-mode).

此句可译为：一个日本女人，Mari Matsunaga，发明了一种不同的访问无线网络的方法，称为信息模式。

[2] She convinced the wireless subsidiary of the former Japanese telephone monopoly that her approach was right, and in February 1999, NTT DoCoMo (literally: Japanese

Telephone and Telegraph Company everywhere you go) launched the service in Japan.

此句可译为:她让以前日本电信垄断运行商的无线子公司相信她的方法是正确的,1999年2月,NTT DoCoMo(字面意思是:伴你行日本电话电报公司)在日本启动了无线服务。

[3] It also had most of the world's telecom companies drooling over its financial success, especially in light of the fact that WAP appeared to be going nowhere.

此句可译为:由于它成功地赚到了钱,所以令世界上大多数电信公司都垂涎三尺,尤其是在WAP似乎无法进行下去的情况下。to be going nowhere 走投无路。

[4] The transmission system consists of two separate networks: the existing circuit-switched mobile phone network (somewhat comparable to D-AMPS), and a new packet-switched network constructed specifically for i-mode service.

此句可译为:传输系统是由两个分离的网络组成的:现有的电路交换的移动电话网络(与D-AMPS类似)以及一个专门为i-mode服务而构建的新的分组交换网络。

[5] NTT DoCoMo heavily advertises i-mode devices as better mobile phones rather than wireless Web terminals, even though that is precisely what they are.

此句可译为:NTT DoCoMo花大力气来宣传i-mode设备是更好的移动电话,而不是无线网络终端,尽管它们的的确确是无线网络终端。

[6] In keeping with this model of i-mode being a service, the handsets are not user programmable, although they contain the equivalent of a 1995 PC and could probably run Windows 95 or UNIX.

此句可译为:为了与i-mode的这种模式保持一致,这些手持机不是用户可编程的,尽管它们相当于内含了一台1995年时候个人计算机,也许还可以运行Windows 95或者UNIX。

[7] The major categories on the official menu include e-mail, news, weather, sports, games, shopping, maps, horoscopes, entertainment, travel, regional guides, ringing tones, recipes, gambling, home banking and stock prices.

此句可译为:在官方菜单上的主要类别包括电子邮件、新闻、天气、体育、游戏、购物、地图、星象预测、娱乐、旅游、地区指南、铃声、医药处方、赌博、家庭银行和股票价格。

[8] The service is somewhat targeted at teenagers and people in their 20s, who tend to love electronic gadgets, especially if they come in fashionable colors.

此句可译为:这些服务瞄准的是十多岁的青少年和二十多岁的年轻人,他们比较喜欢电子设备,特别是具有时尚色彩的电子设备。

who tend to love electronic gadgets 为非限定性定语从句。

[9] Current handsets have CPUs that run at about 100 MHz, several megabytes of Flash ROM, perhaps 1 MB of RAM, and a small built-in screen.

此句可译为:现在的手持机的配置如下:CPU的速率大约为100 MHz,几兆字节的闪存,可能有1 MB的RAM以及一个小的内置屏幕。

Exercises

Mark the following statements with T (true) or F (false) according to the text.

(1) A Japanese woman, Mari Matsunaga, invented a different approach to the

wireless Web called i-mode. ( )

(2) The i-mode system has three major components: a new transmission system, a new handset, and a new language for Web page design. ( )

(3) I-mode uses the packet-switched network so there is no billing for connect time. ( )

(4) NTT DoCoMo heavily advertises i-mode devices as better wireless Web terminal. ( )

(5) Most customers think of their i-mode devices as mobile phones with enhanced services. ( )

(6) In keeping with this model of i-mode being a service, the handsets are user programmable. ( )

(7) The i-mode handsets contain the equivalent of a 1995 PC and could probably run Windows 95 or UNIX. ( )

(8) The most popular application is e-mail, which allows up to 500 B messages. ( )

(9) On-screen navigation is done with the mouse. ( )

(10) I-mode requires the screen to be at least 120 pixels×160 pixels. ( )

Translating Skill 13

专有名词的翻译(二)

3. 公司名

公司名一般由两部分组成:公司名称＋表示公司的词,如 company（Co.）, Limited（Ltd.）, corporation（Corp.）, incorporation（Inc.）,另外还有 business, enterprise, organization, establishment, system 等,有些公司名称不带任何"公司"字样,或省略或免用,但仍可根据其性质译为"××公司"。

Western Union Telegraph Company	西联电报公司
American Satellite Corporation	美国卫星公司
Northern Radio Company Inc.	北方无线电公司
Central Signals Establishment	中央信号公司
Bharat Electronics Limited	巴拉特电子有限公司

公司名前半部是主体,可采用意译。

为从名字上看出公司性质,尽可能意译。

Electronic Tele-Communications Inc.	电子电信公司
Electronic Data System Corporation	电子数据系统公司
Preformed Line Products Company	预制线路产品公司

音译,人名地名和难以意译的词可音译。

Bell South Corporation	贝尔南方公司
Fujitsu Limited	富士有限公司
Summa Four Inc.	萨默 IV 公司

不译,部分公司可直接用缩略名。

AT&T	ATT 公司
3M	3M 公司
FAC	FAC 公司

4. 商标名

商标名的编制虽不免带有一定的随意性,汉译却仍然要持严谨态度,切不可见音译音,见意译意,主观臆测,随手拈来。除必须遵循翻译的一般规律外,还要考虑到商标本身固有的特点,这里提出若干要点。

(1) 约定俗成。凡已有的并已认可的商标汉译一般不要另找译词,沿用即可。

Toshiba	东芝
Siemens	西门子
Motorola	摩托罗拉

(2) 注意商标特征。商标设计一般要考虑 4 个要素:简短易记,发音响亮,具有专利性,译成外文不产生歧义。这些可作为商标汉译的依据。如一个好的商标一般不超过 3 个音节,且首字母常发硬音或含有硬音(C,K,G,Q,X),汉译要考虑原设计的用意。

Casio	卡西欧
Kodak	柯达
Cannon	佳能

(3) 用地名、人名、单位名或其他专有名词作商标的,一般采用原有译词。

Bell	贝尔(人名)
Oxford	牛津(地名)
Cornell	康奈(美国大学名)

(4) 体现原名内涵。计算机商标常常带有高技术气息,而通信商标则往往联想到"通"、"远"、"达"等字眼,汉译时要予以考虑。

OPCOM	光通(光通信公司商标)
FITEL	飞达(光纤通信公司商标)

但 Apple 只能译成"苹果"。这是原设计者的意图,目的是要用这种老幼皆知的水果冲淡苹果高科技的神秘。

Exercises to Translating Skill

Translate the following names into Chinese.

(1) West Coast of America Telegraph Co., Ltd.

(2) Hongkong Telephone Co., Ltd.

(3) Nippon Telegraph and Telephone

(4) Mainichi Broadcasting System

(5) Capital Wireless Incorporation
(6) Cable and Wireless
(7) Telesciences Transmission System
(8) Data Communications Ltd.
(9) Nynex DPL Company
(10) Ericsson Telecom AB
(11) Third World
(12) Universal Post Union
(13) News Week
(14) Uncle Sam
(15) White House
(16) The Houses of Parliement
(17) Ku Klux Klan
(18) International Telecommunication Union
(19) Asian-Pacific Broadcasting
(20) The First World War Union

Unit 14　WLAN

Although Ethernet is widely used, it is about to get some competition. Wireless LANs are increasingly popular, and more and more office buildings, airports, and other public places are being outfitted with them.

尽管以太网已经非常普及了,但是,它仍然会面临竞争。无线局域网正在日渐普及,越来越多的办公楼、机场和其他的公共场合配备了无线局域网。

Text A

Wireless LANs: 802.11

Almost as soon as notebook computers appeared, many people had a dream of walking into an office and magically having their notebook computer be connected to the Internet. Consequently, various groups began working on ways to accomplish this goal. The most practical approach is to equip both the office and the notebook computers with short-range radio transmitters and receivers to allow them to communicate.[1] This work rapidly led to wireless LANs being marketed by a variety of companies.[2]

The trouble was that no two of them were compatible. This proliferation of standards meant that a computer equipped with a brand X radio would not work in a room equipped with a brand Y base station. Finally, the industry decided that a wireless LAN standard might be a good idea, so the IEEE committee that standardized the wired LANs was given the task of drawing up a wireless LAN standard.[3] The standard it came up with was named 802.11. A common slang name for it is WiFi. It is an important standard and deserves respect, so we will call it by its proper name, 802.11.

The proposed standard had to work in two modes:

(1) In the presence of a base station;

(2) In the absence of a base station.[4]

In the former case, all communication was to go through the base station, called an access point in 802.11 terminology. In the latter case, the computers would just send to one another directly. This mode is now sometimes called ad hoc networking. A typical example is two or more people sitting down together in a room not equipped with a wireless LAN and having their computers just communicate directly.

The protocols used by all the 802 variants, including Ethernet, have a certain commonality of structure. The physical layer corresponds to the OSI physical layer fairly well, but the data link layer in all the 802 protocols is split into two or more sublayers.[5] In 802.11, the MAC (medium access control) sublayer determines how the channel is allocated, that is, who gets to transmit next.[6] Above it is the LLC (logical link control) sublayer, whose job is to hide the differences between the different 802 variants and make them indistinguishable as far as the network layer is concerned.[7]

The 1997 802.11 standard specifies three transmission techniques allowed in the physical layer. The infrared method uses much the same technology as television remote controls do. The other two use short-range radio, using techniques called FHSS and DSSS. Both of these use a part of the spectrum that does not require licensing (the 2.4 GHz ISM band). Radio-controlled garage door openers also use this piece of the spectrum, so your notebook computer may find itself in competition with your garage door.[8] Cordless telephones and microwave ovens also use this band. All of these techniques operate at 1 or 2 Mbit/s and at low enough power that they do not conflict too much.[9] In 1999, two new techniques were introduced to achieve higher bandwidth. These are called OFDM and HR-DSSS. They operate at up to 54 Mbit/s and 11 Mbit/s, respectively. In 2001, a second OFDM modulation was introduced, but in a different frequency band from the first one.

That 802.11 is going to cause a revolution in computing and Internet access is now beyond any doubt. Airports, train stations, hotels, shopping malls and universities are rapidly installing it. Even upscale coffee shops are installing 802.11 so that the assembled yuppies can surf the Web while drinking their lattes. It is likely that 802.11 will do to the Internet what notebook computers did to computing: make it mobile.[10]

Words and Expressions

WLAN (Wireless LAN) *abbr.* 无线局域网
notebook computer 笔记本电脑
magically [ˈmædʒikli] *adv.* 如魔法般地,用魔法地
consequently [ˈkɔnsikwəntli] *adv.* 所以,因此
accomplish [əˈkʌmpliʃ] *v.* 达到(目的),完成(任务),实现(计划)
equip [iˈkwip] *v.* 装备,配备;(智力、体力上)使有准备
short-range [ˈʃɔːtˈreindʒ] *adj.* 不能到达远处的;短射程的
a variety of 各种各样的,品类繁多的
proliferation [prəˌlifəˈreiʃən] *n.* 增殖;分叉
base station 基站
IEEE (Institute of Electrical and Electronics Engineers) *abbr.* 电气和电子工程师协会
standardize [ˈstændədaiz] *v.* 使符合标准,使标准化
draw up 草拟
come up with 赶上,提出,拿出
slang name 俗名

in the absence of 缺乏……时
terminology [ˌtəːmiˈnɔlədʒi] n. 术语
commonality [kɔməˈnæliti] n. 共同或普通的性质或状态
correspond [ˌkɔriˈspɔnd] v. 符合，协调；通信；相当，相应
correspond to 与……一致，符合
sublayer [ˈsʌbleiə] n 下（低，次，内）层，亚层，子层
split [split] v. 分裂，分离
OSI (open system interconnect reference model) abbr. 开放式系统互联参考模型
MAC (medium access control) abbr. 介质访问控制
LLC (logical link control) abbr. 逻辑链路控制
indistinguishable [indiˈstiŋgwiʃəbl] adj. 不能辨别的，不能区别的
infrared [ˌinfrəˈred] adj. 红外线的
television remote controls 电视机遥控器
cordless [kɔːdlis] adj. 不用电线的
conflict [ˈkɔnflikt, kənˈflikt] n. 冲突，争论 v. 冲突，抵触
upscale [ˈʌpskeil] adj. 迎合高层次消费者的，（商品）质优价高的
latte [ˈlaːtei] n. 拿铁咖啡

Notes

[1] The most practical approach is to equip both the office and the notebook computers with short-range radio transmitters and receivers to allow them to communicate.

此句可译为：最为实际的一条途径是，在办公室和笔记本计算机上安装上短距离的无线发射器和接收器，从而允许它们之间进行通信。

to equip both the … 不定式做表语；equip sth. with 用……装备起来，使装备。

[2] This work rapidly led to wireless LANs being marketed by a variety of companies.

此句可译为：这项工作很快导致了无线局域网的诞生，并且有一些公司还将产品推广到了市场上。

lead to 导致；a (considerable, great, wide) variety of 各种各样的，品类繁多的。

[3] Finally, the industry decided that a wireless LAN standard might be a good idea, so the IEEE committee that standardized the wired LANs was given the task of drawing up a wireless LAN standard.

此句可译为：最后，工业界认为，建立无线局域网的标准可能是解决这个问题的好办法。所以，原来制定有线局域网标准的 IEEE 委员会承担了拟定无线局域网标准的任务。

that a wireless LAN standard might be… 是一个宾语从句。that standardized the wired LANs 是定语从句，修饰先行词 the IEEE committee。

[4] In the presence of a base station; 有基站的模式；

In the absence of a base station. 无基站的模式。

[5] The physical layer corresponds to the OSI physical layer fairly well, but the data link layer in all the 802 protocols is split into two or more sublayers.

此句可译为：其中物理层与 OSI 的物理层对应得非常好,但是,在所有的 802 协议中,数据链路层都被分成了两个或者更多个子层。

correspond to(= correspond with)与……一致,符合

[6] In 802.11, the MAC (medium access control) sublayer determines how the channel is allocated, that is, who gets to transmit next.

此句可译为：在 802.11 中,介质访问控制子层确定了信道的分配方式,也就是说,它决定了下一个该由谁传输数据。

MAC (medium access control),介质访问控制

[7] Above it is the LLC (logical link control) sublayer, whose job is to hide the differences between the different 802 variants and make them indistinguishable as far as the network layer is concerned.

此句可译为：介质访问控制子层上面是逻辑链路控制子层,它的任务就是隐藏 802 各个标准之间的差异,使得它们对于网络层而言都是一致的。

whose job is to hide the differences between the different 802 variants and make them indistinguishable as far as the network layer is concerned. 这是一个由 whose 引导的非限制性定语从句,补充说明逻辑链路控制的作用。LLC (logical link control),逻辑链路控制。

[8] Radio-controlled garage door openers also use this piece of the spectrum, so your notebook computer may find itself in competition with your garage door.

此句可译为：无线电控制的垃圾门自动开关也使用了这部分频谱,所以你可能会发现你的笔记本在与你的垃圾门竞争频段。

in competition with 与……竞争。

[9] All of these techniques operate at 1 or 2 Mbit/s and at low enough power that they do not conflict too much.

此句可译为：所有这些技术都工作在 1 Mbit/s 或者 2 Mbit/s 的速率上,并且功率非常低,因此一般不会有严重的冲突。

that they do not conflict too much 是一个定语从句,修饰先行词 power,在翻译的时候单独处理为一个句子——因此一般不会有严重的冲突。

[10] It is likely that 802.11 will do to the Internet what notebook computers did to computing: make it mobile.

此句可译为：可以这样说,802.11 对于互联网所做的事情,实际上也相当于笔记本计算机对于计算机技术所起到的作用一样:让它移动起来。

Exercises

1. Put the following phrases into English.

(1) 无线局域网　　　　　　　　(6) 以太网
(2) 发射器　　　　　　　　　　(7) 物理层
(3) 接收器　　　　　　　　　　(8) 数据链路层
(4) 介质访问控制　　　　　　　(9) 子层
(5) 逻辑链路控制　　　　　　　(10) 802.11 协议

2. Put the following phrases into Chinese.

(1) surf the Web
(2) the most practical approach
(3) short-range radio transmitters
(4) proliferation of standards
(5) a wireless LAN standard
(6) the 802 variants
(7) the infrared method
(8) television remote control
(9) cordless telephones
(10) Internet access

3. Translate the following sentences into Chinese.

(1) In the former case, all communication was to go through the base station, called an access point in 802.11 terminology. In the latter case, the computers would just send to one another directly.

(2) Wireless LANs are increasingly popular, and more and more office buildings, airports and other public places are being outfitted with them.

(3) Even upscale coffee shops are installing 802.11, so that the assembled yuppies can surf the Web while drinking their lattes.

(4) That 802.11 is going to cause a revolution in computing and Internet access is now beyond any doubt. Airports, train stations, hotels, shopping malls and universities are rapidly installing it.

(5) This proliferation of standards meant that a computer equipped with a brand X radio would not work in a room equipped with a brand Y base station.

(6) The other two use short-range radio, using techniques called FHSS and DSSS. Both of these use a part of the spectrum that does not require licensing (the 2.4 GHz ISM band).

(7) This work rapidly led to wireless LANs being marketed by a variety of companies.

(8) It is an important standard and deserves respect, so we will call it by its proper name, 802.11.

(9) In 802.11, the MAC (medium access control) sublayer determines how the channel is allocated, that is, who gets to transmit next.

(10) Above it is the LLC (logical link control) sublayer, whose job is to hide the differences between the different 802 variants and make them indistinguishable as far as the network layer is concerned.

4. Translate the following paragraphs into Chinese.

(1) The next step up in wireless networking are the wireless LANs. These are systems in which every computer has a radio modem and antenna with which it can communicate with other systems. Often there is an antenna on the ceiling that the machines talk to. However, if the systems are close enough, they can communicate directly with one another in a peer-to-peer configuration. Wireless LANs are becoming increasingly common in small offices and homes, where installing Ethernet is considered too much trouble, as well as in older office buildings, company cafeterias, conference

rooms and other places. There is a standard for wireless LANs, called IEEE 802.11, which most systems implement and which is becoming very widespread.

(2) Why would anyone want wireless networks? A common reason is the portable office. People on the road often want to use their portable electronic equipment to send and receive telephone calls, faxes, and electronic mail, surf the Web, access remote files, and log on to remote machines. And they want to do this from anywhere on land, sea or air. For example, at computer conferences these days, the organizers often set up a wireless network in the conference area. Anyone with a notebook computer and a wireless modem can just turn the computer on and be connected to the Internet, as though the computer were plugged into a wired network. Similarly, some universities have installed wireless networks on campus so students can sit under the trees and consult the library's card catalog or read their e-mail.

Text B

New Wireless LAN Standard

With portable computers and wireless LANs, users can enjoy greater productivity while away from their desks, whether they are in conference rooms, public areas or remote offices. Until recently, however, wireless LANs were too slow for most enterprise applications. Based on the IEEE 802.11 standard, they ran at 1~2 Mbit/s.

Now a new high-rate extension to the standard, 802.11b, lets wireless networks support data rates up to 11 Mbit/s.

Ratified in 1997, the original 802.11 standard united the wireless industry by defining a low-level protocol architecture that worked with conventional upper-layer enterprise protocol stacks.[1] Also, 802.11 maintained compatibility with the three most popular radio transmission types: direct sequence spread spectrum frequency-hopping spread spectrum and infrared.[2] Essentially, this new architecture added intelligence at the MAC Layer 2 and at the Physical (PHY) Layer 1, fostering cooperation between the two layers in performing the critical tasks involved with initiating and maintaining wireless communications.[3]

For instance, to ensure reliability of the wireless link, the MAC and PHY work together to determine if a clear path exists before they start a transmission.

During transmission, they employ special collision-avoidance and arrival-acknowledgement techniques that are not required in wired Ethernet LANs.[4]

In September 1999, the IEEE approved a new designation, known as 802.11b, as the high-rate extension to 802.11. Intended to retain the error-correction, security, power-management and other advantages of the original, the new 802.11b standard adds a key ingredient—a technique for increasing bandwidth to 11 Mbit/s.

Called complementary code keying (CCK) the technique works only in conjunction with the DSSS technology specified in the original standard. It does not work with frequency-hopping or infrared transmissions.[5]

What CCK does is to apply sophisticated mathematical formulas to the DSSS codes, permitting the codes to represent a greater volume of information per clock cycle. The transmitter is now able to send multiple bits of information with each DSSS code, enough to make possible the 11 Mbit/s of data rather than the 2 Mbit/s in the original standard.

The 802.11b standard benefits users by delivering wireless Ethernet speeds of 11 Mbit/s that can reliably support everyday business applications, e-mail, Internet and server network access.

With support from the new Wireless Ethernet Compatibility Alliance, founded by 3Com, Lucent, Nokia and several other companies in the wireless LAN business, the new standard will also promise certified interoperability across multivendor platforms.[6]

Finally, the 802.11b standard serves as a rallying point for vendors and users clamoring for a simplified wireless LAN landscape.

Vendors can now focus on a single, high-speed standard, and users can cut through the clutter of wireless options by focusing on a standard that delivers multivendor interoperability and the performance to meet their application needs.

Words and Expressions

productivity [ˌprɔdʌk'tiviti] n. 生产力；生产率
remote [ri'məut] adj. 偏僻的
enterprise ['entəpraiz] n. 企业(或事业)单位
ratify ['rætifai] v. 正式批准，使正式生效
stack [stæk] n. 整齐的一叠(堆) v. 叠成堆，堆放于
compatibility [kəmpæti'biliti] n. [计] 兼容性
essentially [i'senʃəli] adv. 本质上，基本上
HPY (Physical) abbr. 物理的
error-correction 纠错
ingredient ['in'ɡri:diənt] n. 成分，因素
CCK (complementary code keying) abbr. 互补码键控
frequency-hopping 跳频
formula ['fɔ:mjulə] n. 公式；规则
volume ['vɔlju:m] n. 量；大量
Wireless Ethernet Compatibility Alliance 无线以太网兼容性联盟
multivendor [ˌmʌlti'vendə] n. 多厂商
rally ['ræli] n. 集会 v. 集合；恢复，振作
clamor ['klæmə] v. 喧嚷；大声的要求
interoperability ['intərˌɔpərə'biləti] n. 互用性，协同工作的能力

Notes

[1] Ratified in 1997, the original 802.11 standard united the wireless industry by defining a low-level protocol architecture that worked with conventional upper-layer enterprise protocol stacks.

此句可译为：最初的 802.11 标准是在 1997 年提出的，通过定义能与常规的上层企业协议组一起工作的低级协议体系结构，把无线行业团结起来了。

that worked with conventional … 是一个定语从句，修饰先行词 low-level protocol architecture。

[2] Also, 802.11 maintained compatibility with the three most popular radio transmission types: direct sequence spread spectrum, frequency-hopping spread spectrum and infrared.

此句可译为：802.11 也保持了与 3 种最流行的无线电传输方式直接顺序扩频、跳频扩频和红外线的兼容性。

direct sequence spread spectrum 直接顺序扩频，frequency-hopping spread spectrum 跳频扩频。

[3] Essentially, this new architecture added intelligence at the MAC Layer 2 and at the Physical (PHY) Layer 1, fostering cooperation between the two layers in performing the critical tasks involved with initiating and maintaining wireless communications.

此句可译为：本质上，这种新的体系结构在介质接入控制层（第二层）和物理层（第一层）增加了智能，建立这两层之间在执行涉及开始和保持无线通信的关键任务时的协作关系。

[4] During transmission, they employ special collision-avoidance and arrival-acknowledgement techniques that are not required in wired Ethernet LANs.

此句可译为：在传输过程中，它们采用有线以太网不需要的、特殊的避免碰撞和到达应答技术。

collision-avoidance 避免碰撞，arrival-acknowledgement techniques 到达应答技术。

[5] Called complementary code keying (CCK) the technique works only in conjunction with the DSSS technology specified in the original standard. It does not work with frequency-hopping or infrared transmissions.

此句可译为：此项技术叫做互补码键控，它只与原标准中规定的直接顺序扩频技术一起工作，不能用跳频或红外传输方式工作。

CCK（complementary code keying）互补码键控，frequency-hopping 跳频。

[6] With support from the new Wireless Ethernet Compatibility Alliance, founded by 3Com, Lucent, Nokia and several other companies in the wireless LAN business, the new standard will also promise certified interoperability across multivendor platforms.

此句可译为：由 3Com、Lucent、Nokia 和其他几家有无线局域网业务的公司组成的"无线以太网兼容性联盟"支持新标准，此标准也有望实现跨多厂商平台的互用性。

founded by 3Com, Lucent, Nokia … 过去分词短语做定语，Wireless Ethernet Compatibility Alliance 无线以太网兼容性联盟。

Exercises

Mark the following statements with T (true) or F (false) according to the text.

(1) Now a new high-rate extension to the standard, 802.11b, lets wireless networks support data rates up to 1 Mbit/s. ( )

(2) The original 802.11 standard was ratified in 1997. ( )

(3) Wireless Ethernet Compatibility Alliance was founded by 3Com, Lucent, Nokia and several other companies in the wireless LAN business. ( )

(4) During transmission, they employ special collision-avoidance and arrival acknowledgement techniques that are required in wired Ethernet LANs. ( )

(5) 802.11 maintained compatibility with the three most popular radio transmission types: direct sequence spread spectrum, frequency-hopping spread spectrum and infrared. ( )

(6) Complementary Code Keying (CCK) works with frequency-hopping or infrared transmissions. ( )

(7) The three most popular radio transmission types are direct sequence spread spectrum, frequency-hopping spread spectrum, and infrared. ( )

(8) The 802.11b standard serves as a rallying point for vendors and users clamoring for a simplified wireless LAN landscape. ( )

(9) The 802.11b standard benefits users by delivering wireless Ethernet speeds of 11 Mbit/s. ( )

(10) CCK applies sophisticated mathematical formulas to the DSSS codes, permitting the codes to represent a greater volume of information per clock cycle. ( )

Translating Skill 14

否定的处理

同每一种语言一样,英语也有自己的否定表达方式。由于使用的方式及词汇、语法手段与汉语有所差异,所以翻译时应灵活地从正反两方面处理。

1. 完全否定

英语中表示完全否定的词有 no(没有),none(没有人、无一物、一点也不),not(不),never(从来不、决不),neither(两者都不),nor(也不)和 no 与其他词组成的合成词等。由上述词构成的否定句一般仍为汉语否定句,可直译。

例如:

No defect did we find in these circuits.

在这些电路中,我们没有发现任何缺陷。

Videophone service will spread from the office to the home in the not far distance future.

在不久的将来,可视电话业务将会从办公室扩展到家庭。

Nothing in the world moves faster than light.

世界上没有任何东西比光速更快。

2. 部分否定

英语中的部分否定通常是由 not 与 all,both,every,always,many 等词连用构成的。通常译为"不都是"、"不全是"、"并非"、"不总是"、"不多"等。

例如:

All that glitters is not gold.

发光的不都是金子。

Every amplifier can not be dependable.

并非每个放大器都可靠。

I do not have much experience in operating microcomputer.

我并没有多少操作微机的经验。

3. 双重否定

在句子中出现两次否定,主要是为了强调,翻译时应变为肯定句。常见的词组有:no…not (no)(没有……没有),without…nor(没有……就不),not…until(直到……才),not…but(没有……不),never…without(每逢……总是),no…other than(不是……正是)等。

例如:

There is no grammatical rule that does not have exceptions.

语法规则都有例外。

You cannot be too careful in performing an experiment.

做实验越仔细越好。

Heat can never be converted into a certain energy without something lost.

热能转换成某种能量时总是有些损耗。

4. 意义否定

英语中有很多含有否定意义的词和词组,一般可翻译成否定意义。这些词和词组可以是动词、名词、形容词、副词、连词和介词等。

例如:

The operator must have missed the notice and instruction on the instrument.

操作人员一点没有看到仪器上的注意事项和须知。

One of the advantages of optical fibers is freedom from direct effect of interfering radio transmission.

光纤的优点之一就是不受无线电传输干扰的直接影响。

Our knowledge of propagation phenomena at optical wavelength is from perfect.

我们对光波传播现象的认识还很不全面。

It's hardly a possibility to mention all the kinds of applications electronic computers.

将电子计算机的应用种类列举齐全几乎是不可能的。

Unless there is motion, there is no work.
没有运动就没有功。
But for air and water, nothing could live.
没有空气和水,什么也不能活。

Exercises to Translating Skill

Translate the following phrases into Chinese.

(1) at no time
(2) by no means
(3) in no account
(4) have nothing in common
(5) more often than not
(6) under no circumstances
(7) not a bit
(8) not a quarter
(9) not amount too much
(10) not to speak of
(11) nothing but
(12) nothing less than
(13) spare no pains
(14) to say nothing of
(15) come to nothing
(16) there is no (little) doubt
(17) make no difference
(18) nothing else but

Unit 15　Networks Applied Technology

As you know, E-mail and World Wide Web are the two killer apps for the Internet. But in this unit, we'll discuss the unprecedented growth of the home networking. How many people in 1990 predicted that nearly any individual has a computer in his home for Internet access? It is worth devoting some time to pointing out why people are interested in computer networks and what they can be used for.

众所周知,电子邮件和万维网是互联网的两个杀手锏应用。但是在这个单元里我们将要讨论的是以超乎想象的速度在增长的家庭网络应用。在1990年的时候又有多少人会预见到几乎每个人家里都拥有一台计算机并且用它上网呢？我们值得花一点时间来说明为什么人们对于计算机网络感兴趣以及计算机网络可以用来做些什么？

Text A

Home Networking

In 1977, Ken Olsen was president of the Digital Equipment Corporation, then the number two computer vendor in the world (after IBM). When asked why Digital was not going after the personal computer market in a big way, he said: "There is no reason for any individual to have a computer in his home." History showed otherwise and Digital no longer exists.[1] Why do people buy computers for home use? Initially, for word processing and games, but in recent years that picture has changed radically. Probably the biggest reason now is for Internet access. Some of the more popular uses of the Internet for home users are as follows:

Access to remote information.
Person-to-person communication.
Interactive entertainment.
Electronic commerce.[2]

Access to remote information comes in many forms. It can be surfing the World Wide Web for information or just for fun. Information available includes the arts, business, cooking, government, health, history, hobbies, recreation, science, sports, travel and many others.[3]

The second broad category of network use is person-to-person communication, basically the 21st century's answer to the 19th century's telephone.[4] E-mail is already used on a daily basis by millions of people all over the world and its use is growing rapidly.

It already routinely contains audio and video as well as text and pictures.

Any teenager worth his or her salt is addicted to instant messaging. This facility, derived from the UNIX talk program in use since around 1970, allows two people to type messages at each other in real time.[5] A multiperson version of this idea is the chat room, in which a group of people can type messages for all to see.

Our third category is entertainment, which is a huge and growing industry. The killer application here (the one that may drive all the rest) is video on demand. A decade or so hence, it may be possible to select any movie or television program ever made, in any country, and have it displayed on your screen instantly.[6] New films may become interactive, where the user is occasionally prompted for the story direction (should Macbeth murder Duncan or just bide his time?) with alternative scenarios provided for all cases.[7] Live television may also become interactive, with the audience participating in quiz shows, choosing among contestants and so on.

Our fourth category is electronic commerce in the broadest sense of the term. Home shopping is already popular and enables users to inspect the on-line catalogs of thousands of companies. Some of these catalogs will soon provide the ability to get an instant video on any product by just clicking on the product's name. After the customer buys a product electronically but cannot figure out how to use it, on-line technical support may be consulted.

Another area in which e-commerce is already happening is access to financial institutions.[8] Many people already pay their bills, manage their bank accounts, and handle their investments electronically. This will surely grow as networks become more secure.

One area that virtually nobody foresaw is electronic flea markets (e-flea). On-line auctions of second-hand goods have become a massive industry. Unlike traditional e-commerce, which follows the client-server model, on-line auctions are more of a peer-to-peer system, sort of consumer-to-consumer.[9]

No doubt the range of uses of computer networks will grow rapidly in the future, and probably in ways no one can now foresee. After all, how many people in 1990 predicted that teenagers tediously typing short text messages on mobile phones while riding buses would be an immense money maker for telephone companies in 10 years?[10] But short message service is very profitable.

Words and Expressions

APP (application) *n.* [计] 应用
predict [pri'dikt] *v.* 预知, 预言, 预报
radically ['rædikəli] *adv.* 根本上, 以激进的方式
routinely [ruː'tiːnli] *adv.* 例行公事地
addict to 耽溺于……, 热爱

multiperson [ˌmʌlti'pə:sn] n. 多人
Macbeth n. 麦克白
Duncan n. 邓肯
scenario [si'nɑ:riəu] n. 剧情说明书，剧本，某一特定情节
figure out 解决，断定，领会到
e-commerce(electronic commerce) n. 电子商务
foresee [fɔ:'si:] v. 预见，预知
e-flea (electronic flea markets) n. 电子跳蚤市场，电子二手货市场
client-server 客户服务器
Peer-to-Peer n. 对等，对等网络
tediously ['ti:diəsli] adv. 沉闷地，冗长而乏味地
immense [i'mens] adj. 极广大的，无边的，＜口＞非常好

Notes

[1] History showed otherwise and Digital no longer exists.
此句可译为：历史证明这是错误的，所以 DEC 公司不再存在了。
DEC (Digital Equipment Corporation) (美)数字设备公司。

[2] Some of the more popular uses of the Internet for home users are as follows:
Access to remote information.
Person-to-person communication.
Interactive entertainment.
Electronic commerce.
此句可译为：现在最主要的理由可能是为了访问互联网。对于家庭用户而言，互联网的几个最流行的用途是：
访问远程信息。
个人之间的通信。
交互式娱乐。
电子商务。

[3] Information available includes the arts, business, cooking, government, health, history, hobbies, recreation, science, sports, travel and many others.
此句可译为：获取到的信息多种多样，包括艺术、商务、烹饪、政府、健康、历史、爱好、娱乐、科学、运动、旅游等。

[4] The second broad category of network use is person-to-person communication, basically the 21st century's answer to the 19th century's telephone.
此句可译为：第二类广泛的网络应用是个人对个人的通信，基本上是 21 世纪对 19 世纪的电话的回应。
person-to-person communication 个人对个人的通信。

[5] This facility, derived from the UNIX talk program in use since around 1970, allows two people to type messages at each other in real time.

此句可译为：这种应用是从 UNIX 上的 talk 程序(差不多从 1970 年以来一直在使用)演变过来的,它允许两个人相互之间实时地输入消息。

derived from…过去分词短语做定语。

[6] A decade or so hence, it may be possible to select any movie or television program ever made, in any country, and have it displayed on your screen instantly.

此句可译为：因此,大约再过 10 年左右,你可能可以选择任何一部电影,或者任何一个国家的电视节目,然后让它立即显示在你的屏幕上。it may be possible to do sth. 可能做……。

[7] New films may become interactive, where the user is occasionally prompted for the story direction (should Macbeth murder Duncan or just bide his time?) with alternative scenarios provided for all cases.

此句可译为：新的电影可能变成交互式的,看电影的时候用户偶尔可以提示一下故事的发展方向(麦克白应该杀死邓肯,还是应该等待时机?),电影片子为各种可能的选择提供了相应的场景。

[8] Another area in which e-commerce is already happening is access to financial institutions.

此句可译为：在电子商务应用中另一个领域是允许直接访问金融机构。

[9] Unlike traditional e-commerce, which follows the client-server model, on-line auctions are more of a peer-to-peer system, sort of consumer-to-consumer.

此句可译为：传统的电子商务使用了客户-服务器模型,而在线拍卖更多地是一种对等系统,也是一种顾客对顾客的系统。

e-commerce 电子商务；client-server 客户-服务器；peer-to-peer 对等；consumer-to-consumer 顾客对顾客,常缩写为 C2C。

[10] After all, how many people in 1990 predicted that teenagers tediously typing short text messages on mobile phones while riding buses would be an immense money maker for telephone companies in 10 years?

此句可译为：毕竟,在 1990 年的时候又有多少人会预见到,10 年之后那些坐在公共汽车上频频发送冗长短消息的青少年会给电话公司带来巨额的利润呢？

that 引导从句做宾语。

Exercises

1. Put the following phrases into English.

(1) 计算机网络　　　　　　(6) 个人之间的通信
(2) 电子商务　　　　　　　(7) 在线技术支持
(3) 在线拍卖　　　　　　　(8) 远程学习
(4) 交互式娱乐　　　　　　(9) 聊天室
(5) 访问远程信息　　　　　(10) 即时消息

2. Put the following phrases into Chinese.

(1) access to remote information (6) live television
(2) word processing (7) home shopping
(3) person-to-person communication (8) traditional e-commerce
(4) short message service (9) the on-line catalogs
(5) electronic flea markets (10) client-server model

3. Translate the following sentences into Chinese.

(1) There is no reason for any individual to have a computer in his home.

(2) Initially, for word processing and games, but in recent years that picture has changed radically.

(3) A multiperson version of this idea is the chat room, in which a group of people can type messages for all to see.

(4) E-mail is already used on a daily basis by millions of people all over the world and its use is growing rapidly.

(5) A decade or so hence, it may be possible to select any movie or television program ever made, in any country, and have it displayed on your screen instantly.

(6) Live television may also become interactive, with the audience participating in quiz shows, choosing among contestants and so on.

(7) This will surely grow as networks become more secure.

(8) On-line auctions of second-hand goods have become a massive industry.

(9) Using computer networks, manufacturers can place orders electronically as needed.

(10) Telemedicine is only now starting to catch on but may become much more important.

4. Translate the following paragraphs into Chinese.

(1) Many companies is doing business electronically with other companies, especially suppliers and customers. For example, manufacturers of automobiles, aircraft, and computers, among others, buy subsystems from a variety of suppliers and then assemble the parts. Using computer networks, manufacturers can place orders electronically as needed. Being able to place orders in real time (i. e., as needed) reduces the need for large inventories and enhances efficiency.

(2) Computer networks may become hugely important to people who are geographically challenged, giving them the same access to services as people living in the middle of a big city. Telelearning may radically affect education; universities may go national or international. Telemedicine is only now starting to catch on (e. g., remote patient monitoring) but may become much more important. But the killer application may be something mundane, like using the webcam in your refrigerator to see if you have to buy milk on the way home from work.

Text B

E-Mail

E-mail is one of the two killer apps for the Internet. Everyone from small children to grandparents now uses it.

Electronic mail, or e-mail, as it is known to its many fans, has been around for over two decades. Before 1990, it was mostly used in academia. During the 1990s, it became known to the public at large and grew exponentially to the point where the number of e-mails sent per day now is vastly more than the number of snail mail (i. e., paper letters). [1]

E-mail, like most other forms of communication, has its own conventions and styles. In particular, it is very informal and has a low threshold of use. People who would never dream of calling up or even writing a letter to a Very Important Person do not hesitate for a second to send a sloppily-written e-mail. [2]

E-mail is full of jargon such as BTW (by the way), ROTFL (rolling on the floor laughing), and IMHO (in my humble opinion). Many people also use little ASCII symbols called smileys or emoticons in their e-mail. [3]

The first e-mail systems simply consisted of file transfer protocols, with the convention that the first line of each message (i. e., file) contained the recipient's address. [4] As time went on, the limitations of this approach became more obvious.

(1) Sending a message to a group of people was inconvenient. Managers often need this facility to send memos to all their subordinates.

(2) Messages had no internal structure, making computer processing difficult. For example, if a forwarded message was included in the body of another message, extracting the forwarded part from the received message was difficult. [5]

(3) The originator (sender) never knew if a message arrived or not.

(4) If someone was planning to be away on business for several weeks and wanted all incoming e-mail to be handled by his secretary, this was not easy to arrange.

(5) The user interface was poorly integrated with the transmission system requiring users first to edit a file, then leave the editor and invoke the file transfer program. [6]

(6) It was not possible to create and send messages containing a mixture of text, drawings, facsimile and voice. [7]

As experience was gained, more elaborate e-mail systems were proposed. In 1982, the ARPANET e-mail proposals were published as RFC 821 (transmission protocol) and RFC 822 (message format). [8] Minor revisions, RFC 2821 and RFC 2822, have become Internet standards, but everyone still refers to Internet e-mail as RFC 822.

In 1984, CCITT drafted its X. 400 recommendation. After two decades of competition, e-mail systems based on RFC 822 are widely used, whereas those based on X.400 have disappeared.

Words and Expressions

academia [ˌækəˈdemik] *n.* 学术界
exponential [ekspəuˈnenʃəl] *n.* 指数 *adj.* 指数的，幂数的
vastly [ˈvɑːstli, ˈvæstli] *adv.* 广大地，许多，巨额地
snail mail 传统邮件，纸质邮件
threshold [ˈθreʃhəuld] *n.* 开始，开端，极限
hesitate [ˈheziteit] *v.* 犹豫，踌躇，不愿
sloppily-written 随意书写的
jargon [ˈdʒɑːɡən] *n.* 行话，术语
ASCII (American Standard Code for Information Interchange) *abbr.* 美国信息互换标准代码
smiley [ˈsmaili] *n.* 微笑图标
emoticon [iˈməutikɔn] [计] 由字符组成的图释，也称作 smiley，由 emotion 和 icons 合成
recipient [riˈsipiənt] *adj.* 容易接受的，感受性强的 *n.* 收件人
subordinate [səˈbɔːdinət] *n.* 下属，下级
forwarded message 被转发的信息
originator [əˈridʒəneitə] *n.* 发信方
file [fail] *n.* 文档
invoke [inˈvəuk] *v.* 调用，恳求
elaborate [iˈlæbərət/ -reit] *adj.* 精心制作的，详细阐述的
RFC Internet 标准（草案）

Notes

[1] During the 1990s, it became known to the public at large and grew exponentially to the point where the number of e-mails sent per day now is vastly more than the number of snail mail (i.e., paper) letters.

此句可译为：在整个20世纪90年代，它一下子变得普及起来，并且呈指数地增长，以至于现在每天发送的电子邮件数量远远超过了传统邮件（snail mail，纸质邮件）信函的数量。

[2] People who would never dream of calling up or even writing a letter to a Very Important Person do not hesitate for a second to send a sloppily-written e-mail.

此句可译为：那些从来没有梦想过给某个大人物打一个电话或者只是写一封信的人，也可以毫不犹豫地给他发一封随意书写的电子邮件了。

who would never dream of calling up or even writing a letter to a Very Important Person… 是定语从句，修饰先行词 people。

[3] Many people also use little ASCII symbols called smileys or emoticons in their e-

mail.

此句可译为:很多人还在他们的电子邮件中使用一些被称为微笑图标(smiley)或情绪图标的小巧的 ASCII 符号。

called smileys or emoticons 过去分词短语做定语修饰 symbols。

[4] The first e-mail systems simply consisted of file transfer protocols, with the convention that the first line of each message (i. e., file) contained the recipient's address.

此句可译为:第一个电子邮件系统只是简单地由一些文件传输协议组成,同时也遵从约定:每个消息(即文件)的第一行包含了收信人的地址。

that the first line of each message 是定语从句,修饰先行词 convention。

[5] For example, if a forwarded message was included in the body of another message, extracting the forwarded part from the received message was difficult.

此句可译为:例如,如果一个被转发的消息包含在另外一个消息中,则难以从收到的消息中提取出被转发的部分。

[6] The user interface was poorly integrated with the transmission system requiring users first to edit a file, then leave the editor and invoke the file transfer program.

此句可译为:用户界面与传输系统集成得不好,它要求用户先编辑一个文件,然后退出编辑器并调用文件传输程序。

[7] It was not possible to create and send messages containing a mixture of text, drawings, facsimile and voice.

此句可译为:不可能创建和发送混合了文本、图片、传真和语音的消息。

containing a mixture of text, drawings, facsimile, and voice 是现在分词短语做定语。

[8] In 1982, the ARPANET e-mail proposals were published as RFC821 (transmission protocol) and RFC 822 (message format).

此句可译为:1982 年,ARPANET 的电子邮件提案被作为 RFC 821(传输协议)和 RFC 822(消息格式)发表。

ARPANET ARPA 网。

Exercises

Mark the following statements with T (true) or F (false) according to the text.

(1) E-mail is one of the two killer apps for the Internet. (   )

(2) Before 1990, e-mail was known to the public at large and grew exponentially to the point where the number of e-mails sent per day now is vastly more than the number of snail mail (i. e., paper) letters. (   )

(3) Electronic mail, or e-mail, as it is known to its many fans, has been around for over two decades. (   )

(4) E-mail has not its own conventions and styles. (   )

(5) People who would never dream of calling up or even writing a letter to a Very Important Person do not hesitate for a second to send a sloppily-written e-mail. (   )

(6) E-mail is very formal and has a high threshold of use. ( )

(7) In 1982, the ARPANET e-mail proposals were published as RFC821 (transmission protocol) and RFC 822 (message format). ( )

(8) In 1984, CCITT drafted its X.400 recommendation. ( )

(9) The first e-mail systems simply consisted of file transfer protocols, with the convention that the first line of each message (i.e., file) contained the sender's address. ( )

(10) Now e-mail systems based on RFC 822 are widely used. ( )

Translating Skill 15

And 引导的句型(一)

在学习英语的过程中,and 是大家十分熟悉和经常使用的一个连词,用来连接词、短语和句子,它最基本的意义相当于汉语的"和"、"与"、"并且"。但在实际翻译的过程中,特别是在连接两个句子时,它的译法很多,表达的意义不尽相同,如果不考虑 and 前后成分之间的逻辑关系,只用这几种译法生硬套用,未免造成理解上的失误,把整个句子搞错。

1. And 表示因果

In 1945 a new type of aeroplane engine was invented, it was much lighter and powerful than earlier engines, and enabled war planes to fly faster and higher than ever.

1945 年发明了一种新型的飞机发动机。它比早期发动机要轻得多,功率也要大得多,因此采用这种发动机的军用飞机比以往任何时候都飞得更快、更高。

2. And 表示目的

It was later shown that the results of this work were by no means the ultimate, and further work has been put in hand and to provide closer control and more consistent operation in this area.

后来发现,这项研究工作的结果绝非已做定论,而进一步的研究工作已开始,以便在这方面提供较严密的控制和较稳定的操作。

3. And 表示承接

The next usual step is to decide on the location of the filter and the choice may be influenced by some factors.

通常下一步是确定过滤器的位置,而位置的选择要受某些因素的影响。

4. And 表示原因

Laser is incredibly deadly, and in the blink of an eye, it can destroy the enemy's outer space communications satellites, shutting down much of their advanced intelligence system.

激光的杀伤力难以置信,因为它能在一瞬间摧毁敌人设置在外层空间的通信卫星,使其大部分的先进情报系统不能工作。

Exercises to Translating Skill

Translate the following sentences into Chinese.

(1) Laser is widely used for developing many new kinds of weapons, and it penetrates almost everything.

(2) In many ways, computer is more superior than human brain, and human can rule it.

(3) The solution was to place many filters in the system and hope for the best.

(4) But since a digital signal is made up of a string of simple pulses, noise stands out and easily removed.

(5) Security is a broad topic and covers a multitude of sins.

Unit 16　Microwave Communication

Microwave communication describes a traditional transmission technology that benefits from an inherently robust lifecycle. Known for its rapid deployment capability, low cost and flexible application potential, it has been widely deployed in a range of communication contexts spanning fixed, mobile and private networks. The global scale of 3G/WiMAX[1] construction has delivered with it the latest application scenario for microwave communication, the specific features of which have evolved in alignment with technological development and shifting market pattern.

微波通信描述了一个传统的传输技术,这个技术受益于固有的强大的生命周期。它以快速部署能力、低成本和灵活的应用潜力而著称,已被广泛部署在一系列通信环境中,跨越了固定、移动和专用网络。使用最新的微波通信应用方案的 3G/WiMAX 全球范围的建设已经交付使用,其特性随着技术的发展和不断变化的市场格局而演变。

Text A

Networking Microwave Communication[2]

In Europe, the leading operator, British Telecom[3] (BT), is currently working to establish a suitable wireless edge access solution for its 21st century network. The new, highly efficient, and cost-effective microwave transport network is set to offer significant cost savings for BT, in which Ethernet, SDH[4] and PDH[5] will integrate to improve the network availability and flexibility.

In Pakistan, the GSM network of the mobile operator, Ufone[6], currently serves tens of millions of users. The sustained and rapid increase in new service provision has prompted a wave of transmission construction, central to which is the rapid and large scale deployment of microwave stations across the nation.

Booming consumer demand is yielding both opportunities and challenges for traditional microwave technology. Underpinned by point-to-point signal transmission between a transmission point and a receptor point, the pairing of which is referred to as a "hop", the traditional system cannot be networked on its own. [7] As a consequence, service transference, grooming or convergence necessitates equipment cascading, external equipment cross-connections or digital multiplexers.

These measures incur the detriment of additional construction and maintenance costs. Equipment cascading requires a large number of manually connected cables, as well as digital distribution Frames (DDFs) or Optical Distribution Frames (ODFs). The realization of uniform microwave and external equipment management demands a hub[8] to connect the network management (NM) interfaces of various pieces of microwave equipment at a convergence node. If external cross-connection equipment, digital multiplexers and microwave equipment derive from different manufacturers, additional data communication equipment must be installed to facilitate NM information interworking. The implementation of these measures serves to inhibit economic viability.

If a traditional point-to-point microwave is networklized, however, such problems can be solved. Huawei has thus developed the new concept of networklized microwaves in which cross-connection is adopted within microwave equipment. Specifically, if an external cable connection is changed to the automatic cross-connection of internal buses, and the microwave links are configured to act as optical transmission equipment lines and tributaries, microwave equipment becomes networklized.

Analog microwave communication systems originated in the 1950s and their development over subsequent decades has witnessed evolution from analog to digital and from PDH to SDH. Higher modulation efficiency, greater bandwidth, longer transmission distances, and enhanced reliability denote continual progress that remains essentially market driven.

In the nascent networklized microwave system, microwave links are considered as lines and tributaries of optical transmission equipment, which eradicates the weakness of point-to-point microwaves. The split-mount microwave model, for instance, is composed of indoor and outdoor units (IDUs and ODUs) and antennas. The IDU accesses a service signal, prompting baseband processing, multiplexing and IF modulation. The signal is then sent to the ODU for RF[9] processing, before being finally transmitted by the antenna.

All digital processing operations are performed in the IDU. Functionally equivalent to an optical transmission equipment set, the IDU provides service grooming and multi-service access, and can be utilized to construct a ring network. The platform can also access 2 Mbit/s PDH, 155 Mbit/s SDH, and gigabit Ethernet service signals.

To support multi-service transport, microwave IDUs inherit the advanced and mature strengths of MSTP platforms. In addition to TDM services, they can carry Ethernet and ATM services through encapsulation and mapping, and provide higher-rate optical interfaces to achieve hybrid networking with optical transmission equipment. The microwave IDUs are managed by the same optical transmission equipment NMS, thus fulfilling end-to-end service grooming and management and actualizing a truly uniform transport network.

Words and Expressions

inherently [in'hiərəntli] adv. 天性地，固有地

rapid ['ræpid] adj. 短时间发生的；急速的，迅速的，快的；险峻的
potential [pə'tenʃəl] adj. 潜在的；可能的 n. 潜力，潜能
spanning ['spæniŋ] n. 跨度；拉线；[数]生成，长成
alignment [ə'lainmənt] n. 结盟
significant [sig'nifikənt] adj. 重要的；有意义的；意味深长的
flexibility [ˌfleksə'biliti] n. 灵活性，弹性，适应性，柔韧性
sustain [səs'tein] v. 支持，承受；维持；经受
prompt [prɔmpt] adj. 迅速的 v. 激起，促进；提示 n. 提示，提示的内容
booming ['bu:miŋ] adj. 兴旺的，繁荣的；轰隆作响的
yield [ji:ld] v. 生产，获利；屈服；弯下去 n. 投资收益，生产量
underpin [ˌʌndə'pin] v. 从下头支持，支撑
convergence [kən'və:dʒəns] n. 收敛，汇聚，汇合点
multiplexer ['mʌltiˌpleksə] n. 多路（复用）器
incur [in'kə:] v. 招致，遭受，惹起
detriment ['detrimənt] n. 损伤，损害物
cascading [kəs'keidiŋ] n. 级串联
manufacturer [ˌmænju'fæktʃərə] n. 制造商
facilitate [fə'siliteit] v. 促进，帮助，使……容易
inhibit [in'hibit] v. 抑制，阻止；使不能
origin ['ɔridʒin] n. 起源；出身
witness ['witnis] v. 目击，见证；证明；为（宗教信仰）做见证
denote [di'nəut] v. 表示；象征
essentially [i'senʃəli] adv. 本质上，本来
tributary ['tribjutəri] n. 支流 adj. 支流的
antenna [æn'tenə] n. 天线
modulation [ˌmɔdju'leiʃən] n. 调音，调节，转调，抑扬
eliminate [i'limineit] v. 除去，剔除，忽略；淘汰
manual ['mænjuəl] adj. 手工的，体力的 n. 指南，手册；键盘
relay [ri'lei] v. 中继
via ['vaiə] prep. 经由，通过
inherit [in'herit] v. 继承；遗传
encapsulation [inˌkæpsju'leiʃən] n. 封装
mapping ['mæpiŋ] n. 映射
uniform ['ju:nifɔ:m] adj. 一致的，统一的

Notes

[1] WiMAX (worldwide interoperability for microwave access)，即全球微波互联接入。WiMAX 也叫 802.16 无线城域网或 802.16。WiMAX 是一项新兴的宽带无线接入技术，能提供面向互联网的高速连接，数据传输距离最远可达 50 km。WiMAX 还具有 QoS 保障、传

输速率高、业务丰富多样等优点。WiMAX 的技术起点较高,采用了代表未来通信技术发展方向的 OFDM/OFDMA、AAS、MIMO 等先进技术,随着技术标准的发展,WiMAX 逐步实现宽带业务的移动化,而 3G 则实现移动业务的宽带化,两种网络的融合程度会越来越高。

[2] 本文摘自 http://www.huawei.com。

[3] British Telecom 英国电信(集团),简称 BT,原为英国国营电信公用事业,由英国邮政总局管理,1981 年 10 月 1 日脱离英国皇家邮政,变成独立的国营事业。在英国保守党柴契尔夫人执政下,1984 年向市场出售 50% 公股,成为民营公司。该公司始终是全英最大电信设施硬件的营运者。英国电信在全球 170 个国家设有营业点或办事处,2006 年全球营收约为 390 亿美元。目前海外营业处的营业额占该集团总营业额的三分之一。

[4] SDH(synchronous digital hierarchy,同步数字体系),根据 ITU-T 的建议定义,是不同速度的数位信号的传输提供相应等级的信息结构,包括复用方法和映射方法,以及相关的同步方法组成的一个技术体制。SDH 采用的信息结构等级称为同步传送模块 STM-N (synchronous transport,$N=1,4,16,64$),最基本的模块为 STM-1,4 个 STM-1 同步复用构成 STM-4,16 个 STM-1 或 4 个 STM-4 同步复用构成 STM-16,4 个 STM-16 同步复用构成 STM-64,甚至 4 个 STM-64 同步复用构成 STM-256。SDH 采用块状的帧结构来承载信息。

[5] 在数字传输系统中,有两种数字传输系列,一种叫"准同步数字系列"(plesiochronous digital hierarchy),简称 PDH;另一种叫"同步数字系列"(synchronous digital hierarchy),简称 SDH。采用准同步数字系列(PDH)的系统,是在数字通信网的每个节点上都分别设置高精度的时钟,这些时钟的信号都具有统一的标准速率。尽管每个时钟的精度都很高,但总还是有一些微小的差别。为了保证通信的质量,要求这些时钟的差别不能超过规定的范围。因此,这种同步方式严格来说不是真正的同步,所以叫做"准同步"。

[6] Ufone 是全球知名跨国运营商 Etisalat 在巴基斯坦的子公司,是巴基斯坦第二大的无线服务运营商,由于业务运营成功,Ufone 用户数增长十分迅速,其母公司 Etisalat 是全球领先的跨国运营商。

[7] Underpinned by point-to-point signal transmission between a transmission point and a receptor point, the pairing of which is referred to as a "hop", the traditional system cannot be networked on its own.

此句可译为:传统的系统为基础,以发射机和接收机之间的点到点信号传输为基础,其中的配对被称为"跳",传统系统不能自己组网。

句中的 which 引导非限定性状语从句,修饰先行词"transmission"。

[8] HUB 是一个多端口的转发器,在局域网中得到了广泛的应用。大多数的时候它用在星型与树型网络拓扑结构中,以 RJ45 接口与各主机相连(也有 BNC 接口)。

[9] RF(radio frequency)射频,简称 RF。射频就是射频电流,它是一种高频交流变化电磁波的简称。每秒变化小于 1 000 次的交流电称为低频电流,大于 10 000 次的称为高频电流,而射频就是这样一种高频电流。RF 无线射频识别是一种非接触式的自动识别技术,它通过射频信号自动识别目标对象并获取相关数据。识别工作无需人工干预,可以工作于各种恶劣环境。

Exercises

1. Put the following phrases into English.

(1) 设备制造商   (6) 数字多路复用器
(2) 快速部署   (7) 混合组网
(3) 发射机   (8) 端到端
(4) 业务转移   (9) 点到点
(5) 交叉连接   (10) 微波链路

2. Put the following phrases into Chinese.

(1) low cost   (6) maintenance costs
(2) private networks   (7) manually connected cables
(3) cost-effective   (8) digital distribution frames
(4) microwave stations   (9) optical distribution frames
(5) equipment cascading   (10) information interworking

3. Translate the following sentences into Chinese.

(1) Microwave communication describes a traditional transmission technology that benefits from an inherently robust lifecycle.

(2) The new, highly efficient, and cost-effective microwave transport network is set to offer significant cost savings for BT.

(3) To support multi-service transport, microwave IDUs inherit the advanced and mature strengths of MSTP platforms.

(4) In the nascent networklized microwave system, microwave links are considered as lines and tributaries of optical transmission equipment, which eradicates the weakness of point-to-point microwaves.

(5) Higher modulation efficiency, greater bandwidth, longer transmission distances, and enhanced reliability denote continual progress that remains essentially market driven.

(6) Analog microwave communication systems originated in the 1950s and their development over subsequent decades has witnessed evolution from analog to digital and from PDH to SDH.

(7) Huawei has thus developed the new concept of networklized microwaves in which cross-connection is adopted within microwave equipment.

(8) If a traditional point-to-point microwave is networklized, however, such problems can be solved.

(9) These measures incur the detriment of additional construction and maintenance costs.

(10) Booming consumer demand is yielding both opportunities and challenges for traditional microwave technology.

4. Translate the following paragraphs into Chinese.

(1) Compared with traditional point-to-point microwave, the networklized microwave delivers the following technical advantages: a single IDU supports multiple microwave directions, thus eliminating the need for a manual cable connection at relay or convergence nodes. Hybrid networking can be attained through the integration of wireless microwave and wired transmission. Service convergence and grooming can be executed via embedded add-drop multiplex (ADM).

(2) Microwave transmission refers to the technology of transmitting information or energy by the use of radio waves whose wavelengths are conveniently measured in small numbers of centimeters; these are called microwaves. Microwaves are widely used for point-to-point communications because their small wavelength allows conveniently-sized antennas to direct them in narrow beams, which can be pointed directly at the receiving antenna.

Text B

Understanding Microwave Communication Frequencies[1]

The term "Microwave" is a broad term that covers the UHF (ultra high frequency with frequencies between 300 MHz and 3 GHz) to the EHF (extremely high frequency with frequencies between 30 GHz and 300 GHz). Licensed microwave links and unlicensed wireless Ethernet bridges[2] typically operate in the SHF (super high frequency with frequencies between 3 GHz and 30 GHz) and the EHF bands. Fig. 16-1 is a microwave communication tower.

Fig. 16-1 Microwave Communication Tower

A general rule of thumb is that lower the frequency the farther the signal will travel. Also lower frequencies the lower the throughput and higher the frequency the higher the throughput. Again this is in general terms and depends on the wireless radio hardware used.

The terms "unlicensed wireless bridge" and "licensed microwave link" refer to the radio frequency spectrum characteristics set by the US Federal Communications Commission (FCC) or equivalent national government regulatory body. Licensed products require regulatory approval before deployment while license-exempt products can be deployed without any regulatory approval.

Licensed microwave link frequencies used for wireless backhaul in a point to point wireless backhaul operate 6 GHz, 11 GHz, 18 GHz, 23 GHz bands and the 80 GHz millimeter wave E-band. Unlicensed wireless Ethernet bridges, used in point to point wireless bridges, point to multipoint wireless bridges, or wireless mesh configurations, typically operate in 900 MHz, 2.4 GHz, 5.3 GHz, 5.4 GHz, or 5.8 GHz frequencies. There is also the 60 GHz millimeter wave band that is used for point to point gigabit wireless bridges.

There are registered frequencies that many think are licensed but are actually unlicensed, like the 3.65 GHz WiMAX band used for point to multipoint wireless backhaul and the 4.9 GHz public safety band. These registered bands do provide some protection against interference but only require local users to coordinate with one another on frequency channel coordination. This is often confused by public safety organizations that think the 4.9 GHz band is for exclusive use by local law enforcement. Anyone can register the use of the 4.9 GHz band as long as it's used for some form of public safety, such as video backhaul.

Licensed microwave wireless radio systems are typically built and designed for long term solutions. Point to point licensed microwave links are true fiber replacement systems and offer full duplex wireless communications for both Ethernet and TDM[3]. The licensed wireless bridge hardware is designed to provide carrier grade performance (high bandwidth and low latency). Because a microwave link is licensed and is not to inject and interference on other licensed microwave backhaul operators in the area they must have LOS (line of sight) and not cause heavy multipath. This is a common question of why licensed microwave radios don't use OFDM[4] or MIMO[5] and why they can't be used in NLOS (non line of sight) applications. In a NLOS wireless link application unlicensed wireless backhaul radios that use OFDM or MIMO take advantage of multipath for their connectivity.

Microwave communication using unlicensed wireless Ethernet bridge systems have been an extremely popular choice for outdoor wireless backhaul. The unlicensed spectrum of 5 GHz (5.3 GHz, 5.4 GHz and 5.8 GHz UNII[6] bands) became a primary selection by many end users and outdoor wireless installation VAR[7]'s, because of their flexibility, cost effectiveness, rapid ROI[8] and quick deployments. Many outdoor wireless manufactures started introducing "value line" point to point wireless Ethernet bridges using 802.11[9] chipsets. Basically, the same radio boards found in WiFi access points put into an outdoor enclosure and using outdoor wireless antennas. The new 802.11n[10] based wireless backhaul radios use OFDM and MIMO taking advantage of multipath, especially helpful in NLOS applications. The major issue with unlicensed wireless Ethernet bridges is potential wireless interference.

Words and Expressions

frequency [ˈfriːkwənsi] *n.* 频繁；频率
ultra [ˈʌltrə] *adj.* 超，过激的，极端的 *n.* 过激论者，急进论者
license [ˈlaisns] *n.* 许可证，执照，特许；放纵 *v.* 发许可证给，特许
throughput [ˈθruːput] *n.* 产量，吞吐量
spectrum [ˈspektrəm] *n.* 系列，范围；光谱；[科] 频谱
regulatory [ˈregjulətəri] *adj.* 管理的，控制的，调整的
backhaul 回程，又称"回传"，通信线路的返回路程
mesh [meʃ] *n.* 网孔，网状物
gigabit [ˈdʒigəbit] *n.* 吉比特，千兆比特
register [ˈredʒistə] *v.* 登记，记录，注册，挂号 *n.* 登记簿，记录；暂存器
coordinate [kəuˈɔːdineit, kəuˈɔːdinit] *v.* (使)协调，(使)一致 *adj.* 同等的，等位的
exclusive [iksˈkluːsiv] *adj.* 排外的；独占的；唯一的；奢华的
video [ˈvidiəu] *n.* 录像，视频 *adj.* 视频的，录像的
interference [ˌintəˈfiərəns] *n.* 干扰；妨碍
multipath *n.* 多路 *adj.* 多路的
connectivity [kəˈnektiviˌti] *n.* [计] 连通性
enclosure [inˈkləuʒə] *n.* 附件；围墙，围绕

Notes

[1] 本文摘自 http://www.aowireless.com，Alpha Omega Wireless 公司网站，Joe Wargo。

[2] Bridge，网桥，可将两个相似的网络连接起来，并对网络数据的流通进行管理。它工作于数据链路层，不但能扩展网络的距离或范围，而且可提高网络的性能、可靠性和安全性。但在这里，考虑到上下文的意思，笔者将其意译为"通信系统"或"传输系统"，全文都做此理解。

[3] TDM 就是时分复用模式。时分复用是指一种通过不同信道或时隙中的交叉位脉冲，同时在同一个通信媒体上传输多个数字化数据、语音和视频信号等的技术。

[4] OFDM (orthogonal frequency division multiplexing)，正交频分复用技术，实际上 OFDM 是 MCM (multi-carrier modulation)，多载波调制的一种。其主要思想是将信道分成若干正交子信道，将高速数据信号转换成并行的低速子数据流，调制到在每个子信道上进行传输。正交信号可以通过在接收端采用相关技术来分开，这样可以减少 ICI(子信道之间的相互干扰)。每个子信道上的信号带宽小于信道的相关带宽，因此每个子信道上的可以看成平坦性衰落，从而可以消除符号间干扰。而且由于每个子信道的带宽仅仅是原信道带宽的

一小部分,信道均衡变得相对容易。

[5] MIMO (multiple-input multiple-out put) 系统是一项运用于 802.11n 的核心技术。802.11n 是 IEEE 继 802.11b/a/g 后全新的无线局域网技术,速度可达 600 Mbit/s。同时,专有 MIMO 技术可改进已有 802.11a/b/g 网络的性能。该技术最早是由 Marconi 于 1908 年提出的,它利用多天线来抑制信道衰落。在第四代移动通信技术标准中被广泛采用。例如,IEEE 802.16e (WiMAX),长期演进(LTE)。MIMO 有时被称作空间分集,因为它使用多空间通道传送和接收数据。只有站点(移动设备)或接入点(AP)支持 MIMO 时才能部署 MIMO。

[6] UNII (unauthorized national information infrastructure),未被授权的国家信息基础设施。

[7] 增值经销商(VAR)是增加现有产品的功能或服务的公司,然后作为一个集成的产品或完整的"承包"解决方案加以转售(通常是最终用户)。这种做法通常发生在电子行业。例如,一个 VAR 可能在提供硬件时捆绑软件应用。

[8] ROI (return on investment),投资回报率(ROI)是指通过投资而应返回的价值,它涵盖了企业的获利目标。利润和投入的经营所必备的财产相关,因为管理人员必须通过投资和现有财产获得利润。又称会计收益率、投资利润率。

[9] 802.11 是 IEEE 最初制定的一个无线局域网标准,主要用于解决办公室局域网和校园网中,用户与用户终端的无线接入,业务主要限于数据存取,速率最高只能达到 2 Mbit/s。

[10] IEEE 802.11n,2004 年 1 月 IEEE 宣布组成一个新的单位来发展新的 802.11 标准。资料传输速度估计将达 540 Mbit/s(需要在物理层产生更高速度的传输率),此项新标准应该要比 802.11b 快 50 倍,而比 802.11g 快 10 倍左右。802.11n 也将会比目前的无线网络传送到更远的距离。802.11n 增加了对于 MIMO (multiple-input multiple-output) 的标准。MIMO 使用多个发射和接收天线来允许更高的资料传输率。MIMO 使用了 Alamouti 编码方案来增加传输范围。

Exercises

Mark the following statements with T (true) or F (false) according to the text.

(1) Higher the frequency the farther the signal will travel.　　　　　　(　　)

(2) Higher the frequency the higher the throughput.　　　　　　　　(　　)

(3) E-band is the licensed microwave link frequencies used for wireless backhaul in a point to point wireless backhaul.　　　　　　　　　　　　　　　　　(　　)

(4) Unlicensed wireless Ethernet bridges cannot operate 5.3 GHz and 5.4 GHz frequencies.　　　　　　　　　　　　　　　　　　　　　　(　　)

(5) The 60 GHz millimeter wave band can be used for point to multipoint gigabit wireless bridges.

(6) The 4.9 GHz public safety band is licensed.　　　　　　　　　　(　　)

(7) The unlicensed spectrum of 5 GHz became a primary selection by many end users.

　　　　　　　　　　　　　　　　　　　　　　　　　　　　(　　)

(8) Licensed microwave wireless radio systems are typically built and designed for long term solutions. ( )

(9) Microwave covers the UHF to the EHF. ( )

(10) Unlicensed wireless Ethernet bridges typically operate with frequencies between 3 MHz and 30 GHz. ( )

Translating Skill 16

And 引导的句型(二)

5. And 表示对照

Motion is absolute, and stagnation is relative.

运动是绝对的,而静止是相对的。

6. And 表示结果

Operators found that the water level was too low so they turned on two additional main coolant pumps, and too much cold water flowing into the system caused the steam to condense, further destabilizing the reactor.

操作人员发现冷却水的水位过低,就启动了另外两台主冷却泵,结果过量的冷却水进入系统使蒸汽冷凝,反应堆因而更不稳定。

7. And 表示条件

Even if a programmer had endless patience, knowledge and foresight, storing every relevant detail in a computer, the machine's information would be useless, and the programmer knew little how to instruct it in what human beings refer to as commonsense reasoning.

即使一名编程员很有耐心、知识和预见,把每一个有关细节都存入计算机,如果他不懂得怎样按人类的常识推理去对计算机下达指令,机器里的信息也还是没有用处的。

8. And 表示递进

The electronic brain calculates a thousand time quicker, and more accurately than is possible for the human being.

电脑的运算速度比人所能达到的要快 1 000 倍,而且更准确。

9. And 表示转折

While industrial laser today are most often used for cutting, welding, drilling and measuring, and the laser's light can be put to a much different use: separating isotopes to produce nuclear fuel.

虽然今天的工业激光器经常用于切割、焊接、钻孔和测量,但激光可以有其他不同的用处,即分离同位素以生产核燃料。

10. And＝With

In addition, a plug-in fault diagnostic unit and signal monitoring system is normally supplied with the drive to enable any drive alarm or control signal to be checked and monitored.

此外,一个带有信号监控系统的插入式故障诊断器通常装有驱动装置,以便能校验可监控任何驱动报警信号或控制信号。

Exercises to Translating Skill

Translate the following sentences into Chinese.

(1) As Intel estimated, personal computers used in American households will attain 50 million sets in one to two years, and by the end of 1995 or 1996, personal computers will override TV sets in production.

(2) Keep your face to the sunshine, and you cannot see your shadow.

(3) The phone of the future will be more mobile, do a lot of different tasks and be part of a complex, far-reaching information network.

(4) There will always be some things that are wrong, and that is nothing to be afraid of.

(5) Only a few might be needed by one organization, and the specialized model might not do anyone else any good.

(6) Ethernet uses a bus topology and relies on the form of access known as CSMA/CD to regulate traffic on the main communication line.

附录1 电子信息常用缩略语

AAON (ATM Active Optical Network)	ATM 有源光网络
AC (Alternating Current)	交流（电）
ADC (Analog to Digital Converter)	模/数转换器
ADM (Adaptive Delta Modulation)	自适应增量调制
ADM (Add-Drop Multiplexer)	上、下话路复用器
ADPCM (Adaptive Differential Pulse Code Modulation)	自适应差分脉冲编码调制
AMPS (Advanced Mobile Phone Service)	高级移动电话业务（北美）
APON (ATM Passive Optical Network)	无源光网络
ASCII (American Standard Code for Information Interchange)	美国信息交换标准码
ASIC (Application Specific Integrated Circuit)	专用集成电路
ATM (Asynchronous Transfer Mode)	异步传输模式
AT&T (American Telephone & Telegragh Company)	美国电话电报公司
AV (Audio Video)	音视频
BCD (Binary Coded Decimal)	二进制编码的十进制数
BCR (Bi-directional Controlled Rectifier)	双向晶闸管
BiCMOS (Bipolar CMOS)	双极 CMOS
B-ISDN (Broad Integrated Service Digital Network)	宽带综合业务数字网
BPL (Broadband over Power Line)	电力线宽带
bps (bit per second)	每秒位数
BTB/C (Branch Target Buffer/Cache)	分支目标缓冲
BZ (buzzer)	蜂鸣器，蜂音器
CATV (Cable Television)	有线电视
CCD (Charge-Coupled Device)	电荷耦合器件
CCIR (International Radio Communications Consultative Committee)	国际无线通信咨询委员会
CCITT (Consultative Committee in Telegraphy and Telephony)	国际电报电话咨询委员会
CCTV (Closed-Circuit Television)	闭路电视
CD (Compact Disc)	光盘
CISC (Complex Instruction Set Computer)	复杂指令集计算机
CMOS (Complementary Metal Oxide Semiconductor)	互补金属氧化物半导体
CNNIC (China Network Information Center)	中国网络信息中心

CO (Central Office)	中心交换局
COB (Cache On Board)	板载集成缓存
COD (Cache on Die)	芯片内集成缓存
CPU (Central Processing Unit)	中央处理单元
CPGA (Ceramic Pin Grid Array)	陶瓷针型栅格阵列
DAST (Direct Analog Store Technology)	直接模拟存储技术
DAT (Digital Audio Tape)	数字音频磁带
DBS (Direct-broadcast Satellite)	直播卫星
DC (Direct Current)	直流电
DCS (Digital Communication System)	数字通信系统
DCC (Digital Cross Connection)	数字交叉连接
DCS (Digital Cross-connect Switch)	数字交叉连接交换
DCT (Discrete Cosine Transform)	离散余弦变换
DDR (Dual Data Rate)	双倍数据速率
DMA (Direct Memory Access)	直接存储器存取
DP (Dial Pulse)	拨号脉冲
DRAM (Dynamic Random Access Memory)	动态随机存储器
DSL (Digital Subscriber Line)	数字用户线
DSP (Digital Signal Processing)	数字信号处理
DTL (Diode-transistor Logic)	二极管晶体管逻辑
DVD (Digital Video Disc)	数字式视频光盘
DVM (Digital Voltmeter)	数字电压表
EC (Embedded Controller)	微型控制器
ECC (Error Correction Code)	纠错码
ECC (Error Check Correction)	错误检查纠正
ECG (Electrocardiograph)	心电图
ECL (Emitter Coupled Logic)	射极耦合逻辑
EDI (Electronic Data Interchange)	电子数据交换
EDO (Extended Data Out)	扩展数据输出
EIA (Electronic Industries Association)	电子工业联合会
EIDE (Enhanced Integrated Drive Electronics)	增强型集成驱动电子设备
EMI (Electromagnetic Interference)	电磁干扰
EMC (Electromagnetic Compatibility)	电磁兼容性
EPROM (Erasable Programmable Read Only Memory)	可擦可编程只读存储器
EEPROM (Electrically EPROM)	电可擦可编程只读存储器
ESD (Electro-Static Discharge)	静电放电
ETSI (Europe Telecommunication Standard Institution)	欧洲电信标准学会
EW (Electronic Warfare)	电子战
FCC (Federal Communication Committee)	美国联邦通信委员会

FDD (Frequency Division Duplex)	频分复用
FDDI (Fiber Distributed Data Interface)	光纤分布式数字接口
FDMA (Frequency Division Multiple Access)	频分多路接入
FEC (Forward Error Correction)	前向纠错
FET (Field-Effect Transistor)	场效应晶体管
FM (Frequency Modulation)	调频
FPGA (Field Programmable Gate Array)	现场可编程门阵列
FS (Full Scale)	满量程
FSK (Frequency Shift Keying)	频移键控
GAL (Generic Array Logic)	通用阵列逻辑
GND (Ground)	接地,地线
GPRS (General Packet Radio Service)	通用分组无线业务
GPS (Global Positioning System)	全球定位系统
GSM (Global System for Mobile Communications)	环球移动通信系统
GSM-MAP (GSM-Mobile Application Part)	GSM 移动应用部分
HCMOS (High Density CMOS)	高密度互补金属氧化物半导体
HDSL (High Bit-Rate Digital Subscriber Line)	高比特速率数字用户线
HDTV (High-definition Television)	高清晰度电视
HF (High Frequency)	高频
HFC (Hybrid Fiber Coaxial Network)	混合光纤同轴网络
HTL (High Threshold Logic)	高阈值逻辑电路
IC (Integrated Circuit)	集成电路
ID (International Data)	国际数据
IDE (Integrated Drive Electronics)	集成驱动电子设备
IDLC (Integrated Digital Loop Carrier)	综合数字环路载波
IDSL (ISDN Digital Subscriber Line)	ISDN 数字用户线
IEEE (Institute of Electrical & Electronic Engineers)	电气和电子工程师协会
IF (Intermediate Frequency)	中频
IGBT (Insulated Gate Bipolar Transistor)	绝缘栅双极型晶体管
IGFET (Insulated Gate Field Effect Transistor)	绝缘栅场效应晶体管
I/O (Input/Output)	输入/输出
IS- (Interface Specification-)	接口规范(IS-136,IS-95A,IS-95B)
IT (Information Technology)	信息技术
JFET (Junction Field Effect Transistor)	结型场效应晶体管
LAN (Local Area Network)	局域网
LASCS (Light Activated Silicon Controlled Switch)	光控可控硅开关
LB (Linear Burst)	线性突发
LCD (Liquid Crystal Display)	液晶显示器

LDR (Light Dependent Resistor)	光敏电阻
LED (Light Emitting Diode)	发光二极管
LMDS (Local Microwave Distribution System)	本地多点分配系统
LNA (Low-noise Amplifier)	低噪放大器
LO (Local Oscillator)	本机振荡器
LRC (Longitudinal Redundancy Check)	纵向冗余(码)校验
LSB (Least Significant Bit)	最低有效位
LSI (Large Scale Integration)	大规模集成电路
MCT (MOS Controlled Gyrator)	场控晶闸管
MIC (MICrophone)	话筒,微音器,麦克风
MIS (Management Information System)	管理信息系统
MLS (Microwave Landing System)	微波着陆系统
MMDS (Multichannel Multipoint Distribution Service)	多点多通道分配业务
MOSFET (Metal Oxide Semiconductor FET)	金属氧化物半导体场效应晶体管
MPEG (Moving Picture Expert Group)	活动图像专家组
MW (Micro Wave)	微波
N (Negative)	负
NLOS (Near Line Of Sight)	近距离视距
NMOS (N-channel Metal Oxide Semiconductor FET)	N 沟道 MOSFET
NMT (Nordic Mobile Telephone)	北欧移动电话
NTC (Negative Temperature Coefficient)	负温度系数
OC (Over Current)	过电流
OCB (Overload Circuit Breaker)	过载断路器
OCS (Optical Communication System)	光通信系统
OFDM (Orthogonal Frequency Division Multiplexing)	正交频分复用
OLT (Optic Line Terminal)	光纤线路终端
ONU (Optic Network Unit)	光网络单元
OV (Over Voltage)	过电压
PAL (Programmable Array Logic)	可编程阵列逻辑
PAM (Pulse Amplitude Modulation)	脉冲幅度调制
PAPR (Peak-to-Average Power Ratio)	峰均功率比
PBX (Private Branch Exchange)	用户交换机
PC (Pulse Code)	脉冲码
PCM (Pulse Code Modulation)	脉冲编码调制
PDA (Personal Data Assistant)	个人数据助手
PDC (Personal Digital Cellular)	个人数字蜂窝(日本)
PDH (Plesiochronous Digital Hierarchy)	准同步数字序列
PDM (Pulse Duration Modulation)	脉宽调制

PF (Power Factor)	功率因数
PFM (Pulse Frequency Modulation)	脉冲频率调制
PG (Pulse Generator)	脉冲发生器
PI (Proportional-integral(controller))	比例积分(控制器)
PID (Proportional-integral-differential(controller))	比例积分微分(控制器)
PIN (Positive Intrinsic-negative)	光电二极管
PLD (Phase-locked Detector)	同相检波
PLD (Phase-locked Discriminator)	锁相解调器
PLL (Phase-locked Loop)	锁相环路
PM (Phase Modulation)	相位调制
PMOS (P-channel Metal Oxide Semiconductor FET)	P 沟道 MOSFET
PPM (Pulse Phase Modulation)	脉冲相位调制
PROM (Programmable Read Only Memory)	可编程只读存储器
PUT (Programmable Unijunction Transistor)	可编程单结晶体管
PWM (Pulse Width Modulation)	脉宽调制
QAM (Quadrature Amplitude Modulation)	正交幅度调制
QoS (Quality of Service)	服务质量
QPSK (Quadrature Phase Shift Key)	正交相移键控
RAM (Random Access Memory)	随机存储器
RBF (Radial-Basis Function)	径向基函数
RF (Radio Frequency)	射频
RFI (Radio Frequency Interfere)	射频干扰
RISC (Reduced Instruction Set Computing)	精简指令集计算机
RP (Resistance Potentiometer)	电位器
RTL (Resistor Transistor Logic)	电阻晶体管逻辑(电路)
SA (Switching Assembly)	开关组件
S-CDMA (Synchronous-code Division Multiple Access)	同步码分多址
SCR (Silicon Controlled Rectifier)	可控硅整流器
SDH (Synchronous Digital Hierarchy)	同步数字序列
SDRAM (Synchronous Dynamic Random Access Memory)	同步动态随机存取存储器
SDSL (Symmetric Digital Subscriber Line)	对称数字用户线
SNR (Signal to Noise Ratio)	信噪比
SoC (System-on-Chip)	嵌入式系统
SOI (Silicon-on-Insulator)	绝缘体硅片
SOM (Self-organizing Map)	自组织特征映射
SONET (Synchronous Optical Network)	同步光网络
SP (Shift Pulse)	移位脉冲
SR (Silicon Rectifier)	硅整流器

SRAM (Static Random Access Memory)	静态随机存储器
SSL (Security Socket Layer)	安全套接层
SSR (Solid-state Relay)	固体继电器
SSR (Switching Select Repeater)	中断器开关选择器
SSS (Silicon Symmetrical Switch)	硅对称开关,双向可控硅
SSW (Synchro-switch)	同步开关
TACS (Total Access Communication System)	全接入通信系统(英国)
TDD (Time Division Duplex)	时分复用
TDMA (Time Division Multiple Access)	时分多路接入
TAT (Turn Around Time)	周转时间
TTL (Transistor-transistor Logic)	晶体管-晶体管逻辑
TV (Television)	电视
UART (Universal Asynchronous Receiver Transmitter)	通用异步收发器
ULOS (Unobstructed Line of Sight)	无障碍视距
VCO (Voltage Controlled Oscillator)	压控振荡器
VC (Virtual Container)	虚拟容器
VD (Video Decoders)	视频译码器
VDSL (Very High Bit-rate Digital Subscriber Line)	甚高比特速率数字用户线
VF (Video Frequency)	视频
VHDL (Very High Speed IC Hardware Description Language)	极高速集成电路硬件描述语言
VGA (Video Graphic Array)	视频图像阵列
VLSI (Very Large Scale Integration)	超大规模集成电路
VOD (Video on Demand)	视频点播
VoIP (Voice-over-IP)	IP 语音
VPN (Virtual Private Network)	虚拟专用网
VRAM (Video RAM)	视频随机存取存储器
xDSL (A,H,I,S,V-DSL)	数字用户线
WDM (Wavelength Division Multiplexing)	波分复用
WiFi (Wireless Fidelity)	无线保真
WLAN (Wireless Local Area Network)	无线局域网
WMAN (Wireless Metropolitan Area Networks)	无线城域网
WPAN (Wireless Personal Area Network)	无线个人域网
WYSIWYG (What You See Is What You Get)	所见即所得

附录 2 课文参考译文

Unit 1 电路与电气元件

Text A

电路

电流

电流是指电荷粒子的流动。在铜线里面,电流由叫做电子的微小负电荷粒子运载。在电流开始流动之前,电子是随机任意漂移的。当电流流动时,电子开始朝一个相同的方向移动。电流的大小取决于每秒经过的电子数量多少。

电流由符号 I 表示,度量单位为安培。1 安培表示每秒有 6.24×10^{18} 个电子穿过导线的任何一个位置。这表示每秒有比 6 百万百万百万还多的电子穿过。

在电路中,电流经常用毫安表示,即千分之一安培。

电压

在手电筒电路中,是什么让电流流动呢?答案是电池单元提供一个"推力"让电流在电路中环行。

每个电池单元都提供一个推力,这叫做它的电势差,或者叫电压。电压由符号 U 表示,度量单位是伏特。

通常,每个电池单元提供 1.5 V 的电压。2 个电池单元串联就提供 3 V 电压,3 个电池单元串联就提供 4.5 V 电压。如图 1-1 所示。

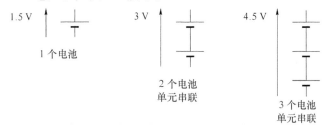

图 1-1 电池单元串联

电池单元串联

哪种电池排列可以让灯泡最亮?灯泡是设计成工作在特定电压下的,但是当其他条件相同时,电压越高,灯泡就越亮。

严格来说,一个电池包括 2 个以上的电池单元。它们可以串联,就像用在手电筒电路中那样,但是它们也可以并联,如图 1-2 所示。

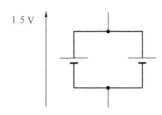

图 1-2 电池单元并联

电池单元并联

单个电池单元可以长时间提供小电流,或者短时间提供大电流。把电池单元串联可以提高电压,但不会影响电池单元的使用寿命。另一方面,如果电池单元是并联,电压就保持在 1.5 V,但是电池寿命延长一倍。

一个手电筒灯泡需要 300 mA 电流,一个 C 型碱性电池可以供电超过 20 个小时直到耗尽。

电阻

手电筒电路的某些部分会限制或阻止电流的流动。电路大部分由厚金属导体组成,使得电流可以轻易流动。这些部分都是低电阻,包括弹簧,开关簧片和灯泡连接。但是灯泡的灯丝,是由非常细的金属线构成,它比电路的其他部分更不容易传导电流,也具有更高的电阻。

灯丝的电阻 R 度量单位是欧姆。如果电池的电压是 3 V(两个 C 型的电池单元串联)灯泡电流是 300 mA,或者 0.3 A,那么灯丝的电阻是多少?
计算如下

$$R=\frac{U}{I}=\frac{3}{0.3}=10\ \Omega$$

R 是电阻,U 是穿过电灯泡的电压,I 是电流。

在这里,10 Ω 是电灯丝通电以后的电阻。

在电路中电阻值可以由几欧姆到几千欧姆甚至几兆欧姆变化。设计成具有特定电阻值的电子元件叫做电阻器。

Text B

电气元件

电阻器

电阻器是一种电子器件,它能阻碍电流的流动。在电阻器中流过的电流与加在电阻两端的电压成正比,与电阻的阻值成反比,这就是欧姆定律,可以用公式表示成 $I=\dfrac{U_R}{R}$。电阻器一般是线性器件,它的(伏安)特性曲线形成一条直线。

电阻器常用作限流器,限制流过器件的电流以防止器件因流过的电流过大而烧坏。电阻器也可用作分压器,以降低其他电路的电压,如晶体管偏置电路。电阻器还可用作电路的负载。

电容器

电能可以储存在电场里,能储存电能的元件叫电容器。

一个简单的电容器是由被介质隔开的两块金属板组成的。如果电容器连接到电池上,电子将从电池的负极流出堆积在与负极相接的极板上。同时与电源正极相接的极板上的电子将离开极板流入电池正极,这样两极板上就产生了与电池上相等的电位差。我们就说电容充上了电。

用一根导线连接电容器的两个极板,电容就会放电。电子从一个极板通过导线向另一个极板运动去恢复电中性。

电感器

当电流流过电感器时,电感器周围就有电磁场,电感器是以电磁场的形式暂时储存电磁能量的电子器件。而且,电感器是由不同尺寸的导线绕制的,电感器有不同的圈数,这些都会影响线圈的直流电阻。以后你将学到在交流电路中电阻对电感工作的影响。

在《业余无线电手册》中有满足所需的技术条件绕制线圈的详尽资料。有许多便宜的特殊滑动尺允许你设定所需要的参数,确定电感器的圈数、线圈长度、线圈直径等,这些都是你达到预想结果所必需的。

Unit 2 测量工具

Text A

仪表测量什么?

仪表就是测量仪器。安培表测量电流,电压表测量两点的电势差(电压),欧姆表测量电阻。万用表把所有这些功能和其他一些功能包括在一起。

模拟万用表

一个模拟万用表顺着表盘刻度移动指针。切换量程的模拟万用表非常便宜,但是对初学者来说不太容易读准,特别是电阻测量。万用表的移动非常精密,所以摔万用表就很容易造成损坏。

两种类型(数字和模拟)的万用表各有自己的优势。像电压表,数字的要更好,因为内电阻要高很多,1 MΩ 或者 10 MΩ。模拟万用表在类似的量程内电阻在 200 kΩ。但另一方面,观测模拟显示的指针移动来跟踪缓慢的电压变化要更容易。

作为安培表使用的时候,一个模拟万用表的电阻非常低,因此很敏感,可以量至 50 μA。更昂贵的数字万用表能够大于等于这个性能。

数字万用表要更先进,而传统的模拟万用表注定要被淘汰。

数字万用表

万用表为电子工程师而设计和量产。甚至最简单和最廉价的型号也可能包括你不会用到的功能。数字万用表通常以数字形式输出在一个液晶显示屏上。

图 2-1 是一个可变量程的万用表。

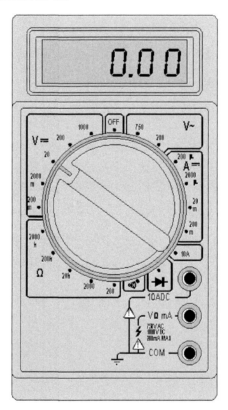

图 2-1 可变量程万用表

中间的旋钮有很多个位置,你必须选择一个来匹配你的测量。例如,如果万用表被选到 20 V 直流,那么 20 V 就是你可以量的最大电压。有时候这个被称为 20 V 满刻度偏转。

对一些有电源最大为 20 V 的电路,且包括所有你可能搭建的电路来说,20 V 直流电压量程最为有用。直流量程在万用表上由"V＝"读出。有时候,你要测量一些更低的电压,这时候,2 V 或者 200 mV 量程就更合适。

Text B

示 波 器

示波器是一种看见信号电压的电子测试设备。通常显示一个或多个电势差(纵轴)对时间或者其他电压(横轴)的二维图像。示波器是用途最多和使用最广泛的电子仪器之一。

示波器被广泛使用在需要观察电子信号的准确波形的情况下。除了信号的振幅以外,示波器还可以测量频率,显示失真和两个相关信号间的相对时差。示波器被用在科学、医疗、工程、通信和工业中。通用示波器被用作维护电子设备和实验室工作,特殊用途的示波器可以用于调节汽车的点火系统,或者显示心脏跳动的波形。

一开始所有的示波器用阴极射线管显示器作为显示单元,但是现代的数字示波器使用高速的数-模转换器和计算机化的显示屏和信号处理。示波器外设模块可以把通用笔记本或台式计算机变成有用和灵活的测试设备。

使用实例

在示波器上的李萨如图形如图 2-2 所示,x 和 y 输入之间有 90°相差。

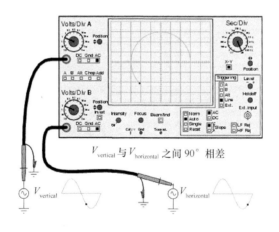

图 2-2 示波器上的李萨如图形,x 和 y 输入之间有 90°相差

示波器的一个最常用的用途是解决电子设备的故障。示波器的一个优势是可以图形化显示信号:当电压表显示一个完全未料到的电压时,示波器也许能揭示电路在振荡。在其他一些情形下,一个脉冲的准确形状是很重要的。

例如,在一件电子设备中,内部器件(电子感应龙头,电子振荡器,放大器)的连接可以由预期的信号来探测。这时示波器只是作为一个简单的信号跟踪器。如果预期的信号缺失或者不正确,前述的某些器件就没有正常工作。由于很多错误出现在一个故障部分,所以每次测量可以证明一个复杂设备里的半数器件要么工作正常,要么由于故障而不正常工作。

一旦故障器件被发现,进一步的探测通常可以告诉有经验的技术人员具体哪一个元件出错。在故障元件被替换之后,整个单元可以恢复使用,或者至少把下一个故障排查出来。

示波器的另一个用途是检查新设计的电路。通常一个新设计的电路会由于设计错误而不正常,比如错误的电压水平,电子噪声等。数字电子设备通常由时钟操作,所以一个同时显示时钟信号和依赖于时钟的测试信号的双重跟踪示波器很有用。"存储示波器"在"捕获"导致错误操作的罕见电子事件时也很有用。

示波器的另外一个用途就是在软件工程师为电子设备编程的时候。通常示波器是在软件运行时观测电子设备正常与否的唯一方式。图2-3为示波器应用图例。

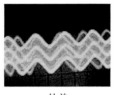
外差

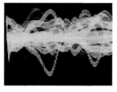
交流电电子噪声

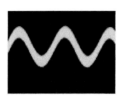
调幅信号

图 2-3　示波器应用图例

Unit 3　电子器件

Text A

电子元件

电子电路主要由电子元件的互连组成。电子元件被分成两大类:有源和无源。无源元件提供的能量少于它们自身吸收的能量,有源元件提供的能量大于它们自身吸收的能量。

真空管

真空管由抽成真空的玻璃膜组成,这种玻璃膜包含几个金属电极。一种简单的双极管(二极管)由阴极和连接能量供应的正极端的阳极组成。阴极是一个小金属管,由灯丝加热而释放电子;阴极释放的电子向阳极移动,阳极也称作板极,是一个围绕阴极的金属圆筒。如果阳极施加交流电压,电子仅在交流电的正半周期流向阳极。在交流电的负半周,阳极阻止电子的流动,从而没有电流经过真空管。仅在交流电的正半周允许交流电流通过的二极管称作整流管,通过的电流叫直流。在阴极阳极之间插入一个栅格,此栅格由螺旋的金属线组成,施加一个负电压给栅格,从而可以控制真空管的电流。当栅格是负电压时,它阻止电子的移动,仅有少部分的电子可以从阴极发射出来到达阳极。这样的管子叫做真空三极管,它可以当放大器使用。栅极电压的微小变化(如因无线和声音产生的),将造成从阴极到阳极或连接阳极的电子回路中电子流的巨大变化。

晶体管

晶体管由半导体制成。半导体是硅和锗这样的材料,经过掺杂,即加入微量的外部元素,使内部的自由电子过剩或者不足。前一种类型的半导体叫N型半导体,后一种类型的半导体叫 P 型半导体。将 N 型半导体和 P 型半导体结合在一起就形成了二极管。当这个二极管连接上电池,使 P 型材料为正,N 型材料为负时,电子就会被电池的负极排斥而毫无阻止地进入 P 区,因为 P 区缺少电子。当电池反接时,要到达 P 区的电子经过 N 区非常困难,因为 N 区已经填充了大量自由电子,电流几乎为零。1948 年发明了双极型晶体管,它可以替代三极真空管。它由三层掺杂材料组成,两个 PN 结可以配置成 P-N-P 或 N-P-N 型晶体管。其中一个 PN 结连接上电池使其有电流通过(正向偏置),另一个 PN 结以相反的方向连接上电池(反向偏置)。如果用一个外加信号使晶体管的正偏 PN 结中的电流发生变化,反偏 PN 结中的电流将相应地跟着变化。这个原理可以用来构建放大器,正向偏置结的小信号可以引起反向偏置 PN 结中电流大的变化。

另一种类型的晶体管是场效应管。由于双重电场的作用,这种晶体管可以阻断或吸引电荷。场效应管可以实现电流的放大,它的工作方式和真空管的栅格控制类似。由于非常小能量的信号可以控制大能量信号,因此场效应管具有比三极管更高的工作效率。

Text B

半导体二极管

半导体二极管是含有一个 PN 结的二端器件。半导体二极管的一般电路符号及相关的 PN 结特性如图 3-1 所示。

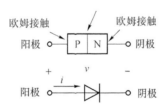

图 3-1 半导体二极管电路符号

一般说来,二极管的应用可以根据二级管工作的 3 个区域进行分类(图 3-2)。作为开关和整流应用时,它涉及了反向偏置和正向偏置区域的转换。在这些应用中必须小心地选择反向击穿电压足够大的二级管以防止不希望的反向击穿。反向击穿区域主要是作为参考电压应用。这时二极管是根据反向击穿时的电压值来选择的。

典型的半导体二极管特性如图 3-2 所示。

二极管是我们所遇到的正常工作区域的中间部分为明显非线性的第一个网络元件。基尔霍夫电流定律(KCL)和基尔霍夫电压定律(KVL)都可以使用,这是因为它们的适用性与网络元件是线性还是非线性无关。然而我们必须小心地使用叠加原理、戴维南等效原理和诺顿等效原理,因为这些方法明显地只适用于线性网络。

一种普遍有效的方法,是把线性网络与非线性元件分开,使用图解法求出非线性元件的电压和电流。为了说明这种图解方法,来看一下图 3-3。一个非线性元件,二极管,连接到一个任意复杂的网络上。这个网络仅含线性电阻元件和电源。网络的线性部分可用戴维南等效网络代替,如图 3-4 所示。

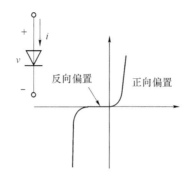

图 3-2　二极管三个工作区典型特性示意图

图 3-3　常见非线性网络

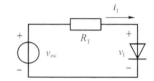

图 3-4　戴维南等效电路代替线性网络

解法的第一步是把线性网络与非线性网络分开,如图 3-5 所示,然后确定 v_D 和 i_D 的关系,即非线性元件的 v-i 特性。这个特性可以通过实验测量获得或厂商提供的数据等其他来源获得,并画出相关曲线如图 3-6 所示。解法的第三步是找出 v_L 与 i_L 之间的关系,即线性网络的 v-i 特性。从图 3-5 得出:

$$v_L = v_{oc} - i_L R_T \tag{3-1}$$

式中 v_{oc} 和 R_T 是线性网络的戴维南等效电压和等效电阻,然后将式(3-1)画在有非线性元件的 v-i 特性曲线图上,因为等式(3-1)是 v_L 与 i_L 之间的线性关系。画出来是一条直线。确定这条直线只需计算出直线上的两个点。两个方便的点是直线与坐标轴在 $v_L=0$ 和 $i_L=0$ 时的相交点,这分别相当于在线性网络的端口处短路和开路。因为 $v_L=0$,从式(3-1)得出:

$$i_L = v_{oc}/R_T \quad v_L = 0 \tag{3-2}$$

而从 $i_L=0$ 得出

$$v_L = v_{oc} \quad i_L = 0 \tag{3-3}$$

直线与 x 轴和 y 轴相交的点和由它们得到的直线如图 3-6 所示。可以看出直线的斜率为 $1/R_T$,因此当 R_T 的值很小时,这条直线接近于垂直;而 R_T 值很大时,这条直线变为水平。

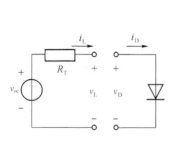

图 3-5　分开线性网络与非线性网络

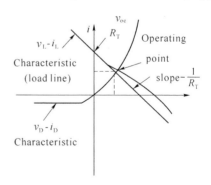

图 3-6　相关曲线图

如果非线性元件与线性网络连接,如图 3-4 所示,我们就会得到由电路连接形成的下达电路约束

$$v_L = v_D = v_1 \quad i_L = i_D = i_1$$

从图 3-6 可以看出,只有一个点的值满足 $v_L = v_D$ 和 $i_L = i_D$,这个点就是两条 $v\text{-}i$ 特性曲线的交点。因此所求的 v_1 和 i_L 的值就是这个交点的电压和电流值,而且能从图上直接读出。

画在图 3-6 中的线性的 $v\text{-}i$ 特性是负载线,因为它代表线性网络对非线性元件呈现出的所有可能的负载的轨迹。交点 $v_1\text{-}i_L$ 常常被称为非线性元件的工作点或 Q 点。

Unit 4 集成电路

Text A

集成电路

现代固体电子学产生了集成电路。随着半导体时代的到来,已有可能把包括电阻器、电容器、电感器、二极管和晶体管在内的完整电子电路建造在一片硅片或者锗片上。其他物质,特别是金属氧化物,用于制造集成电路。结果便产生一种比铅笔橡皮擦也许还要小的组件,但它却能容纳一个复杂的系统,而就在几十年前这种系统会占用整个一间屋子。

集成电路有多种分类方法。不论是模拟式还是线性式,集成电路都连续工作,并包括诸如运算放大器这样的器件。数字式集成电路主要用于计算机、电子计数器、频率合成器和数字仪表。双极集成电路采用双极晶体管技术。互补金属氧化物半导体集成电路仅需极弱电流,正变得越来越普遍。单片集成电路整体制造在一片半导体材料上,其他器件可以在单一组件中使用二片或二片以上单片。

集成电路有多种组件。最常见的可能是双列直插式。其他封装方法有管脚在一边的单列直插式组件和管脚分布在两边、三边和四边的扁平组件。

8 脚的 555 定时器芯片(图 4-1)使用在许多项目中,流行的型号有 NE555。大多数电路指定使用"555 集成电路芯片",NE555 就适用。555 的输出端引脚 3 的拉电流和灌电流可达 200 mA。这比大多数的芯片都大而且足够去驱动发光二极管、继电器和低电流电灯。想产生大电流时你可以连接一个晶体管来放大电流。

图 4-1 555 定时器芯片

556(图 4-2)是被放置在 14 个引脚的插座下的两个 555 的组合版本。这两个定时器共享同一个电源脚。

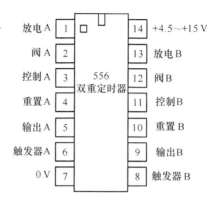

图 4-2　556 定时器芯片

可编程集成电路微控制器(图 4-3)是一个计算机式芯片。它们有一个处理器和存储器，可用来根据输入来运行程序从而控制输出。因此它们能够很容易地完成一些要几个传统的集成电路芯片才能实现的复杂功能。

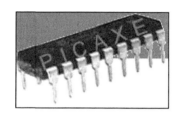

图 4-3　可编程集成电路微控制器

集成电路所能达到的微型化程度可能存在着一个理论限度。一些专家认为目前已接近这一限度，而另一些专家认为仍有可能取得进一步微型化。

除大功率应用外，集成电路部件正迅速取代所有电子装备中的分立元件。数字集成电路组件功率通常额定为 1 W 或更小些，线性集成电路部件额定功率达 10 W。集成电路组件的应用可能将会继续增长，原因在于其体积小、重量轻、成本低、耗能小，性能优异而可靠。

Text B

集成电路应用

集成电路通常被称为芯片，它们是被固化在微小的半导体(硅)芯片中的复杂电路。这个芯片用带有引脚的塑料插座包着，每个引脚间隔 0.1 英寸(2.54 mm)，可插在电路试验板上。插座下一些非常精细的导线将芯片与引脚相连。

引脚号（图 4-4）

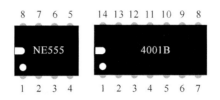

图 4-4 引脚号

集成电路芯片的引脚号从靠近槽口或圆点处开始以逆时针方向排列，图 4-4 显示了一个 8 脚和 14 脚的集成电路芯片，但对所有尺寸的芯片引脚命名的规则都是一样的。

芯片座（双列直插式插座）（图 4-5）

集成电路芯片很容易被焊接时的热量所损坏，并且它们短引脚不受散热片的保护。因此采用芯片座作为替代，严格地说叫双列直插式插座，它可安全地被焊接到电路板上。当所有的焊接工作完成后，再把芯片嵌入到插座中。仅在焊接时才使用芯片插座，在电路试验板是不使用的。

图 4-5 芯片座

商业上生产的电路板通常是在没有芯片插座的情况下直接将芯片焊接到板上的，通常这项工作都是由动作非常快的机械设备完成的。不要试图自己去这样做，因为你很可能会损坏芯片且通过电焊移出芯片时不可避免地会损坏它。

将芯片从插槽中移出

如果你要将芯片移出，可用一个小平口螺丝刀轻轻地把芯片从插座中拔出。将螺丝刀的叶片插入芯片和插座，然后轻轻地转动螺丝刀从而将芯片的两端小心地水平地起翘。注意要分别在两端口起翘，否则会将引脚弄弯甚至折断。

资料手册

大多数的集成电路都有资料手册，上面给出了产品等级和功能方面的详细信息。有些情况下还给出了参考电路。大量带有符号和缩写的信息会使初学者感到资料手册难以理解。但对于有经验的使用者来说，资料手册是很值得一看的，因为它包含了大量的有用信息和测试电路。

可编程集成电路微控制器的编程

对于初学者来说，可编程集成电路微控制器的编程是一件很困难的事情，但是现在有许多使这个过程简单化的系统。PICAXE 就是一个非常好的例子，因为它使用了标准的计算机来对 PIC 编程。除了下载数据线，它不再需要其他专门的设备了。程序可在简单版本的 BASIC 中编写或使用流程图。由于 PICAXE 编程软件和大量的文件可免费下载，在教学和家庭中使用这个系统是非常理想的。

如果你由于从未编写过程序而认为 PIC 不适合你，那么请看 PICAXE 系统。它可以通过使用一些简单的 BASIC 命令来开始，并且还有许多对初学者非常理想的方案可作为工具。

Unit 5　数字信号处理器

Text A

数字信号处理器

　　数字信号处理器 DSP 是一种特殊用途的中央处理器,它提供超快速的指令序列,例如移位叠加、乘法和加法,这些指令序列常用在数学密集型信号处理应用软件中。

　　然而,DSP 与典型的微处理器是不相同的。微处理器通常是运行大型软件的通用设备。大多数情况下没有实时计算的要求,工作速度也较慢,它们通过选择动作过程,然后在响应下一条用户命令之前等待完成目前的工作。另一方面,DSP 经常被用来作为一种建立在另一块设备中的嵌入式控制器或处理器,并致力于单组任务的实现。在这种环境下,DSP 协助通用微处理器主机工作。

　　数字信号处理算法通常需要在一组数据上快速、反复地进行大量的数学运算。信号(可能来自音频或视频传感器)不断地进行模数转换、数字操作,然后转换回模拟形式。许多 DSP 应用有延迟限制,也就是说想要系统工作,DSP 操作必须在一定时间内完成,延迟(或批量)处理是不可行的。

　　大多数通用微处理器和操作系统能够成功实现 DSP 算法,但是由于电源和空间的限制,并不适合用在便携设备上,如手机和掌上电脑。然而,一个专门的数字信号处理器,往往会提供一种低成本的解决方案,具有更好的性能、更低的延迟,而且不需要专门冷却或大型电池。

　　为了进行数字信号处理,数字信号处理器的结构进行了专门优化。由于信号处理很少是一个系统的唯一任务,大多数数字信号处理器也支持一些作为应用处理器或微控制器的功能。

数字信号处理

　　数字信号处理是一种将来自现实世界的信号(通常模拟形式)转换成数字数据,然后可以对其进行分析的技术。以数字形式进行分析,是因为一旦信号被简化成数字,相较于模拟形式而言,它的成分会更容易被分离、分析和重新排列。

　　最终,当 DSP 完成其工作,数字数据可以转换回模拟信号,以改善其质量。例如,一个 DSP 可以从信号中过滤噪声、消除干扰、放大有用频段且抑制其他频段、加密信息、或将一个复波分解成频谱分量。这个处理过程必须是实时的,往往非常迅速。例如,音响设备处理高达 20 kHz 声音信号(每秒 20 000 次),需要 DSP 每秒执行几亿次操作。

DSP 的类型

因为不同的应用有不同的频率范围,也就需要不同的 DSP。根据动态范围和数字宽度对 DSP 进行分类,数字宽度是在应用过程中必须处理的宽度。这个数字是处理器的数据宽度(操作的位数)和它所执行的算术类型(定点或浮点)。例如,32 位处理器比 24 位处理器具有更宽的动态范围,24 位处理器又比 16 位处理器具有更宽的范围。浮点芯片比定点设备具有更宽的范围。

每种类型的处理器都与应用的特定范围相适合。16 位定点 DSP 用于语音级的系统,如手机,因为它们的声音频率范围相对狭窄。高保真立体声有一个较宽的频率范围,需要 16 位模/数转换器和一个 24 位定点 DSP。图像处理,3D 图像和科学仿真有非常宽的动态范围,需要一个 32 位浮点处理器。

使用

DSP 芯片在音卡、传真机、调制解调器、蜂窝无线电话、大容量硬盘和数字电视中使用。据德州仪器统计,世界上 70% 的数字蜂窝电话使用 DSP 作为其引擎,无线应用方面也有所增加,这个数字只会增加不会减少。数字信号处理被应用于许多领域,包括生物医药、声纳、雷达、地震、语音和音乐处理、图像和通信。

Text B

数字信号处理器的结构

DSP 算法通常在循环中花费大部分的执行时间。这意味着,同一组程序指令将不断地从程序存储器传递到 CPU。超级哈佛结构能充分利用这种情况,凭借包含在 CPU 中的指令高速缓存。这是一个很小的存储器,其中包含约 32 条最近的程序指令。该存储器第一次通过一个循环写入指令,程序指令必须通过程序存储器总线传送。这导致较慢的操作,因为系数的冲突,提取系数也必须沿着这条路径。然而,在另外的循环执行中,程序指令可从指令高速缓存中提取。这意味着所有的存储器到 CPU 的信息传输可以在一个周期内完成:经过数据存储器总线系数传输输入信号采样、经过程序存储器总线传输系数和经过指令高速缓存传输程序指令。用该领域的行话,这种高效的数据传输被称为高内存访问带宽。

图 5-1 展示了更加详细的 SHARC 架构的视图,显示 I/O 控制器连接到数据存储器。这显示信号如何输入和输出系统。例如,SHARC 系列 DSP 同时提供串行和并行通信端口。这些都是非常高速度的连接。例如,在 40 MHz 时钟速度,有 2 个串行端口,每个都在 40 Mbit/s 运行,而 6 个并行端口,每个提供 40 MB/s 的数据传输。当所有 6 个并行端口一起使用时,数据传输速率是惊人的 240 MB/s。

这类高速 I/O 是 DSP 的关键特征。首要目标是在得到下一个采样之前将数据输入、执行数学运算并输出数据。其他一切都是次要的。一些 DSP 板上都有模/数和数/模转换器,具有混合信号的功能。然而,所有的 DSP 都可以通过串行或并行端口连接外接转换器。

现在让我们看看里面的 CPU。在图的上方是两个标记为数据地址发生器 (DAG) 的方块,一个(方块)代表两个存储器之一。这些(方块)控制着送往程序和数据存储器的地址,具体规定信息读自何方、写往何处。在简单一点的微处理器中,这个任务是处理程序定序器的固有部分,并且对于程序员是透明的。然而,DSP 使用循环缓冲区,并从有效地管理额外硬件中受益。这就避免了需要使用宝贵的 CPU 时钟周期,以保持数据的存储轨道。例如,在 SHARC DSP 中两个 DAG 各可控制 8 个循环缓冲区。这意味着每个 DAG 拥有 32 个变量(每个缓冲区 4 个),再加上所需的逻辑。

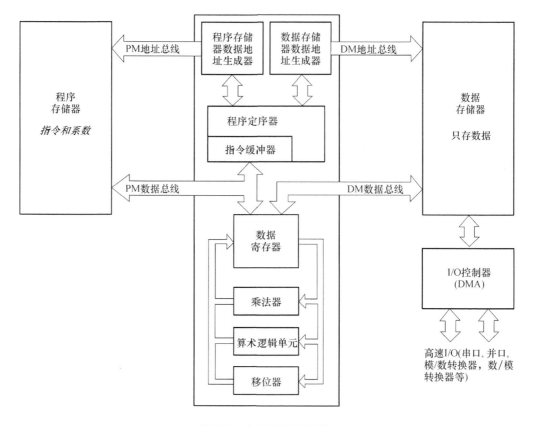

图 5-1 典型的 DSP 结构

数学处理被分成 3 个部分,一个乘法器,一个算术逻辑单元(ALU)和一个桶形移位器。乘法器从两个寄存器中取出乘数的值,将它们相乘,并将结果放入另一个寄存器中。ALU 执行加法、减法、绝对值、逻辑运算(与,或,异或,非)、定点和浮点格式之间的转换,以及类似的功能。基本的二进制操作由桶形移位器执行,如平移、旋转、提取和存入段等。SHARC 系列的一个强大功能是可以并行访问乘法器和算数运算单元。在一个时钟周期,来自 0~7 号寄存器的数据可以传递到乘法器,来自 8~15 号寄存器的数据可以传递到 ALU,两个结果返回给 16 个寄存器中的任何一个。

Unit 6 电源

Text A

电源

电源是一种生产电供电子装备使用的装置,或者是一种将公用电源转换成适用于电子装备形式的装置。电源一般分成电池或变压器/整流器/滤波器电路。一台发电机或一组光生伏打电池也可用作电源。

直流电源根据电压输出、供电量以及不定负载条件下保持稳压的能力来分类。在选择一种电源用于一件特定的电子仪器时这些参数都必须考虑到。电压必须正确,电源必须能输送必需的电流,电压必须在负载阻抗或电阻变化时保持在一定范围内。然而无需使用比需要精确得多的电源。例如,在一条仅 10 mA 的电路上使用 20 A 电源会使效率很低。

电源电压可以低到 1 V 或更低,也可以高到成千上万伏。供电量可以仅仅是几毫安,也可以是几百安。电源保持近于稳定电压的能力称为稳压,而在其他情况中,稳压不需要精确。

一些电子器件具有内装电源。大部分无线电接收机、磁带录音机、高保真度放大器及其他用户电器都有适合于电流要求的内装电源。然而,另有一些设备需要外部电源。许多商用电源有各种专门用途。

设计成输入交流电、产生直流电的电源必须包含一个变压器、一个整流器、一个滤波器,可能还要一个稳压电路。变压器把公用电压转换成适当电压,供设备使用;整流器把交流电转换成脉动直流电;滤波器把脉动直流电转换成几乎是纯直流电。

Text B

电源的种类

电源的种类很多。大多数电源的作用是将高电压交流电变为能给电子电路和其他设备使用的低电压电源。电源由一系列的部件组成,每个执行一种特定的功能。

例如,图 6-1 是一个 5 V 的稳压电源。

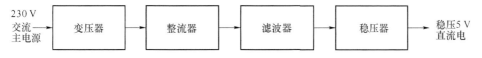

图 6-1 稳压电源模块图

每一部分详细介绍如下:

(1) 变压器——把高电压交流电源降为低电压交流电。

(2)整流器——把交流变为直流,但直流输出大小变化。
(3)滤波——把变化很大的直流电过滤成脉动很小的直流电。
(4)稳压器——消除脉动,把直流输出恒定。

双电源

一些电子电路需要带有正、负和零输出电源电压。这种电源叫双电源,因为它好像两个普通的电源连在一起。

双电源有3个输出,例如,一个±9 V的电源有+9 V,0 V和-9 V输出。

整流器

有几种连接二极管组成整流器把交流电变为直流电的方法,桥式整流器是最重要的整流装置,它产生全波的变化直流电。单个的二极管可以用作整流器,但它只能把交流电的正半波变成半波的变化直流电。

滤波

滤波由并联在直流电源端的大电解电容执行,大电解电容可作为储存器。当从整流器输出的变化的直流电压下降时,电容给输出端供电。图6-2表示没有经过滤波的变化直流电(虚线)和经过滤波的直流电(实线)。在变化的直流电的峰值处,电容迅速充电,当电容把电流供给输出端,电容放电。

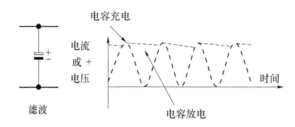

图6-2 没有经过滤波的变化直流电和经过滤波的直流电

注意滤波明显地把平均直流电压提高到接近峰值。

由于电容放电时,电容电压有点下降,会产生一个较小的脉动电压,滤波效果并不完美。

稳压器

集成电压稳压器可提供固定的(一般为5 V,12 V和15 V)或可调的输出电压。它们可以根据允许流过的电流最大值来分类。负电压稳压器主要用在双电源上。绝大多数的稳压器含有过流("过载")、过热自动保护。

表6-3 稳压器

Unit 7 同步数字系列

Text A

同步数字系列(SDH)

自从同步数字系列(SDH)和同步光网络(SONET)在1990年由标准组织提出后,它对光纤电信网络性能与成本的变革起到了促进作用。

SDH提供了一个具有独立运营商和复杂信号结构的传输网络,这种信号结构具有丰富的性能特点,结果产生了新的网络应用,在新的网络拓扑结构中使用了新的设备,运营系统管理比以前我们在传输网络中看到的更加强大。

多路复用技术允许综合稍不同步的速率,被称为准同步,由此产生了准同步数字序列(PDH)。

SDH与SONET的定义是指一组具有不同容量、能够传输数字信号的光纤传输率。这种新的复用方法应该是同步的,并非像PDH那样基于位间隔,而是基于字间间隔,如同由64 kbit/s到主速率1 544 kbit/s (1.5 Mbit/s)和2 048 kbit/s (2 Mbit/s)的复用结构那样。这一点已被人们广泛接受。

SDH新标准起初出现在SONET系统,由美国的Bellcore起草,随后经历了多次修改,才以新的面貌出现,并与国际SDH兼容。SDH与SONET出现于1988—1992年之间。

SONET是美国国家标准学会(ANSI)制定的标准,它能够承载类似北美PDH的位速率系统:1.5/6/45 Mbit/s和2 Mbit/s(在美国被称为E-1系统)。SDH包括了大部分SONET标准,而且是一个国际性的标准。

SDH是国际电报电话咨询委员会(CCITT)/国际电信联盟技术规范(ITU-TS)定义的一种,它用于全球范围内并是与SONET兼容的网络节点接口(NNI);它是两种用户网络接口(UNI)(用户连线),并在格式上支持宽带综合业务数字网(BISDN)的U参考点接口。

SDH标准原被定义在155.52 Mbit/s速率内传输1.5/2/6/34/45/140 Mbit/s,并正计划在155.52 Mbit/s整数倍速率内,承载其他类型的信息量,如异步转移模式(ATM)和互联网协议(IP)。SONET的基本传输单位是51.84 Mbit/s,但为了承载140 Mbit/s的信息量,SDH是基于它的3倍速率,即155.52 Mbit/s(155 Mbit/s),来传输的。

通过合适的选择,SDH子系统与SONET子系统能相互兼容,因此,业务交互工作是可能的,而告警与管理运行通常在SDH与SONET系统之间不能交互工作。对于某些性能而言,只有在某些情况下,在SDH系统供应商以及略微更常见的SONET系统供应商之间,这种交互工作才有可能。

尽管SONET和SDH原是为光纤传输系统设计的,但SDH无线系统的存在,可与

SONET 与 SDH 两者的速率兼容。

目前在公共网中,几乎所有正在安装的新的光纤传输系统都在使用 SDH 或 SONET。人们希望它能够主导未来数十年的数据传输,正如它的前身 PDH 主导了 20 多年数据传输一样。2005 年以后,长途电话系统的比特速率很快会达到 40 Gbit/s,与此同时,155 Mbit/s 及其以下速率的传输系统将深入地渗透到接入网络。

Text B

SDH 的组织结构

SDH 可应用于所有传统的电信应用领域。因此,SDH 有可能使电信网的结构衍变成为一个统一的网络。SDH 为这个网络提供了单一的、通用的标准,这就意味着由不同厂家供应的设备可以直接互联起来。

现在,就让我们来看看网络的"组件"以及它们的构成方式。这些网络单元均已由 CCITT 的标准所定义,并提供复用或交换的功能。

线路终端复用单元(LTM)可接受一批支路信号并将它们复用至适当的 SDH 速率的光载体上,即 STM-1,STM-4 或 STM-16。输入的支路信号可以是现有的 PDH 信号,例如 2 Mbit/s、34 Mbit/s 和 140 Mbit/s,也可以是较低速率的 SDH 信号。LTM 形成了由 PDH 网络到 SDH 的主入口。

分插复用单元(ADM)是一种特殊类型的终端复用单元,它是以"贯通"模式运行的。在 ADM 中,可以从"贯通"信号中上、下话路。ADM 通常在 STM-1 和 STM-4 的接口速率下工作并能上、下多种支路信号,即 2 Mbit/s、34 Mbit/s 或 140 Mbit/s 的信号。

ADM 的功能是 SDH 的主要优势之一,因为在 PDH 网络中,完成类似功能需要一套硬布线的背对背的终端设备。

同步数字交叉连接单元(DXC)将成为新的同步数字系列的基石。它们能对传输信道起到半永久交换的作用,并可在从 64 kbit/s 直至 STM-1 速率的任何级别上进行交换。一般地,这种单元具有 STM-1 或 STM-4 的接口。DXC 可以在软件控制下迅速地重构电路,以提供数字租用线路或变带宽的其他业务。

为清晰起见,在 STM-1 中的一帧可用一个二维的图形表示(图 7-1)。该二维结构由 9 行、270 列个方框组成。每个方框代表同步信号中的一个 8 位字节。在二维图的左上角有 6 个成帧字节,这些成帧字节起着标志作用,它使帧中的任何字节极易被确定位置。

信号比特按这样的次序传送:首先传送第一行,传输次序由左到右。当帧中的最后一个字节(即位于第 9 行第 270 列的字节)被传送之后,就再重复整个次序——又从下一帧的 6 个成帧字节开始。

一个同步传输帧是由两个不同的,并可直接接入的两部分——虚容器部分和段开销部分组成。虚容器主要用于通过网络来传送用户信息,而段开销提供了支持和维护同步网络节点间传输虚容器(VC)所需要的开销,例如告警监视、误码检测和数据通信信道。

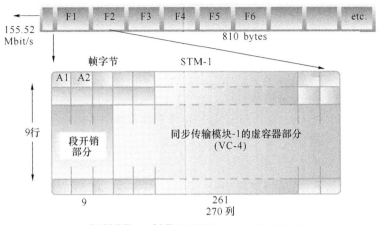

图 7-1 同步传输模块-1 的同步传输帧示意图

Unit 8 密集波分复用

Text A

密集型波分复用

密集型波分复用(DWDM)最初是指在 1 550 nm 波段内复用的光信号,以便能够控制掺铒光纤放大器(EDFAs)的容量(和成本),这对于波长约 1 525~1 565 nm(C 波段)的波,或 1 570~1 610 nm(L 波段)的波是有效的。掺铒光纤放大器最初是开发来取代 SONET/SDH 光电光(OEO)再生器的,实际上它们已经过时了。掺铒光纤放大器可以放大在其操作范围内的任何光信号,不论调制比特率是多少。就多波长信号而言,只要掺铒光纤放大器有足够的泵能量提供给它,它能放大可以复用进其扩增/放大带(虽然信号密度受到调制格式选择限制)的许多光信号。因此,掺铒光纤放大器能通过取代连接两端的唯一设备使单信道光连接以比特率升级,同时保留现有的掺铒光纤放大器或通过长途路线的一系列掺铒光纤放大器。此外,使用掺铒光纤放大器的单波连接同样可以以合理的费用升级到波分复用(WDM)连接。因此,在可以复用到 1 550 nm 波段的许多信道中,掺铒光纤放大器的成本是可以控制的。

在现阶段,一个基本的 DWDM 系统包含几个主要部分。

1. 密集型波分复用终端复用器

实际上,该终端复用器对于它所携带的每个波长信号都有一个波长转换收发器。波长转换收发器接收输入的光信号(即来自于客户层的 SONET/SDH 或其他信号),把信号转换成电力网域,并转发使用1 550 nm波段激光的信号。

2. 一个中间的光终端,或光分插复用器

这是一个远程扩增/放大站点,它能放大也许要跨过长达140 km或更长距离才能到达远程站点的多波信号。

3. 密集型波分复用终端多路解调器

该终端多路解调器把多波信号转换成单波信号并在客户层系统(如 SONET/SDH)的独立光纤上输出它们来进行检测。

4. 光监控信道

这是掺铒光纤放大器放大波段(在1 510 nm、1 620 nm、1 310 nm或其他专有波长)以外的附加波。该光监控信道传输多波长光信号信息,以及在光终端或掺铒光纤放大器站点上的远程条件。这也通常用于远程软件升级和用户(即网络运营商)的网络管理信息。

由于波长间隙更紧密,所以 DWDM 系统必须保持比普通波分复用(CWDM)所需要的更稳定的波长或频率。DWDM系统需要光传送器的高精密温度控制来防止只有几个千兆赫的非常狭窄的频带发生漂移。此外,由于DWDM技术提供了更大的最大容量,因此在通信体系中,它也往往被用于比CWDM更高的层次上,例如在骨干互联网上,因此它有较高的调制率,从而创造一个有着高性能水平的较小的密集型波分复用设备市场。体积更小和性能更好这些因素导致了 DWDM 系统通常比 CWDM 昂贵得多。

DWDM 传输系统最近的革新包括热插拔和软件可调的收发器模块,能操作40频道或80频道。这大大减少了对离散零件可插拔模块的需要,少数可插拔设备可处理各种波长的光线。

Text B

密集型波分复用——波长转换器,复用转发器和可重构光分插/增减复用器

波长转换器

在这一阶段,应该讨论有关波长转换器的一些细节,因为这将澄清目前 DWDM 技术作为一项额外的光传输层所发挥的作用。它也将有助于描述这种系统在过去的10多年间演变的轮廓。

如上所述,波长转换器原来是用来把客户层信号的波长转换为一个在1 550 nm 波段内的密集波分复用系统的内部波长(注意,甚至在1 550 nm 内的外部波长很可能也需要转换,因为它们几乎肯定会没有所需的频率稳定度公差,也不会有系统的掺铒光纤放大器所必需的光功率)。

但是,在20世纪90年代中期,波长转换器就迅速采取了额外的信号再生功能。转换器中的信号再生迅速从1R,2R,3R演变为高架监测多比特率3R再生器。这些差异概述如下。

1R 转发/中继。

基本上,早期的转换器是"无用输入和无用输出",因为它们所输出的信号几乎是收到

的光信号的一个模拟"复制",基本上没有信号清理。这限制了早期的DWDM系统的覆盖范围,因为信号必须先交给一个客户层接收器(可能来自不同供应商),然后信号质量大大下降。信号监测基本上限于如接收功率这样的光域参数。

2R 重新定时,重新传输。

这种类型的转换器不是很常见,它利用一个准数字施密特触发方式来进行信号清理。一些最基本的信号质量监测工作由传送器来完成,这些传送器基本上要考虑模拟参数。

3R 重新定时,重新传输,重新形成。

3R 转发器是全数字化的,通常可以查看 SONET/SDH 层架空部分,如字节 A1 和 A2,以确定信号质量的好坏。许多系统将提供 2.5 千兆转发器,这通常意味着转发器是能够在 OC-3/12/48 信号,并可能在千兆/吉比特以太网上完成 3R 再生的,且通过监测 SONET/SDH 层架空部分字节来报告信号的好坏度。许多转发器,将能够在两个方向执行完整的多速率 3R。一些厂商提供 10 个千兆转发器,这将执行速率等于和超过 OC-192 的层架空监测。

复用转发器

对于复用转发器来说,不同的供应商有不同的称谓。它主要是把较低速率信号的一些相对简单的时分复用转换为系统内的较高速率载波。(一个常见的例子就是它能接受 4OC-48s,然后输出一个单一的在 1 550 nm 波段内的 OC-192 信号)。最近的复用转发器设计吸收了更多的时分复用(TDM)功能,在某些情况下,无需传统的 SONET/SDH 传输设备。

可重构光分插复用器

如上所述,DWDM 系统中的中间光放大站可允许某些波长的信道的减少和增加。2006 年 8 月所配置的大多数系统是很少这样做的,因为增加或降低波长需要手动插入或更换波长选择卡。这是昂贵的,并且在一些系统中要求所有主动流量都要从 DWDM 系统中去除,因为插入或去除特殊波长卡中断了多波长光信号。

有了可重构光分插/增减复用器(ROADM)

网络运营商可以通过发送软命令来进行远程重构复用器的操作。ROADM 的这种体系结构使得波长的降低或增加不会使直通信道发生中断。各种商用 ROADM 都采用了多种技术方法,采用哪些技术方法则取决于成本、光功率和灵活性等方面的折中考虑。

Unit 9　嵌入式系统

Text A

嵌入式系统概述

计算机系统随处可见。它们从本质上分成两个不同的类别。首先,最明显的是台式电脑。当我们谈计算机时，这是首先出现在我们脑海中的机器。台式电脑的设计灵活，满足广泛用户的需求。终端用户可以通过仅仅改变应用程序来改变一台台式电脑的功能。一会儿你可以将它作为一个文字处理器来使用，一会儿你可以将它作为一个 MP3 播放器或游戏机来使用。

第二类计算机是嵌入式计算机（或嵌入式系统），一个被嵌入到更大的电子系统，并重复实现特定功能，系统用户往往完全无法识别的计算机。如果你问一个人家里有多少台计算机，他可能会将台式电脑和笔记本电脑计算在内。然而，计算机总是被嵌入到各种日常用品中。事实上，他可能有超过 20 台计算机，隐藏或嵌入到洗衣机、电视机、数码相机、手机、烤箱、空调、DVD 播放机等电器中。与台式电脑不同，嵌入式计算机通常专用于特定的任务。

嵌入式系统是一个被开发来控制一个或几个专用功能的计算机系统，并且终端用户不能以在台式电脑上编程的方式来对该系统进行编程。

用户可以选择功能，但不能通过添加或更换软件来更改系统的功能。例如，一个可编程的数字温度调节器有一个专门监测和控制周围环境温度的嵌入式系统。您可以选择设置所需的低温和高温，但你恰恰不能改变其作为温度控制器的功能。嵌入式系统的软件通常称为固件，并包含在系统的非易失性内存中。

在大多数情况下，嵌入式系统是用来取代应用程序特定的电子消费产品。通过这样做，绝大多数系统功能封装在运行系统的固件中，并有可能通过改变固件来改变和升级系统，同时保持相同的硬件。这使生产成本降得更低，因为许多不同的系统可以共享相同的硬件基础，而功能由加载在其上的固件决定。

使用嵌入式计算机来代替专用电子电路的另一个优点是知识产权的保护。如果你的设计是完全基于硬件的，那么设计更加容易被窃取。你需要的是确定电路元件和跟踪在电路板上的轨道。嵌入式系统的硬件可以被识别，但真正提供系统功能的软件却不能，软件可以隐藏起来，而且更难以破解。

现在来讨论数字温度调节器内的嵌入式系统。功能框图如图 9-1 所示。

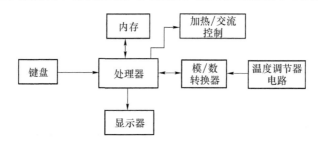

图 9-1　嵌入式系统示例之温度调节器

温度调节器检测其周围的温度（温度传感器），并转换为成比例的模拟电压。处理器不能直接控制这个信号，因此，它通过模-数转换（ADC）过程转换为等效的数字信号。然后处理器将这个温度读数与用户设置的高、低温进行比较，在必要时打开或关闭加热器/交流。用户使用键盘输入的温度设置，该温度保存到内存。该处理器在液晶显示屏上显示设定温度和当前温度。执行监测和控制温度的全部功能的软件存储在内存中。处理器从内存中读取指令并执行。

Text B

嵌入式系统的电源调节

电源是所有嵌入式系统的一个重要方面。没有电力就无法工作。根据应用的类型,有几种电源可供选择。例如,如果系统不需要便携性,它可以使用交流适配器直接从墙壁电源供电。交流适配器很便宜,而且很容易在任何电子商店买到。它们用于给家里的一堆电子小玩意供电,像收音机、应答机、无线路由器等。它们还作为手机充电器。它们将墙上的插座中高压交流电转换为适合在电器中运行的低压直流电。它们通常提供大约在+3.3 V~+12 V范围内的直流输出电压,并提供高达几安培的电流。

嵌入式系统由许多不同的元件组成,这些元件可以在宽泛的供电电源下运转。但一些元件,如模-数转换器,需要一个恒定的电压供应来提供精确的输出,因为模拟信号转换成数字量需要一个参考电压,被称为稳压器的装置用于此目的。它的任务是将各种直流输入电压转换为一个恒定的输出电压。此外,稳压器也最大限度地减少电源噪声,并提供一种由于输入电压的波动对嵌入式系统造成的任何损害的保护。底线是包括稳压器在内的设计始终是完好的。

稳压器的类型

1. 线性稳压器

线性稳压器使用至少一个有源元件(如晶体管),并要求比输出电压更高的输入电压。它们体积小,价格便宜,易于实现,净输出电压噪声低,因此很受欢迎。然而,它们产生大量废热(注意,输入和输出电压之差是通过稳压器下调的),这些废热必须用庞大的散热器来消散。因此,就效率而言,它们不是一个好的选择,尤其是针对电池供电的嵌入式系统。此外,它们只能降低电压,并不能提高输入电压。

2. 开关稳压器

不同于线性稳压器,开关稳压器可以升压(增加),降压(降低),或使输入电压反相。开关稳压器的工作原理是将离散能量包从输入电压源转移至输出。这是在电子开关(通常使用场效应管和一个调节能量转换率的控制器的帮助下完成的。它们用电感或电容作为储能元件,将能量从输入转移至输出。由于按需传递能量,它们较线性稳压器消耗的电源更少,且更加有效。然而其缺点是,它们需要更多的元件(即让它们昂贵),占用更多的空间,且电路设计复杂。这就是为什么它们没有在爱好者中流行起来的原因。此外,电路中的高开关频率会产生远远超过线性稳压器的噪声。

LM78xx 稳压器

市面上有数百个可用的稳压器。最常用的是LM78xx系列的线性稳压器,它由几个公司制造,如仙童半导体公司、Semelab有限公司和意法半导体有限公司。它们通常用TO-220封装,并有一个散热器的金属附着点。零件号标明输出电压。例如,LM7805提供5 V稳压输出,而LM7809提供了一个稳定的9 V输出(如表9-1所示)。它们能提供高达1安培的输出电流,并有过载和短路保护功能。

表 9-1　LM78xx 稳压器

零件号	输入电压范围/V	输出电压/V
LM7805	7～25	5
LM7806	8～25	6
LM7808	10.5～25	8
LM7809	11.5～25	9
LM7810	12.5～25	10
LM7812	14.5～30	12
LM7815	17.5～30	15
LM7818	21～33	18
LM7824	27～38	24

图 9-2 显示了如何使用 LM7805 来获得一个稳压的+5 V 电源。去耦电容(名义上位于 1～47 μF 之间)用于过滤输入和输出电压,它们还帮助消除电源中任何瞬间毛刺。通过调整来自降压变压器的低压交流输出,使用一个二极管桥式整流器获得 LM7805 的输入直流电压。

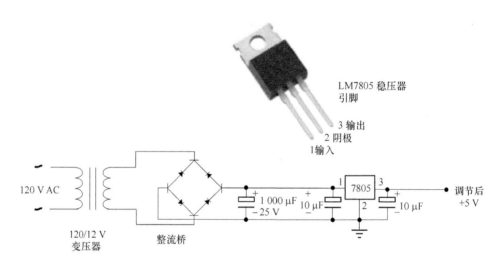

图 9-2　LM7805

Unit 10　可编程逻辑控制器

Text A

梯形逻辑

　　梯形逻辑是用于可编程逻辑控制器（PLC）编程的主要方法。如前所述，梯形逻辑已经发展到模仿继电器逻辑。决定使用的继电器梯形逻辑图是具有战略性意义的。通过选择梯形逻辑作为主要的编程方法，再培训工程师和零售商的资金大大减少。

　　现代控制系统仍包括继电器，但这些继电器很少用于逻辑控制。继电器是一个使用磁场来控制开关的简单装置，如图10-1所示。当在输入线圈施加电压时，所产生的电流产生一个磁场。磁场拉动一个金属开关（或簧片）并吸合触点，关闭开关。线圈通电时，吸合的触点称为常开触点。输入线圈不通电时，吸合常闭触点。在电路原理图中，继电器通常用一个圆圈代表输入线圈。输出触点用两条平行线表示。常开触点用两条竖线表示，并且在输入不通电时，常开触点被释放（不导电）。常闭触点用两条竖线表示，且有一条对角斜线穿过这两条竖线。当输入线圈不通电时，常闭触点被吸合（导电）。

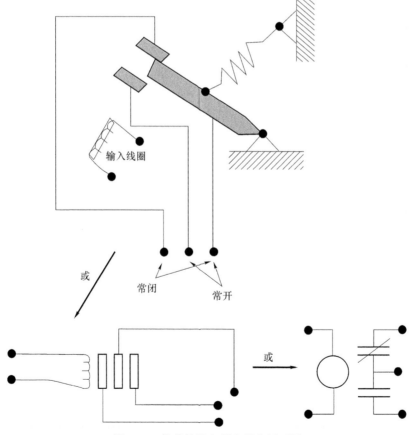

图 10-1　简单的继电器布局和原理图

继电器用来让一个电源关闭另一个电源（通常高电流），同时保持它们隔离。一个简单的继电器控制程序的例子如图10-2所示。在这个系统中左边第一个继电器常闭，当电压加到输入点A时允许电流流过。第二个继电器常开，当电压加到输入点B时，不允许电流流过。如果电流流过前两个继电器，那么电流将流过第三个继电器的线圈，并关闭输出点C的开关。此电路通常被绘制成梯形逻辑形式。逻辑上可以理解为，如果A是关闭且B是打开，则C是打开。

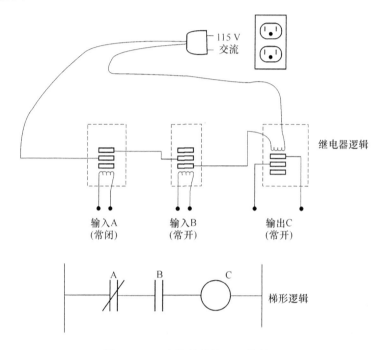

图10-2 一个简单的继电器控制器

图10-2的例子并没有显示整个控制系统，而只显示了逻辑。当我们关注一个PLC时，要考虑它的输入、输出和逻辑。图10-3给出了PLC更完整的表示。这里有两个按钮控制输入。我们可以将输入想象成24 V直流电驱动PLC的继电器线圈。这反过来又驱动一个输出继电器，它开关115 V交流电，这将打开一盏灯。请注意，在实际的PLC系统中输入从来不用继电器，但输出往往是继电器。PLC中的梯形逻辑实际上是一种用户可以输入和更改的计算机程序。两个输入按钮都常开，但PLC里面的梯形逻辑有一个常开触点和一个常闭触点。不要以为PLC的梯形逻辑需要输入或输出相匹配。许多初学者会陷入试图将梯形逻辑匹配输入类型的误区。

许多继电器也有多个输出（开关），这允许一个输出继电器同时也是输入。图10-4所示的电路就是这样一个例子，它被称作自保持电路。在此电路中，电流通过标有A或B的触点流经任一分支电路。当输出点B为打开时，输入点B将只能为打开。如果B是关闭的，而A通电，则B将打开。如果B打开则输入点B将打开，并且即使输入点A关闭，输出点B仍保持打开。B打开后，输出点B将不会关闭。

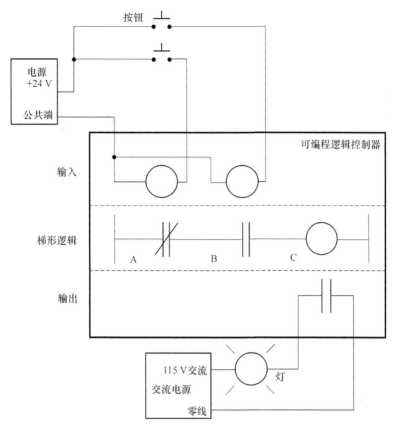

图 10-3 用继电器图解 PLC

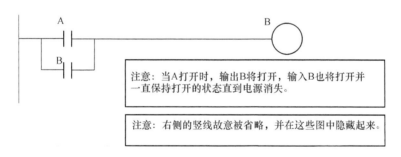

图 10-4 自保持电路

Text B

PLC 编程

最初对 PLC 的编程是基于一种继电器逻辑布线示意图的技术。这消除了教电工、技术员和工程师如何编写计算机程序的需要——但是,这种方法已被大家所接受,而且是现在最常见的 PLC 的编程技术。从图 10-5 中可以看到一个梯形逻辑的例子。为了解释这个图,假想电源是在左手边垂直线一方,我们称之为母线,在右手边的是零线。在图中有两个梯级,并且每个梯级都有输入(两条垂直线)和输出(圆圈)的组合。如果输入以正确的组合方式打开或闭合,能流就会从母线流经输入,驱动输出,并最终到达零线。输入可能来自一个传感器、开关或任何其他类型的传感器。输出是某些可以开启或关闭的 PLC 外部设备,如灯光或电动机。在最高的梯级中,触点是常开和常闭的。这意味着如果输入点 A 是打开并且输入点 B 是关闭的,那么能流将流经输出和驱动它。任何其他输入值的组合将导致输出点 X 被关闭。

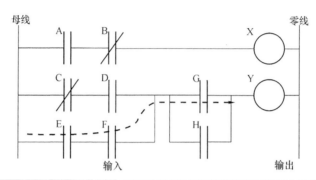

注意:电流需要流经某个输入组合(A、B、C、D、E、F、G、H)来打开输出(X、Y)。

图 10-5 一个简单的梯形图逻辑图

图 10-5 的第二个梯级更复杂,实际上有多种输入组合导致输出 Y 运行。在梯级的最左边的部分,如果 C 是关闭的并且 D 是打开的,能流可能流经顶部。如果 E 和 F 都为真,能流还可能(同时)流经底部。这将使能流一半流过梯级,然后如果 G 或 H 是真,能流将被传送到输出 Y。

还有其他的 PLC 编程方法。其中最早的技术之一涉及助记符指令。这些指令可能直接源自梯形逻辑图,并通过一个简单的编程终端输入到 PLC 中。助记符指令例子如图 10-6 所示。在这个例子中,指令一次自上而下读取一行。第一行 00000 是对输入点 A 的指令输入装载并求反(LDN),这条指令将检查 PLC 的输入点。如果它是关闭的,就记为 1(或真);如果它是打开的,就记为 0(或假)。下一行使用一个输入装载(LD)语句来检查输入。如果输入关闭,它记为 0;如果输入为打开,它还会记为 1(注:这是 LDN 的取反)。逻辑与(AND)语句取出内存中最后的两个数,如果二者都为真,结果是 1,否则结果是 0。这一结果现在取代了那两个被取出的数,并只有一个数在内存中。在 00003 行和 00004 行,这一过程将重复进行,但当这些完成时,现在就有三个数在内存中。最老的数是从 AND 指令获得,新一点的数是从两个 LD 指令获得。00005 行中的 AND 组合了来自最近的 LD 指令,而现在已经有两个数在内存中。逻辑或(OR)指令提取现在保存的两个数,如果任意一个是 1,结果就是 1,否则结果是 0。这一结果将替代那两个数,现在只有一个单一的数在内存中了。最后一个指令是存储输出(ST),将检查最近存储的值。如果是 1,输出将被打开;如果是 0,输出将被关闭。

图 10-6 的梯形逻辑程序等价于助记符程序。即使你用梯形逻辑对一个 PLC 进行了编程,它在使用之前将被 PLC 转换为助记符形式。在过去,助记符编程是最常见的,但现在对用户来说是不常见的,甚至很少看到助记符程序。

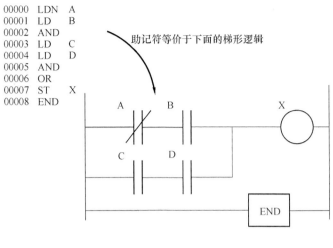

图 10-6 一个助记符程序和等效梯形逻辑图的例子

顺序功能图(SFCs)已经发展出来适应对更先进系统的编程。它们类似于流程图,但强大得多。图 10-7 中的例子就是在做两件不同的事情。阅读这幅图时,从顶部写着"start"的地方开始读,其下方的双重水平线代表有两条路可走。因此,PLC 将分别同时从左右两个分支开始。在左边有两个函数,第一个是 power up 函数。此函数将运行至其判决完成,之后 power down 函数接着运行。在右手边是 flash 函数,它一直运行到其结束为止。这些函数看上去并不明确,但每个函数,例如 power up 可能是一个小的梯形逻辑程序。这种方法和流程图有很大不同,因为它不必沿着单一路径遍历流程图。

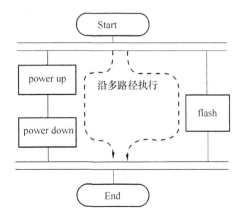

图 10-7 一个顺序功能图范例

Unit 11　第三代移动通信技术

Text A

国际移动通信 2000——全球第三代移动通信标准

国际移动通信 2000（IMT-2000）是国际电信联盟（ITU）使用的一个术语，用来指一套全球统一的第三代移动通信业务与设备的标准。第三代（3G）业务的目的是提供速率达 2 Mbit/s 的宽带无线接入，这将使移动多媒体业务成为可能。1998 年，ITU 向有关方面征集 IMT-2000 的建议，收到了许多基于时分多址（TDMA）和码分多址（CDMA）技术的方案。欧洲电信标准化协会（ETSI）和从事全球移动通信系统（GSMC）业务的公司，如诺基亚、爱立信等基础设备供应商，支持宽带码分多址（W-CDMA）方案，而美国的供应商们，包括高通公司、朗讯科技公司，则支持 CDMA2000 方案。

为照顾各方利益，ITU 提出，IMT-2000 标准以 CDMA 为基础，包括 3 个不同的工作模式。其中每一个工作模式都应当能够工作于全球移动通信系统（GSM）和接口规范-41（IS-41）的网络体系。这 3 个工作模式分别为：

直接序列频分双工模式。该模式基于通用移动通信系统陆地无线接入（UTRA）方案的第一个运行节点，得到了 GSM 网络运营商和设备供应商以及日本无线工业及商贸联合会（ARIB）的支持。

多载波频分双工模式。该模式基于美国电信工业委员会（TIA）的 CDMA2000 方案，得到了美国移动通信网络运营商和设备供应商的支持。

时分双工模式。该模式基于 UTRA 方案的第二个运行节点，不需成对频率的方案已被中国的时分同步码分多址（TD-SCDMA）采用。

ITU 于 2000 年 5 月 8 日至 6 月 3 日期间在土耳其的伊斯坦布尔召开世界无线通信大会，同意开发以上业务。该决议为希望实施 IMT-2000 标准的国家规定了许多全球范围内可供使用的频带。该决议利用现有的移动通信和移动卫星通信的频率分配，为运营商们根据市场情况和国情向 IMT-2000 过渡提供了高度的灵活性。

同时，该决议并未排除使用应用于其他移动通信或分配给其他业务的频带，这是大会达成一致意见的关键因素。就规定频带内 IMT-2000 的许可证发放与设备制造，大会决议作了全球统一的规定。每个国家将根据自身的具体需求确定在其本国范围内实施 IMT-2000 的时机。

IMT-2000 的频率划分有两个阶段。第一个阶段是在 1992 年，IMT-2000 刚开始开发。第二个阶段是最近召开的这次大会。早在 1992 年确定的频带保持不变，因为全世界许多地方已发放的或正在发放的频带使用许可证是以这些频带为基础的。这些频带为 1 885～

2 025 MHz以及2 110～2 200 MHz。其他供IMT-2000陆地移动通信系统使用的还包括806～960 MHz，1 710～1 885 MHz以及2 500～2 690 MHz。所有全球范围内供IMT-2000使用的频带具有相同地位。

Text B

第三代移动通信(3G)的实施和历史

2001年5月，日本最大的移动通信运营商日本电报电话公共公司(NTT DoCoMo)在W-CDMA技术试发布会上推出了世界第一个名为FOMA的第三代移动通信(3G)试商用网络。同年10月1日，该公司推出了世界第一个3G商用网络。2002年1月，世界第二个3G网络由韩国SK电信投入商用。该网络以CDMA2000 1xEV-DO技术为基础。同年5月，韩国行动电话公司(KTF)以EV-DO技术为基础，推出了该国的第二个3G商用网络。由此韩国成为了第一个实现3G网络运营商间相互竞争的国家。

英国电信公司下属的Manx电信公司在马恩岛推出了欧洲第一个3G试商用网络。欧洲第一个3G商用网络由挪威的Telenor电信公司于2001年12月投入运营。因为没有商用手机可供使用，所以该网络也没有付费的客户。这些网络都是基于W-CDMA技术的。

美国的Monet公司以CDMA2000 1xEV-DO技术为基础部署了美国首个3G商用网络，后来，该网络运营商停止了网络的运营。Verizon公司是美国第二个3G网络运营商，该公司于2003年10月发布了同样利用CDMA2000 1xEV-DO标准的3G网络，该网络发展一直很强劲。

2002年2月，m.Net公司在南澳大利亚的阿德莱德建成了南半球的第一个3G试商用示范网络。该网络采用了工作在2 100 MHz频带的通用移动通信系统(UMTS)标准，是2002年世界信息技术大会上发布的一个示范性网络。和记电讯公司于2003年4月发布了澳大利亚第一个名为"三"的3G商用网络。2006年10月，澳大利亚电讯公司(Telstra)推出了澳大利亚规模最大、速度最快的3G网络。该网络名为"下一代"，采用UMTS/高速下行分组接入(HSDPA)标准，工作于850 MHz频带，用来替代澳大利亚的cdmaOne网络。

据全球移动供应商协会(GSA)发表的数据显示，截至2007年12月，已有190个3G网络在40个国家运营，154个HSDPA网络在71个国家运营。在亚洲、欧洲、加拿大和美国，许多电信公司采用W-CDMA技术运营3G通信网络，并得到了大约100个终端设计的支撑。

在欧洲，和记电讯公司的"三"网络于2003年3月开始在英国和意大利大规模地向市场推出3G商用业务。欧盟建议，截至2005年年底，3G运营商的业务应覆盖欧洲80%的人口。

在一些国家，因频谱使用许可费的巨额成本，3G网络的推广被延迟。许多国家的3G网络没有使用与2G相同的无线频谱，因此，移动通信运营商必须建设全新的网络并申请全新的频率使用许可。而美国则不在此列，因为其运营商使用与其他业务相同的频率经营3G业务。由于政府拍卖的频谱使用许可证数量有限和密封投标拍卖方式的影响以及大家在初期阶段热情看好 3G 的发展前景，这就使得频谱使用许可费在一些欧洲国家非常高。3G 网络建设被延迟的其他原因还有新系统的设备更新费用。

　　截至 2007 年 6 月，已有 2 亿个 3G 用户连接上了网络，这只占全世界 30 亿移动电话用户的 6.7%。在最早推出 3G 的国家——日本和韩国，超过一半的用户使用 3G。在欧洲，领先的国家是意大利。该国三分之一的用户过渡到了 3G。从过渡到 3G 的数量来看，其他处于领先位置的国家还包括英国、澳大利亚、奥地利和新加坡。它们过渡到 3G 的用户数量达到了 20%。一个容易引起混淆的统计数字是把 CDMA2000 1xRTT 的用户当作 3G 用户来计算。如果采用这种极具争议的算法，那么 2007 年 6 月全世界共有 4.75 亿 3G 用户，占全部移动电话用户的 15.8%。

Unit 12　非对称数字用户线

Text A

非对称数字用户线（ADSL）

　　人们可以通过不同的途径连接到互联网，可以采用一般的调制解调器、综合服务数字网（ISDN）、办公室的本地局域网、电缆调制解调器和数字用户线（DSL）进行连接。非对称数字用户线（ADSL）是一种高速互联网接入业务，它使用现有的电话铜线来发送和接收数据，其速度远高于传统的拨号方式。采用拨号调制解调器方式最快的速率为 57 kbit/s，在良好的工作条件下通常的运行速率是 53 kbit/s。相比之下，ADSL 允许的数据流速率是 1.5～8 Mbit/s，当然取决于所购买的 ADSL 服务等级。

　　ADSL 使用标准的电话线在数字频率上传送上行和下行数据流，数字频率将这些数据流和电话与传真机使用的模拟信号分开。由于 ADSL 信号是运行在不同的频率上，电话可以正常使用，即使是在用 ADSL 进行网上浏览时也是如此。唯一的要求可能是在每个电话线或传真线上使用便宜的 DSL 滤波器，以去除 ADSL 业务产生的线路"白噪声"。

　　ADSL 中的非对称是指下行数据流速率大于上行数据流速率，下行数据流是从互联网上到你计算机的数据，上行数据流是从你计算机上到互联网的数据。上行数据速率较小是由于网络请求是相当小的数据串，其操作并不需要很大的带宽。

　　当电话公司和其他业务服务商在进入新市场以提供视频和多媒体格式信息时，ADSL 将发挥重要的作用。新的宽带布线还要数十年才会到达所有盼望它的用户，但这些新业务的成功却取决于在最近几年就将它们送往尽量多的用户家中。通过将电影、电视、视频目录、公司局域网和互联网带入家庭和小型商业机构，ADSL 会为电话公司和应用供应商带来市场的活跃并赢利。

ADSL 电路连接电话双绞线两端的 ADSL 调制解调器,并产生 3 个信息通道:一个高速下行信道、一个中速上行信道和一个双工的电话信道,这取决于安装的 ADSL 结构。ADSL 依靠先进的数字信号处理技术和创新算法来将如此大量的信息通过电话双绞线进行传输。此外,在变换设备、模拟滤波器和模-数转换器方面也需要许多先进技术。长距离的电话线使 1 MHz 的信号衰减高达 90 dB,因此要实现大的动态范围、分离通道和维持低噪声,ADSL 调制解调器的模拟部分工作相当尽力。为产生多个通道,ADSL 调制解调器利用下面两种方式之一来划分电话线的可用带宽:频分复用(FDM)或回声抵消。频分复用将一个频带用于上行数据传输,而另一个频带用于下行数据传输,再利用时分复用技术将下行路径分为一个或多个高速通道以及一个或多个低速通道。回声抵消技术安排上行频带与下行频带重叠,通过本地回声抵消来分开两个频带,这种技术在 V.32 和 V.34 调制解调器中广为使用。

Text B

ADSL 的应用

数字用户线(DSL)是一种通过铜质电话线进行数据传输的数据通信技术,其传输速率大于传统的话音频带调制解调器。非对称数字用户线(ADSL)就是 DSL 技术中的一种。同其他 DSL 相比,ADSL 的一个显著特点是一个方向上的数据流量大于另一个方向上的数据流量,即非对称性。从网络到用户方向上的下行带宽远远大于从用户到网络方向上的上行带宽。这种安排很适合多种服务与应用。

作为一种视频点播服务,传送娱乐视频是早期推动 ADSL 发展的服务之一。就传输视频而言,下行方向的高带宽能够支持少量的数字压缩视频信道。另外,在用户到网络的下行方向上,速率相对低得多的一个控制信道给观众提供类似盒式录像机的停止、播放、暂停、快进、快倒等功能。

视频点播依靠一种适合娱乐视频的标准视频压缩技术。这种技术决定了下行视频信道的带宽大小。国际标准化组织(ISO)的活动图片专家组(MPEG)已制定出了视频/音频的存储、播放标准。与交互式视频通信不同,娱乐影片的压缩过程不要求是实时的,而且可在传输之前以"离线"转换、存储的方式进行,但其压缩与解压缩要求具有相当高的解压缩图片质量。MPEG 的标准还包括了高质量立体声的压缩。利用 MPEG 的标准可以把一个娱乐视频及音频声道压缩成一个通信信道带宽仅需 1.5 Mbit/s 的数字数据流,而一个广播电视信道则需要 6 Mbit/s 的带宽。

除视频点播外,将来还可根据用户的需求和所处的位置利用 ADSL 提供许多的服务。另一个很流行的并非常适合非对称通信的应用就是互联网接入。互联网协议(IP)是一个面向连接的包协议。它依靠使用应答包来确认,在大量数据包发出之前发出的数据包能否被正确接收。当用户访问互联网网页时,从互联网到用户的数据占绝大部分。这些数据通常以含有大量图像信息或文档下载的互联网网页的形式出现。在相反方向上,从用户到互联网的数据则主要是应答包和控制包。这些应答包和控制包的数据相对较小,因此它们仅需要很小的信道带宽。但是，上行带宽不可以小到引起应答包不应有的排队时延，因为这会大大减少朝向用户的下行方向的包的吞吐量。上行带宽比率应该要求达到10∶1。将来，由于视频和音频的使用使得网页的内容会越来越丰富，下行带宽的需求也必定会越来越大。

通过 ADSL 提供的其他服务还包括互动游戏、在家网上购物、远程教育等。

Unit 13 无线网络技术

Text A

第二代无线网络

无线应用协议（WAP 1.0）基于一些被公认的国际标准，人们曾经期望它是未来移动商务中的重要工具，但是它失败了。I-mode 只是日本年轻人的电子玩具，一切都是私有的，但是它获得了巨大的成功。接下来将会怎么样呢？每一方都从第一代无线网络中学到了一些东西。WAP 联盟学到了内容方面的教训。没有足够多的网络站点使用你的标记语言，这将是致命的。NTT DoCoMo 则学到了一个与小型手持设备和日本文化紧密相关的私有封闭系统不是一个好的出口产品。双方得出的结论是，要让大量的网络站点采用你的格式来表达它们的内容，那么，一个开放的、稳定的、可被普遍接受的标记语言是非常必要的。格式战争对商业竞争没有任何好处。

这两种服务都将进入到第二代无线网络技术领域中。WAP 2.0 首先出现，所以我们将拿它作为例子来讲述。WAP 1.0 做的有些事情是正确的，这些还将继续下去。首先，WAP可以被承载在不同类型的网络上。第一代使用了电路交换网络，但是分组交换网络是一种选择，即使现在还是这样。第二代系统有可能使用分组交换，例如，通用分组无线业务（GPRS）。另外，WAP 最初的目标是支持各种各样的设备，从移动电话到功能强大的笔记本计算机，现在仍然坚持这个目标。

WAP 2.0 也有一些新的特性，最重要的一些如下。

（1）推（push）模型与拉（pull）模型。

（2）允许将电话集成到应用中。

（3）多媒体消息。

（4）包含 264 个象形文字。

（5）与存储设备之间的接口。

（6）在浏览器中支持插件。

拉模型是指客户请求一个页面并且获得该页面。推模型是指无需请求就可以获得数据，例如，连续地获得股票价格或者交通路况报警信息。

语音和数据开始融合，WAP 2.0 有多种方式来支持它们的融合。前面介绍中的一个例子是 i-mode 能够把一个屏幕图标或者文本链接到一个要呼叫的电话号码上。除了电子邮件和电话以外，WAP 2.0 还支持多媒体信息。

I-mode 中表情符号的广泛流行刺激 WAP 联盟也发明了 264 个它自己的表情符号,其中类别包括动物、器具、衣服、情绪、食物、人体、性别、地图、音乐、植物、体育、时间、工具、汽车、武器和天气。非常有意思的是,该标准只是命名了每个象形文字,而并没有给出实际的位图,可能是担心某一种文化中表达"睡觉"或者"拥抱"的图案冒犯了其他的文化。I-mode 不存在这个问题,因为它只是为一个国家而设计的。

提供一个存储接口并不意味着每部 WAP 2.0 电话都配备一个大硬盘。闪存(Falsh ROM)也是一种存储设备。一个支持 WAP 功能的无线相机可以先将图像临时存储到闪存中,然后再将最好的图像传输到互联网上。

最后,插件能够扩展浏览器的功能。WAP 2.0 还提供了一种脚本语言。

在 WAP 2.0 中也体现了各方面的技术差异。两个最大的技术差异是协议栈和标记语言。WAP 2.0 继续支持老的协议栈,但是也支持标准的,包括传输控制协议(TCP)和超文本传输协议 1.1(HTTP1.1)在内的互联网协议栈。然而,它对 TCP 作了 4 个小的(但是兼容的)修改(以便简化代码):(1)使用固定的 64 KB 窗口,(2)没有慢启动,(3)最大传输单元(MTU)为 1 500 字节,(4)一直略微有所不同的重传算法。

与 WAP 1.0 的另一个技术差异是标记语言。WAP 2.0 支持 XHTML Basic,它是专门为小型无线设备而设计的。由于 NTT DoCoMo 公司也同意支持这个子集,所以,网络站点设计者可以使用这种格式,并且知道他们的页面既可以在固定位置的互联网上正常工作,也可以在所有的无线设备上正常工作。这些决定最终将结束多年来妨碍无线网络工业成长的标记语言格式之争。

Text B

信息模式(i-mode)

当电信运营商和计算机公司的多产业联盟忙于采用超文本标记语言(HTML)的最先进版本打造一个开放标准的时候,在日本,另外一项研发工作也正在进行中。一个日本女人,Mari Matsunaga,发明了一种不同的访问无线网络的方法,称为信息模式(i-mode)。她让以前日本电信垄断运营商的无线子公司相信她的方法是正确的。1999 年 2 月,NTT DoCoMo(字面意思是:伴你行日本电话电报公司)在日本启动了无线服务。3 年内它便拥有了超过 3 500 万日本用户,他们可以访问 40 000 多个特殊的 i-mode 网络站点。由于它成功地赚到了钱,所以令世界上大多数电信公司都垂涎三尺,尤其是在 WAP 似乎无法进行下去的情况下。下面来看一看 i-mode 是什么以及它是如何工作的。

I-mode 系统有 3 个主要部件:新的传输系统、新的手持机以及新的网络页面设计语言。传输系统是由两个分离的网络组成的。现有的电路交换的移动电话网络(与数字先进移动电话系统类似)以及一个专门为 i-mode 服务而构建的新的分组交换网络。语音模式使用电路交换网络,并且按连接时间的分钟数进行计费。I-mode 使用分组交换网络,并且总是在线(类似于 ADSL 或者通过电缆联网),所以并非按连接时间来计费。相反,每个发送的分组都要收费。目前还不可能同时使用这两个网络。

手持机看上去像是附加了小屏幕的移动电话。NTT DoCoMo 花大力气来宣传 i-mode 设备是更好的移动电话,而不是无线网络终端,尽管它们的的确确是无线网络终端。实际上,可能大多数用户根本不知道自己已经在互联网上,他们认为自己的 i-mode 设备是具有增强功能的移动电话。为了与 i-mode 的这种模式保持一致,这些手持机不是用户可编程的,尽管它们相当于内含了一台 1995 年时候的个人计算机,也许还可以运行 Windows 95 或者 UNIX。

当打开 i-mode 手持机的时候,呈现给用户的是一个经官方批准的服务分类列表,共大约 20 个类别的 1 000 多种服务。每个服务实际上是一个小的 i-mode 网络站点,由一家独立的公司来运行。在官方菜单上的主要类别包括电子邮件、新闻、天气、体育、游戏、购物、地图、星象预测、娱乐、旅游、地区指南、铃声、医药处方、赌博、家庭银行和股票价格。这些服务瞄准的是 10 多岁的青少年和 20 多岁的年轻人,他们比较喜欢电子设备,特别是具有时尚色彩的电子设备。目前有超过 40 家公司在出售铃声,仅仅这一事实就足以说明一些问题。最流行的应用是电子邮件,它允许长达 500 字节的消息,因此它可被视为对短消息服务(SMS)的极大改进,因为短消息最多只有 160 字节。另外,游戏也很流行。

现在的手持机的配置如下:CPU 的速率大约为 100 MHz,几兆字节的闪存(Flash ROM),可能有 1MB 的随机存储器(RAM)以及一个小的内置屏幕。I-mode 要求手持机屏幕至少是 72 像素×94 像素,但有些高端的设备具有 120 像素×160 像素。屏幕通常有 8 位颜色,因而允许 256 种颜色。这对于显示照片是不够的,但是对于线条画和简单的卡通来说则足够了。由于没有鼠标,屏幕上的导航操作需要通过箭头键来完成。

Unit 14　无线局域网

Text A

无线局域网:802.11

几乎是在笔记本计算机刚问世的时候,许多人就梦想着一边在办公室里走动,一边还可以让他们的笔记本计算机连接到互联网上。因此,有许多研究组织很早就开始为这个目标而努力了。最为实际的一条途径是,在办公室和笔记本计算机上安装短距离的无线发射器和接收器,从而允许它们之间进行通信。这项工作很快导致了无线局域网(LAN)的诞生,并且有一些公司还将产品推广到了市场上。

问题在于,这些无线 LAN 没有两个是相互兼容的。这种标准分叉现象意味着,如果一台计算机安装了一个 X 品牌的无线发射设备,而房间里安装了 Y 品牌的基站,则这两者相互之间不能协同工作。最后,工业界认为,建立无线 LAN 的标准可能是解决这个问题的好办法。所以,原来制定有线 LAN 标准的电气与电子工程师协会(IEEE)委员会承担了拟定无线 LAN 标准的任务。该委员会制定出来的标准被命名为 802.11。按照通俗的话来说,它被称为基于 IEEE 802.11b 标准的无线局域网(WiFi)。这是一个很重要的标准,值得引起人们的注意,所以我们将使用它的正式名称 802.11。

标准提案中介绍了两种工作模式:
(1) 有基站的模式;
(2) 无基站的模式。

在第一种情况下,所有的通信都经过基站,按照 802.11 的术语,基站称为访问点(access point)。在第二种情况下,计算机相互之间直接发送数据,这种模式有时候也称为无线自组织(ad hoc)网络。一个典型的例子是,两个或者多个人坐在一个房间中,房间里并没有安装无线 LAN,所以他们只好让他们的计算机相互之间直接通信。

包括以太网在内的所有 802 标准,它们所使用的协议在结构上有一个共性。其中物理层与开放式系统互联参考模型(OSI)的物理层对应得非常好,但是,在所有的 802 协议中,数据链路层都被分成两个或者更多个子层。在 802.11 中,介质访问控制(MAC)子层确定了信道的分配方式,也就是说,它决定了下一个该由谁传输数据。MAC 子层上面是逻辑链路控制(LLC)子层,它的任务就是隐藏 802 各个标准之间的差异,使得它们对于网络层而言都是一致的。

1997 年,802.11 标准规定了在物理层上允许 3 种传输技术。红外线方法使用了与电视遥控器相同的技术。其他两种方法使用短距离的无线电波,所用的技术分别称为跳频扩频技术(FHSS)和直接序列扩频技术(DSSS)。这两种技术都用到了一部分不要求许可的频段(2.4 GHz ISM 频段)。无线电控制的垃圾门自动开关也使用了这部分频谱,所以你的笔记本可能会发现它在与你的垃圾门竞争频段。无绳电话和微波炉也使用了该频段。所有这些技术都工作在 1 Mbit/s 或者 2 Mbit/s 的速率上,并且功率非常低,因此一般不会有严重的冲突。1999 年,两种新的技术被引入进来,以便达到更高的带宽。这两种技术称为正交频分复用技术(OFDM)和高速直接序列扩频技术(HR-DSSS)。它们的工作速率分别可以达到 54 Mbit/s 和 11 Mbit/s。2001 年,第二种 OFDM 调制技术又被引入进来,它与第一种 OFDM 调制技术工作在不同的频段上。

毋庸置疑,802.11 将会在计算机和互联网接入领域引发一场革命。机场、火车站、旅馆、购物商场以及大学都在安装无线 LAN,甚至高档的咖啡店也在安装 802.11。这样,顾客在品尝饮料的同时还可以在网上冲浪。可以这样说,802.11 对于互联网所做的事情,实际上也相当于笔记本计算机对于计算机技术所起到的作用一样:让它移动起来。

Text B

新的无线局域网标准

有了便携式计算机和无线局域网,用户在离开其办公桌的时候,不管是在会议室、公共区域还是在远处办公室,都能享有更高的生产效率。然而,时至今日,无线局域网对多数企业应用来说还是太慢。依据 IEEE 802.11 标准,它们运行速度为 1~2 Mbit/s。

现在对此标准的一个新的高速扩展,能让无线网支持高达 11 Mbit/s 的数据速率。

最初的 802.11 标准是在 1997 年提出的,通过定义能与常规的上层企业协议组一起工作的低级协议体系结构,把无线行业团结起来。802.11 也保持了与 3 种最流行的无线电传输方式(直接顺序扩频、跳频扩频和红外线)的兼容性。本质上,这种新的体系结构在介质接入控制(MAC)层(第二层)和物理层(第一层)增加了智能,建立这两层之间在执行涉及开始和保持无线通信的关键任务时的协作关系。

例如,为确保无线链接的可靠性,MAC 层和物理层一起工作,以确定在它们开始传输之前是否有一条清晰的路径。

在传输过程中,它们采用有线以太网不需要的、特殊的避免碰撞和到达应答技术。

1999 年 9 月,IEEE 批准了 802.11b 这个新名称,作为 802.11 的高速扩展。此新的 802.11b 标准在保留原标准的纠错、安全、电源管理和其他优点的情况下,增加了一项关键内容,即把带宽增加到 11 Mbit/s 的技术。

此项技术叫做互补码键控(CCK),它只与原标准中规定的直接顺序扩频(DSSS)技术一起工作,不能用跳频或红外传输方式工作。

CCK 所做的工作是把复杂的数学公式应用于 DSSS 代码,以允许该代码在每个时钟周期表示更多的信息。现在发射机能在每个 DSSS 代码中发送多个信息位,足以实现 11 Mbit/s 的数据传输率,而不是原标准中的 2 Mbit/s。

802.11b 标准给出 11 Mbit/s 的无线以太网速度,给用户带来好处,速度能可靠地支持日常的业务应用、电子邮件、因特网和服务器网络的接入。

由 3Com、Lucent、Nokia 和其他几家有无线局域网业务的公司组成的"无线以太网兼容性联盟"支持新标准,此标准也有望实现跨多厂商平台的互用性。

最后,802.11b 标准起到了把嚷着要简化无线局域网环境的厂商与用户团结起来的作用。

现在,厂商能专注在单一的高速标准上,用户也能通过关注给出多厂商互用性和性能的标准,从一大堆无线网中作出选择,以满足他们的应用需求。

Unit 15　网络实用技术

Text A

计算机网络在家庭中的应用

1977 年的时候,Ken Olsen 是数字设备公司(DEC)的总裁,当时该公司名列全球第二大计算机厂商(仅次于 IBM)。当有人问起"为什么 DEC 不大胆地进军个人计算机市场"的时候,他回答说"没有任何理由让每个人家里都拥有一台计算机"。历史证明这是错误的,所以

DEC 公司不再存在了。为什么人们要为了家用而购买计算机呢？最初，是为了文字处理和游戏，但是，最近几年情况发生了很大的变化。现在最主要的理由可能是为了访问互联网。对于家庭用户而言，互联网的几个最流行的用途如下。

（1）访问远程信息。

（2）个人之间的通信。

（3）交互式娱乐。

（4）电子商务。

访问远程信息可以有许多种方式。浏览网站页面可以是为了获取远程信息，也可以纯粹为了娱乐。获取到的信息多种多样，包括艺术、商务、烹饪、政府、健康、历史、爱好、娱乐、科学、运动、旅游等。

第二类广泛的网络应用是个人对个人的通信，基本上是 21 世纪对 19 世纪的电话的回应。电子邮件已经成为全世界成千百万人日常工作和生活的基础，并且它的使用还在快速地增长。这一类应用中也包括音频和视频以及文本和图片。

十几岁的青少年特别容易沉溺于即时消息应用。这种应用是从 UNIX 上的 talk 程序（差不多从 1970 年以来一直在使用）演变过来的，它允许两个人相互之间实时地输入消息。同样是这种思想，一个多人参与的版本是聊天室应用。在聊天室应用中，一组人可以同时输入消息，并且所有的人都可以看到这些消息。

第三类网络应用是娱乐，娱乐业是一个巨大的，并且还在快速增长的行业。这里的杀手级应用（即可以驱动其他所有应用的关键应用）是视频点播。因此，大约再过 10 年，你可能可以选择任何一部电影，或者任何一个国家的电视节目，然后让它立即显示在你的屏幕上。新的电影可能变成交互式的，看电影的时候用户偶尔可以提示一下故事的发展方向（麦克白应该杀死邓肯，还是应该等待时机？），电影片为各种可能的选择提供了相应的场景。直播电视也可能会变成交互式的，观众可以参与智力竞赛节目，选择参赛对手等。

第四类网络应用是广义的电子商务。家庭购物已经很流行了，它允许用户在家里浏览上千家公司的在线商品目录。对于有些商品，你只要在商品的名字上单击一下鼠标，就可以看到一段关于该商品的录像。如果顾客以电子方式购买了一种商品，但是不清楚怎么使用该商品，那么，他甚至还可以获得在线技术支持。

电子商务应用中另一个领域是允许直接访问金融机构。许多人已经通过电子方式来支付账单、管理银行账户、处理他们的投资。随着计算机网络变得越来越安全，这种业务肯定会继续增长。

另一个几乎人人都没有预料到的领域是电子跳蚤市场。二手货物的在线拍卖已经变成了一个巨大的行业。传统的电子商务使用了客户对服务器模型，而在线拍卖更多地是一种对等系统，也是一种顾客对顾客的系统。

毫无疑问，在将来，计算机网络的使用范围还会持续增长，甚至这种增长的态势是现在无法预测的。毕竟，在 1990 年的时候又有多少人会预见到，10 年之后那些坐在公共汽车上频频发送冗长短消息的青少年会给电话公司带来巨额的利润呢？但事实上，短消息业务确实是非常赢利的。

Text B

电子邮件

电子邮件是互联网的两个杀手锏应用之一。从小孩子到老爷爷,现在每个人都在使用电子邮件。

电子邮件,或者 e-mail,正如它的众多爱好者所知道的那样,已经存在 20 多年了。在 1990 年以前,它主要被用于学术界。在整个 20 世纪 90 年代,它一下子变得普及起来,并且呈指数地增长,以至于现在每天发送的电子邮件数量远远超过了传统邮件(纸质邮件)信函的数量。

与大多数其他通信方式一样,电子邮件有它自己的约定和风格,特别是它非常不拘小节,而且用户的门槛很低。那些从来没有梦想过给某个大人物打一个电话或者只是写一封信的人,也可以毫不犹豫地给他发一封随意书写的电子邮件了。

电子邮件中充满了诸如 BTW(by the way,顺便)、ROTFL(rolling on the floor laughing,笑得满地打滚)和 IMHO(in my humble opinion,恕我直言)等行话。很多人还在他们的电子邮件中使用一些被称为微笑图标或情绪图标的小巧的美国信息交换标准码(ASCII)符号。

第一个电子邮件系统只是简单地由一些文件传输协议组成,同时也遵从约定:每个消息(即文件)的第一行包含了收信人的地址。随着时间的推移,这种方法的局限性日益明显。

(1) 要想给一组人发送一个消息极为不便。经理们常常需要用这种功能给他们所有的下属发送备忘录。

(2) 消息没有内部结构,这使得计算机处理起来非常困难。例如,如果一个被转发的消息包含在另外一个消息中,则难以从收到的消息中提取出被转发的部分。

(3) 发信方(寄信人)永远不知道消息是否到达。

(4) 如果某个人计划因公外出几周,同时希望他的秘书处理所有进来的电子邮件,则这种工作方式很不容易安排。

(5) 用户界面与传输系统集成得不好,它要求用户先编辑一个文件,然后退出编辑器并调用文件传输程序。

(6) 不可能创建和发送混合了文本、图片、传真和语音的消息。

随着经验的积累,人们提出了一些设计更为精巧的电子邮件系统。1982 年,阿帕网的电子邮件提案被作为传输协议(RFC821)和消息格式(RFC822)发表。在此基础上作了较小修订的 RFC2821 和 RFC2822 已经成为互联网标准,但大家仍然把互联网电子邮件称为 RFC822。

1984 年 CCITT 起草了它的 X.400 建议书。经过 20 年的竞争,基于 RFC822 的电子邮件系统得到了广泛的使用,而那些基于 X.400 的系统却已经消失了。

Unit 16　微波通信

Text A

网络微波通信

在欧洲,领先的运营商英国电信(BT),目前正在为其 21 世纪的网络,建立一个合适的无线边缘接入解决方案。设置新的、高效的和符合成本效益的微波传输网络,来为 BT 有效地节省成本,在这个网络中以太网、SDH 和 PDH 将整合,以提高网络的可用性和灵活性。

在巴基斯坦,目前 GSM 网络的移动运营商 Ufone,为几千万用户提供服务。持续快速增长的新业务需求,掀起了一个传输建设的浪潮,首当其冲的就是全国微波站快速且大规模的部署。

对传统的微波技术而言,蓬勃发展的消费需求既是机遇又是挑战。传统的系统为基础,以发射机和接收机之间的点到点信号传输为基础,其中的配对被称为"跳",传统系统不能自己组网。因此,服务转移、疏导或汇聚,需要设备级联、交叉连接的外部设备或数字多路复用器。

这些措施引起额外的建设和维护成本的损害。设备级联需要大量手动连接电缆以及数字配线架(DDFS)或光配线架(ODFs)。统一的微波和外部设备管理的实现需要一个集线器连接汇聚节点中各种微波设备的网络管理(NM)接口。如果外部交叉连接设备、数字多路复用器和微波设备来自不同的制造商,就必须安装额外的数据通信设备,以便于方便网管信息互通。这些措施的实施,旨在抑制经济可行性。

然而,如果传统的点至点微波被网路化,这些问题都可以迎刃而解。因此,华为开发网路化的微波的新概念,在网路化的微波中,在微波设备内进行交叉连接。具体来说,如果外部电缆连接改为内部总线的自动交叉连接,并且微波链路配置作为光传输设备线路和支路,微波设备被网路化。

模拟微波通信系统,起源于 20 世纪 50 年代,并历经了随后的几十年的发展,其发展见证了从模拟到数字以及从 PDH 到 SDH 的演进。更高的调制效率、更大的带宽、更长的传输距离和增强的可靠性表明,不断进步仍然是市场的根本驱动力。

在新兴的网路化的微波系统中,微波链路被视为光传输设备的线路和支路,这根除了点到点微波传输系统的弱点。例如,分体安装式微波模型由室内外单元和天线组成。室内单元访问服务信号,促使基带处理、复用和中频调制。然后发送信号到射频处理的室外单元,最后由天线来发射。

全数字化处理操作都在室内单元中实现。其功能相当于一个光传输设备,室内单元提供业务疏导和多业务接入,并可以用来构建一个环形网。该平台还可以访问的 2 Mbit/s 的

PDH、155 Mbit/s 的 SDH 和千兆以太网服务信号。

为了支持多业务传输，微波室内单元继承了多业务传送平台（MSTP 平台）先进和成熟的优势。除 TDM 业务外，它们可以通过封装和映射承载以太网和异步传输模式（ATM）服务，并提供更高速率的光接口，以实现光传输设备混合组网。微波室内单元由相同的光传输设备网管系统管理，从而实现端到端业务的疏导和管理并实现一个真正统一的运输网络。

Text B

了解微波通信频率

"微波"一词是一个广义的术语，包括特高频（UHF，频率介于 300 MHz 和 3 GHz 之间）到极高频（EHF，频率介于 30 GHz 到 300 GHz 之间）。持照的微波链路和无照的无线以太网系统通常使用超高频（SHF，频率介于 3 GHz 至 30 GHz 之间）和 EHF 波段。图 16-1 为微波通信塔。

图 16-1 微波通信塔

一般的经验法则是频率越低，信号传输得越远。并且，频率越低，吞吐量越低；频率越高，吞吐量越高。另一方面，这是笼统的概念，其取决于所使用的无线电硬件。

"无照的无线系统"和"持照的微波链路"是指由美国联邦通信委员会（FCC）或相应的国家政府监管机构设置的无线电频谱范围。持照产品需要在部署之前通过监管部门的批准，而免照产品的部署不需要任何监管机构的批准。

用于无线回程传输的持照微波链路频率，在一个点到点无线回程传输中，使用 6 GHz、11 GHz、18 GHz、23 GHz 频段和 80 GHz 毫米波 E-波段。无照的无线以太网系统，用于点到点的无线通信、点对多点无线通信、或无线网孔型网，通常使用 900 MHz、2.4 GHz、5.3 GHz、5.4 GHz 或 5.8 GHz 的频段。还有 60 GHz 的毫米波频段，用于点到点千兆无线系统中。

很多人认为有牌照的注册频率，但实际上是无照的，像用于点对多点无线回程传输的 3.65 GHz WiMAX 频段和 4.9 GHz 公共安全频段。这些注册频道确实提供一些保护来抗干扰，却只需要本地用户频道调整彼此配合。这通常被公共安全组织所混淆，他们认为 4.9 GHz 频段是由当地执法独家使用的。只要用于公共安全的领域，如视频回程，任何人都可以注册 4.9 GHz 频段的使用权。

通常持照的微波无线电系统都作为长期解决方案被建立和设计。点对点持照微波链路是真正的光纤替代系统,并为以太网和 TDM 系统提供全双工的无线通信。持牌无线硬件系统提供载波带宽性能(高带宽和低延迟)。由于微波链路是有牌照的,并不会混入和干扰同域中的其他持照的微波回程操作,所以他们必须是视线传输(LOS),且禁止造成严重的多径传输。这就是为什么持牌微波无线电传输不使用 OFDM 和 MIMO 技术以及为什么他们不能在非视距(NLOS)应用中使用的原因。在非视距无线链路应用中,使用 OFDM 和 MIMO 技术的无照无线回程传送系统利用多路径的优势来完成连接。

使用无照无线以太网传送系统的微波通信,已经成为一种非常流行的户外无线回程的选择。无照的 5 GHz 系列(5.3 GHz,5.4 GHz 和 5.8 GHz 的 UNII 频段),由于其灵活性,成本效益,快速的投资回报以及快速部署,成为了许多终端用户和无线室外设备增值经销商的首要选择。许多户外无线制造商开始引入"价值线"——点到点无线以太网传送系统,该系统使用 802.11 标准的芯片。基本上,WiFi 接入节点中相同的无线电路板,被放置在一个室外机壳中,且使用室外无线天线。基于无线回程无线电传送系统的新标准 802.11n,使用 OFDM 和 MIMO 技术,利用了多路径的优势,尤其在 NLOS 应用中非常有益。使用无照无线以太网传送系统的主要问题是潜在的无线干扰。

附录3　练习参考答案

Unit 1

Text A

1. Put the following phrases into English.

(1) electrical components
(2) electronic circuit
(3) drift in random directions
(4) measured in amperes
(5) a flow of charged particles
(6) potential difference
(7) the metal conductors
(8) C-size alkaline cells
(9) connect in series
(10) connect in parallel

2. Put the following phrases into Chinese.

(1) 用于构成电子电路的重要电气元件
(2) 微小负电荷粒子
(3) 由符号 I 表示
(4) 朝一个相同的方向移动
(5) 每秒经过的电子数量多少
(6) 让电流在电路中环行
(7) 工作在特定电压下
(8) 严格地说
(9) 以串联的方式连接
(10) 开关簧片

3. Translate the following sentences into Chinese.

(1) 你也可以了解用于构成电子电路的重要电气元件类型。
(2) 电流是指电荷粒子的流动。
(3) 在电流开始流动之前，电子是随机任意漂移的。
(4) 电流的大小取决于每秒经过的电子数量多少。
(5) 当其他条件相同时，电压越高，灯泡就越亮。
(6) 严格来说，一个电池包括两个或两个以上的电池单元。
(7) 把电池单元串联可以提高电压，但不会影响电池单元的使用寿命。
(8) 电路的大部分由厚金属导体组成，使得电流可以轻易流动。
(9) 设计成具有特定电阻值的电子元件称作电阻器。
(10) 它比电路的其他部分更不容易传导电流，也具有更高的电阻。

4. Translate the following paragraphs into Chinese.

(1) 串联和并联连接

元件的连接方法有两种。

串联连接:每个元件都具有相同的电流。电池的电压被分配在两个电灯上。如果两个电灯是相同的,那么每个电灯上的电压将是电池电压的一半。

并联连接:每个元件有相同的电压。每个电灯两端的电压都是全部的电池电压。电池的电流被分成两部分,分别流过两个电灯。

(2) 电子电路中的电阻值从几欧姆到千欧(几千欧姆)以及兆欧(百万欧姆)不等。所设计的具有特定电阻值的电子元件称为电阻器。

Text B

Mark the following statements with T (true) or F (false) according to the text.

(1) F (2) T (3) F (4) T (5) F (6) T (7) T (8) F (9) T (10) F

Translating Skill 1

Translate the following words or expressions into Chinese.

(1) 不相干的
(2) 非全阵
(3) 不正确字组
(4) 不动的
(5) 不良探测器
(6) 异常函数
(7) 非约束逻辑阵列
(8) 非阻塞信号
(9) 非保护性电缆终端盒
(10) 超群转换设备
(11) 超再生式接受
(12) 超同步卫星
(13) 重复循环电路断路器
(14) 重置载波接受
(15) 已换址信号
(16) 过耦合
(17) 叠加方法
(18) 超时费率
(19) 低压告警
(20) 低电流继电器
(21) 地下电缆托架
(22) 拆线指令
(23) 脱线时间
(24) 不连续性
(25) 去极化
(26) 多路分离器
(27) 非集中式计算机网络
(28) 交叉系统
(29) 超视距传播
(30) 技术转让

Unit 2

Text A

1. Put the following phrases into English.

(1) instruments for measurement

(2) the potential difference (voltage) between two points

(3) analogue multimeters

(4) on a similar range

(5) follow a slowly changing voltage

(6) more expensive digital multimeters

(7) mass produced

(8) a switched range multimeter

(9) appropriate for the measurement

(10) measure smaller voltages

2. Put the following phrases into Chinese.

(1) 独立的测试单元
(2) 把这些功能包括在一起
(3) 顺着表盘刻度移动指针
(4) 观测模拟显示的指针
(5) 大于或等于这个性能
(6) 注定要被淘汰
(7) 液晶显示屏
(8) 满刻度偏转
(9) 以数字形式输出
(10) 电子工程师

3. Translate the following sentences into Chinese.

(1) 仪表是用来显示电子线路当中某种变量程度的仪器。
(2) 切换量程的模拟万用表非常便宜，但是对初学者来说不太容易读准。
(3) 每种类型的仪表各有其优势。
(4) 更昂贵的数字万用表能够大于或等于这个性能。
(5) 传统的模拟型注定要被淘汰。
(6) 万用表为电子工程师而设计和量产。
(7) 甚至最简单和最廉价的信号也可能包括你不会用到的功能。
(8) 你必须选择一个来匹配你的测量。
(9) 观测模拟显示的指针移动来跟踪缓慢的电压变化要更容易。
(10) 万用表的移动非常精密，所以摔万用表就很容易造成损坏。

4. Translate the following paragraphs into Chinese.

(1) 仪表就是测量仪器。安培表测量电流，电压表测量两点的电势差(电压)，欧姆表测量电阻。万用表把所有这些功能和其他一些功能包括在一起。

(2) 万用表为电子工程师设计和量产。甚至最简单和最廉价的信号也可能包括你不会用到的功能。数字万用表通常以数字形式输出在一个液晶显示屏上。

Text B

Mark the following statements with T (true) or F (false) according to the text.

(1) F (2) T (3) F (4) T (5) F (6) T (7) T (8) F (9) T (10) T

Translating Skill 2

Translate the following words or phrases into Chinese.

(1) 交互数据处理
(2) 机间中继线
(3) 互调失真
(4) 逆时针极化波
(5) 反压电池
(6) 地网
(7) 输入
(8) 注入型激光二极管
(9) 介入损耗
(10) 外侧信道
(11) 室外电话
(12) 输出业务量
(13) 二分法检索
(14) 成对编码
(15) 双相线路码
(16) 远距离通信
(17) 远程数据
(18) 远程处理
(19) 光导电管
(20) 光电效应
(21) 光敏记录
(22) 微波中继系统
(23) 微伏/米
(24) 微计算机
(25) 超声检漏器
(26) 紫外衰变
(27) 特高频波段

Unit 3

Text A

1. Put the following phrases into English.

(1) half cycle
(2) rectifier tube
(3) forward bias
(4) reverse bias
(5) field effect transistor
(6) active element
(7) minute amounts of foreign elements
(8) superimposed electric field
(9) a spiral of metal wire
(10) lack of free electrons

2. Put the following phrases into Chinese.

(1) 电子元件
(2) 无源元件
(3) 抽成真空的玻璃膜
(4) 正半周期
(5) 从阴极发射出来的少部分的电子
(6) 栅极电压的微小变化
(7) 电子流
(8) 电池的负极
(9) 双极型晶体管
(10) 自由电子过剩

3. Translate the following sentences into Chinese.

(1) 电子电路主要由电子元件的互连组成。
(2) 真空管由抽成真空的玻璃膜组成,这种玻璃膜包含几个金属电极。

(3) 晶体管由半导体制成。
(4) 将 N 型半导体和 P 型半导体结合在一起就形成了二极管。
(5) 1948 年发明了双极型晶体管,它可以替代三极真空管。
(6) 电子元件被分成两大类:有源和无源。
(7) 如果阳极施加交流电压,电子仅在交流电的正半周期流向阳极。
(8) 可以实现电流的放大,其工作方式和真空管的栅格控制类似。
(9) 场效应管具有比三极管更高的工作频率。
(10) 在交流电的负半周,阳极阻止电子的流动。

4. Translate the following paragraphs into Chinese.

(1) 电子电路主要由电子元件的互连组成。电子元件被分成两大类:有源和无源。无源元件提供的能量少于它们自身吸收的能量,有源元件提供的能量大于它们自身吸收的能量。

(2) 另一种类型的晶体管是场效应管。由于双重电场的作用,这种晶体管可以阻断或吸引电荷。场效应管可以实现电流的放大,它的工作方式和真空管的栅格控制类似。由于非常小能量的信号可以控制大能量信号,因此场效应管具有比三极管更高的工作频率。

Text B

Mark the following statements with T (true) or F (false) according to the text.
(1) F (2) T (3) F (4) T (5) T (6) T (7) T (8) F (9) T (10) T

Translating Skill 3

Translate the following words into Chinese.

(1) 录音电话机
(2) 电视文字广播
(3) 电传打字机
(4) 电传打字
(5) 接线员
(6) 电传软件
(7) 远距离控制
(8) 远摄镜头
(9) 远距离钴疗
(10) 远距离工作
(11) 望远显微镜
(12) 头戴式耳机
(13) 电脑通信
(14) 耳机
(15) 地震检波器
(16) 空中电视台
(17) 电视显像管
(18) 电视电话
(19) (放映录像的)放像机
(20) 蜂窝式便携无线电话

Unit 4

Text A

1. Put the following phrases into English.

(1) modern solid-state electronics
(2) extremely low current demand
(3) monolithic integrated circuits
(4) other housing methods
(5) single in-line package
(6) a theoretical limit
(7) much further miniaturization
(8) discrete components
(9) high-power applications
(10) low power consumption

2. Put the following phrases into Chinese.

(1) 集成电路
(2) 半导体时代
(3) 在一片硅片上建造完整电子电路金属氧化物
(4) 金属氧化物
(5) 低电流电灯
(6) 连续工作
(7) 运算放大器
(8) 频率合成器
(9) 双极集成电路
(10) 可编程集成电路微控制器

3. Translate the following sentences into Chinese.

(1) 现代固体电子学产生了集成电路。
(2) 其他物质,特别是金属氧化物,用于制造集成电路。
(3) 集成电路有多种分类方法。
(4) 数字式集成电路主要用于计算机、电子计数器、频率合成器和数字仪表。
(5) 双极集成电路采用双极晶体管技术。
(6) 集成电路有多种组件。
(7) 集成电路所能达到的微型化程度可能存在着一个理论限度。
(8) 除大功率应用外,集成电路部件正迅速取代所有电子装备中的分立元件。
(9) 集成电路组件的应用可能将会继续增长。
(10) 这两个定时器共享同一个电源脚。

4. Translate the following paragraphs into Chinese.

(1) 除大功率应用外,集成电路部件正迅速取代所有电子装备中的分立元件。数字集成电路组件功率通常额定为1 W或更小些,线性集成电路部件额定功率达10 W。集成电路组件的应用可能将会继续增长,原因在于其体积小、重量轻、成本低、耗能小、性能优异而可靠。

(2) 在电子学中,集成电路(又简称作IC或微电路、微芯片、硅片或者芯片)是制作在半导体材料薄基片上的微型电子电路,它主要由半导体器件以及无源部件组成。当今集成电路几乎被用在所有电子设备上,它给电子世界带来了一场革命。

Text B

Mark the following statements with T (true) or F (false) according to the text.

(1) T (2) T (3) T (4) F (5) T (6) F (7) T (8) T (9) T (10) T

Translating Skill 4

Translate the following expressions into Chinese.

(1) 一半开销、双倍性能。Metheus 公司超新图形加速器。
(2) 去除头疼、仅需一支。(电子笔广告)
(3) 凯丽为您服务。(微机广告)
(4) 传输数据公司飞越宇宙。
(5) 有助于开发您的才干。
(6) 有头脑的人购买,买一送一。(软件广告)
(7) 花小钱、省大时。(电器产品广告)
(8) 我爱用科德克斯 2 382 高速调制解调器——带电脑、功能强、价格低。
(9) 经久耐用
(10) 安全可靠
(11) 使用方便
(12) 甘美可口
(13) 营养丰富
(14) 备有样品、函索即寄
(15) 来料加工
(16) 品质优良
(17) 选料上乘
(18) 性能可靠
(19) 造型美观
(20) 外形美观

Unit 5

Text A

1. Put the following phrases into English.

(1) central processing unit
(2) instruction sequences
(3) responding time
(4) analog-to-digital converter
(5) real-time
(6) dynamic range
(7) ranges of frequencies

(8) cellular phones
(9) modem
(10) signal processing and analysis

2. Put the following phrases into Chinese.

(1) 单周期
(2) 并行操作
(3) 数模转换
(4) 图像处理
(5) 语音识别
(6) 数字信号处理
(7) 信号加密
(8) 高保真信号
(9) 带宽
(10) 过滤噪声

3. Translate the following sentences into Chinese.

(1) 微处理器通常是运行大型软件的通用设备。
(2) 数字信号处理算法通常需要在一组数据上快速、反复地进行大量的数学运算。
(3) 信号(可能来自音频或视频传感器)不断地进行模数转换、数字操作、然后转换回模拟形式。
(4) 大多数通用微处理器和操作系统能够成功实现数字信号处理器算法。
(5) 为了进行数字信号处理,数字信号处理器的结构进行了专门优化。
(6) 数字信号处理是一种将来自现实世界的信号(通常模拟形式),转换成数字数据,然后可以对其进行分析的技术。
(7) 最终,当数字信号处理器完成其工作,数字数据可以转换回模拟信号,以改善其质量。
(8) 这个处理过程必须是实时的,往往非常迅速。
(9) 因为不同的应用有不同的频率范围,也就需要不同的数字信号处理器。
(10) 根据动态范围和数字宽度对数字信号处理器进行分类,数字宽度是在应用过程中必须处理的宽度。

4. Translate the following paragraphs into Chinese.

(1) 首先,让我们看看指令高速缓存器如何提高哈佛结构的性能。基本哈佛设计的一个缺陷是数据存储器总线比程序存储器总线忙。当两个数相乘,两个二进制值(数字)必须通过数据存储器总线,而只有一个二进制值(程序指令)通过以上程序存储器总线。为了改善这一情况,我们开始搬迁部分"数据"到程序存储器。

(2) 例如,我们可能会在程序存储器中存放滤波器系数,同时保持输入信号到数据存储器中(在插图中这个被搬迁的数据称为"辅助数据")。乍一看,这似乎对情况毫无帮助;现在我们必须通过数据存储器总线传送一个值(输入信号采样),但有两个值(程序指令和系数)通过程序存储器总线传送。事实上,如果我们执行任意指令,这种情况将再好不过了。

Text B

Mark the following statements with T (true) or F (false) according to the text.

(1) T (2) F (3) T (4) T (5) F (6) F (7) T (8) F (9) F (10) T

Translating Skill 5

Translate the following words into Chinese.

(1) 声光调制解调器
(2) 宽带压缩
(3) 背射天线
(4) 区段配线电缆
(5) 广播卫星
(6) 换向代码
(7) 交叉点
(8) 数据文件
(9) 双向回波检验
(10) 反馈振荡器
(11) 软件
(12) 硬件
(13) 灵活工作时间
(14) 机架接地
(15) 半波偶极天线
(16) 叉簧挂钩
(17) 键盘发报机
(18) 光波通信
(19) 人孔模板
(20) 网络体系结构

Unit 6

Text A

1. Put the following phrases into English.

(1) the electricity from the utility mains
(2) current-delivering capacity
(3) maintain a constant voltage under varying load conditions
(4) a given piece of electronic apparatus
(5) use a supply of much greater precision than required
(6) remain within a certain range
(7) built-in power supplies
(8) tailored to the requirements of the current
(9) commercially manufactured power supplies
(10) pulsating direct current

2. Put the following phrases into Chinese.

(1) 几乎是纯直流电
(2) 稳压电路
(3) 交流输出
(4) 高保真度放大器
(5) 其他用户电器
(6) 电压输出
(7) 外部电源
(8) 各种专门用途
(9) 保持近于稳定电压
(10) 电源

3. Translate the following sentences into Chinese.

(1) 电源是一种生产电供电子装备使用的装置。
(2) 电源一般分成电池或变压器/整流器/滤波器电路。
(3) 一台发电机或一组光生伏打电池也可用作电源。
(4) 在选择一种电源用于一件特定的电子仪器时,这些参数都必须考虑到。
(5) 然而无需使用比需要精确得多的电源。
(6) 电源电压可以低到 1 V 或更低,也可以高到成千上万伏。
(7) 电源保持近于稳定电压的能力称为稳压。
(8) 一些电子器件具有内装电源。
(9) 然而,另有一些设备需要外部电源。
(10) 滤波器把脉动直流电转换成几乎是纯直流电。

4. Translate the following paragraphs into Chinese.

(1) 一些电子器件具有内装电源。大部分无线电接收机、磁带录音机、高保真度放大器及其他用户电器都有适合于电流要求的内装电源。然而,另有一些设备需要外部电源。许多商用电源有各种专门用途。

(2) 输入交流电、设计产生直流电的电源必须包含一个变压器、一个整流器、一个滤波器,可能还要一个稳压电路。变压器把公用电压转换成适当电压,供设备使用;整流器把交流电转换成脉动直流电;滤波器把脉动直流电转换成几乎是纯直流电。

Text B

Mark the following statements with T (true) or F (false) according to the text.

(1) T (2) T (3) F (4) F (5) T (6) F (7) T (8) F (9) T (10) T

Translating Skill 6

Translate the following expressions into Chinese.

(1) 有源中断站
(2) 呼叫选择器
(3) 被叫单方话终拆线
(4) 自动电话区
(5) 双工电话信道
(6) 占线信号
(7) 局间中继线载波
(8) 空线信号
(9) 全日服务
(10) 群呼
(11) 手机
(12) 头载耳机
(13) 业务繁忙时间
(14) 闲频
(15) 入局设备
(16) 占线
(17) 回线传输
(18) 复式线
(19) 架空地线
(20) 分组交换网

Unit 7

Text A

1. Put the following phrases into English.

(1) network topology (6) long-haul system
(2) bit interleaving (7) network node interface
(3) primary rate (8) user-network interface
(4) bit rate (9) the U reference-point
(5) Internet protocol (10) traffic interworking

2. Put the following phrases into Chinese.

(1) 同步数字系列 (5) 多路复用技术 (9) 基本传输单位
(2) 同步光网络 (6) 综合稍不同步的速率 (10) 光纤传输率
(3) 复杂信号结构 (7) 准同步数字系列
(4) 运营系统管理 (8) 异步转移模式

3. Translate the following sentences into Chinese.

(1) SDH 提供了一个具有独立运营商和复杂信号结构的传输网络,这种信号结构具有丰富的性能特点。

(2) SDH 与 SONET 的定义是指一组具有不同容量、能够传输数字信号的光纤传输率。

(3) SDH 包括了大部分 SONET 标准,而且是一个国际性的标准。

(4) SONET 的基本传输单位是 51.84 Mbit/s,但为了承载 140 Mbit/s 的信息量,SDH 是基于它的 3 倍速率,即 155.52 Mbit/s(155 Mbit/s),来传输的。

(5) 通过合适的选择,SDH 子系统与 SONET 子系统能相互兼容,因此,业务交互工作是可能的。

(6) 告警与管理运行通常在 SDH 与 SONET 系统之间不能交互工作。

(7) 尽管 SONET 和 SDH 原是为光纤传输系统设计的,但 SDH 无线系统的存在,可与 SONET 与 SDH 两者的速率兼容。

(8) 目前在公共网中,几乎所有正在安装的新的光纤传输系统都在使用 SDH 或 SONET。

(9) 人们希望它能够主导未来数十年的数据传输,正如它的前身 PDH 主导了 20 多年数据传输一样。

(10) 2005 年以后,长途电话系统的比特速率很快会达到 40 Gbit/s。

4. Translate the following paragraphs into Chinese.

(1) SDH 定义了话务量接口,这个接口对运营商是独立的。在 155 Mbit/s 的速率上,SDH 既可以用于光和铜线接口,也可在更高的速率上仅用于光接口。在 $n\times 4$ 的序列中,这些较高的速率被定义为是 155.52 Mbit/s 的整数倍率,如 622.08 Mbit/s 和 2 488.32 Mbit/s (2.5 Gbit/s)。为支持网络发展和宽带服务需求,以同样的方法可连续复用到更高的速率,如 10 Gbit/s。它的复用上限,由技术决定,而不像 PDH 那种情况,复用上限要受到缺乏标准的限制。

（2）每个接口速率都包含了支持一定范围内的设备开销和流量载荷容量开销。开销区域与载荷区域可以被完全地填充或部分地填充。使用仅具有部分填充载荷区域的 155 Mbit/s 接口可以支持 155 Mbit/s 以下的速率,如一个无线系统,它的频谱分配限制在使它容量小于全部 SDH 载荷,但是它的终端接口被连接到交叉连接的 155 Mbit/s 接口上。为接入应用,接口有时可用于一个较低速率的同步接口。

Text B

Mark the following statements with T (true) or F (false) according to the text.
（1）F　（2）T　（3）T　（4）T　（5）F　（6）F　（7）T　（8）F　（9）T　（10）T

Translating Skill 7

Translate the following words into Chinese.

（1）声频
（2）二进制数字数据
（3）信道配置和选线数据
（4）直接存取存储装置
（5）磁石式电话交换机
（6）起始电路
（7）脉幅调制
（8）全美电缆公司
（9）电信局
（10）国内无线电报
（11）国际通信卫星
（12）关联信道
（13）通话
（14）通信检波系统
（15）数据模拟计算机
（16）综合信息处理
（17）导航卫星
（18）数字综合电报
（19）长途话务员
（20）话音频带压缩器

Unit 8

Text A

1. Put the following phrases into English.

（1）dense wavelength division multiplexing
（2）erbium doped fiber amplifiers
（3）amplification band
（4）modulation format
（5）terminal multiplexer
（6）terminal demultiplexer
（7）client-layer systems
（8）optical supervisory channel
（9）laser transmitter
（10）transceiver modules

2. Put the following phrases into Chinese.

(1) 密集型波分复用　　　(5) 电力网域　　　(9) 可插拔模块
(2) 光信号　　　　　　　(6) 软件升级　　　(10) 传输系统
(3) 操作范围　　　　　　(7) 稳定的波长或频率
(4) 调制比特率　　　　　(8) 最大容量

3. Translate the following sentences into Chinese.

(1) 掺铒光纤放大器可以放大在其操作范围内的任何光信号,不论调制比特率是多少。

(2) 此外,使用掺铒光纤放大器的单波连接同样可以以合理的费用升级到波分复用连接。

(3) 实际上,该终端复用器对于它所携带的每个波长信号都有一个波长转换收发。

(4) 这是一个远程扩增/放大站点,它能放大也许要跨过长达 140 km 或更长距离才能到达远程站点的多波信号。

(5) 该终端多路解调器把多波信号转换成单信号并在客户层系统的独立光纤上输出它们来进行检测。

(6) 这是掺铒光纤放大器放大波段以外的附加波。

(7) 该振荡器传输多波长光信号信息,以及在光终端或掺铒光纤放大器站点上的远程条件。

(8) 这也通常用于远程软件升级和用户(即网络运营商)的网络管理信息。

(9) 由于波长间隙更紧密,所以 DWDM 系统必须保持比 CWDM 所需要的更稳定的波长或频率。

(10) DWDM 传输系统最近的革新包括热插拔和软件可调的收发器模块,能操作 40 频道或 80 频道。

4. Translate the following paragraphs into Chinese.

(1) 密集型波分复用,或缩写为 DWDM,最初是指在 1 550 nm 波段内复用的光信号,以便能够控制掺铒光纤放大器(缩写为 EDFAs)的容量(和成本),这对于波长约为 1 525～1 565 nm(C 波段)的波,或 1 570～1 610 nm(L 波段)的波是有效的。掺铒光纤放大器最初是开发来取代 SONET/SDH 光电光(OEO)再生器的,实际上它们已经过时了。掺铒光纤放大器可以放大在其操作范围内的任何光信号,不论调制比特率是多少。就多波长信号而言,只要掺铒光纤放大器有足够的泵能量提供给它,它能放大可以复用进其扩增/放大带(虽然信号密度受到调制格式选择限制)的许多光信号。因此,掺铒光纤放大器能通过取代连接两端的唯一设备使单信道光连接以使比特率升级,同时保留现有的掺铒光纤放大器或通过长途路线的一系列掺铒光纤放大器。此外,使用掺铒光纤放大器的单波连接同样可以以合理的费用升级到 WDM 连接。因此,在可以复用到 1 550 nm 波段的许多信道中,掺铒光纤放大器的成本是可以控制的。

(2) 由于波长间隙更紧密,所以 DWDM 系统必须保持比 CWDM 所需要的更稳定的波长或频率。DWDM 系统需要光传送器的高精密温度控制来防止只有几个千兆赫的非常狭窄的频率带发生漂移。此外,由于 DWDM 技术提供了更大的最大容量,因此在通信体系中,它也往往用于比 CWDM 更高的层次上,例如在骨干互联网上。因此有较高的调制率,从而创造一个有着高性能水平的较小的密集波分复用设备市场。体积更小和性能更好这些因素导致了DWDM系统通常比CWDM昂贵得多。

Text B

Mark the following statements with T (true) or F (false) according to the text.

(1) F (2) T (3) F (4) F (5) T (6) F (7) F (8) T (9) T (10) F

Translating Skill 8

Translate the following words into Chinese.

(1) 音量体积 (6) 过载 (11) 工作压力 (16) 输出
(2) 终端 (7) 长度 (12) 转数 (17) 设备
(3) 紧急 (8) 选择器（寻线机） (13) 受话器 (18) 电报
(4) 线圈 (9) 图纸 (14) 专用小交换机 (19) 等效
(5) 地下 (10) 分贝 (15) 毫微秒 (20) 发射机

Unit 9

Text A

1. Put the following phrases into English.

(1) end user (6) analog voltage
(2) desktop computer (7) temperature sensor
(3) embedded computer (8) dedicated function
(4) programmable controler (9) surrounding temperature
(5) intellectual property (10) upgrade the system

2. Put the following phrases into Chinese.

(1) 外围硬件设备 (5) 系统响应时间 (9) 系统内核
(2) 专用计算机系统 (6) 中断延迟 (10) 交流信号
(3) 内嵌电子装置 (7) 开发周期
(4) 实时操作系统 (8) 辅助系统

3. Translate the following sentences into Chinese.

（1）这是当我们谈计算机时首先出现在我们脑海中的机器。
（2）终端用户可以通过仅仅改变应用程序来改变一台台式电脑的功能。
（3）与台式电脑不同,嵌入式计算机通常专用于特定的任务。
（4）用户可以选择功能,但不能通过添加或更换软件来更改系统的功能。
（5）在大多数情况下,嵌入式系统是用来取代应用程序特定的电子消费产品。
（6）使用嵌入式计算机来代替专用电子电路的另一个优点是知识产权的保护。
（7）嵌入式系统的硬件可以被识别,但真正提供系统的功能的软件却不能,软件可以隐藏起来,而且更难以破解。
（8）温度调节器检测其周围的温度（温度传感器）,并转换为成比例的模拟电压。
（9）处理器不能直接控制这个信号,因此,它通过模-数转换过程转换为等效的数字信号。
（10）用户使用键盘输入的温度设置,该温度保存到内存。

4. Translate the following passages into Chinese.

（1）嵌入式系统的核心是中央处理单元或处理器。它是执行软件并给嵌入式系统带来生命的硬件。它也控制所有其他电路的动作。可用于嵌入式系统的处理器有很多种,选择哪一种的主要标准是"它能提供执行系统内的任务所需的处理能力吗?"此外,在为嵌入式系统设计选择处理器时,系统成本、功耗、软件开发工具和组件的可用性也被视为重要因素。

（2）嵌入式系统也有内存,在一个系统中往往有几个不同类型的内存。内存用于存储处理器将运行的软件。它还提供数据存储,如程序变量、中间结果、状态信息和任何在操作中生成的其他数据。内存是任何嵌入式系统的重要组成部分,因为它可能会规定软件是如何设计、编写和开发。

Text B

Mark the following statements with T (true) or F (false) according to the text.
（1）T　（2）F　（3）F　（4）F　（5）T　（6）T　（7）T　（8）F　（9）F　（10）T

Translating Skill 9

Translate the following expressions into Chinese.

（1）一千七百万
（2）二十五亿
（3）五十五
（4）一百
（5）二百五十七
（6）五千四百二十
（7）四十个1伏刻度
（8）十六枚二分邮票
（9）三分之二空间
（10）十分之九的集成电路
（11）十五年
（12）1.5毫安
（13）200米
（14）150伏
（15）237.16开尔文
（16）0.15伏
（17）5%率
（18）0～64摄氏度
（19）－5～＋5伏
（20）25～100 000赫兹

Unit 10

Text A

1. Put the following phrases into English.

(1) normally opened contact
(2) normally closed contact
(3) relay logic diagram
(4) factory assembly lines
(5) mimic logic
(6) parallel lines
(7) input coil
(8) multiple outputs
(9) relay controller
(10) a seal-in circuit

2. Put the following phrases into Chinese.

(1) 机电过程的自动化控制
(2) 磁场
(3) 驱动一个输出继电器
(4) 用继电器图解PLC
(5) 逻辑布线示意图
(6) 电气控制
(7) 机械开关
(8) 等价程序
(9) 切断电源
(10) 可编程控制器

3. Translate the following sentences into Chinese.

(1) 继电器是一个使用磁场来控制开关的简单装置。
(2) 当在输入线圈施加电压时,所产生的电流产生一个磁场。
(3) 常开触点用两条竖线表示,并且在输入不通电时,常开触点被释放(不导电)。
(4) 在这个系统中,左边第一个继电器常闭,当电压加到输入点A时允许电流流过。
(5) 如果电流流过前两个继电器,那么电流将流过第三个继电器的线圈。
(6) 在实际的PLC系统中输入从来不用继电器,但输出往往是继电器。
(7) 许多初学者会陷入试图将梯形逻辑匹配输入类型的误区。
(8) 许多继电器也有多个输出(开关),这允许一个输出继电器同时也是输入继电器。
(9) 在此电路中,电流通过标有A或B的触点流经任一分支电路。
(10) 决定使用的继电器梯形逻辑图是具有战略性意义的。

4. Translate the following paragraphs into Chinese.

(1) 控制工程与时俱进。在过去,人力是控制系统的主要方法。最近电力已用于控制,早期电气控制是基于继电器的。这些继电器不用机械开关来切断或接通电源。使用继电器让简单逻辑来控制结果是普遍的做法。低成本电脑的发展带来了最新的革命——可编程逻辑控制器(PLC)。PLC的出现开始于20世纪70年代,它已成为制造控制最普遍的选择。

(2) 当一个过程被PLC控制时,它用来自传感器的输入信号作出判定并更新输出,以驱动执行器。这个过程是一个真正的将随时间改变的过程。执行器将驱动系统到一个新的状态(或运行模式)。这意味着,控制器受传感器可用性的限制,如果输入无效时,控制器将无法检测状态。

Text B

Mark the following statements with T (true) or F (false) according to the text.
(1) T (2) F (3) T (4) F (5) T (6) F (7) F (8) T (9) F (10) F

Translating Skill 10

Translate the following sentences into Chinese.

(1) 固体加热到足够温度时,它所含的电子就会有一部分离开固体表面而飞逸到周围的空间中去,这种现象称热离子放射。电子管通常就利用这种现象产生自由电子。

(2) 我们知道,电阻的大小是随温度而变化的。用电阻进行测量既精确又方便,因此通常都用电阻的变化来表示温度的变化。

(3) 实验证明,我们通常划分为金属的那些元素,如银、铜、金3种是热和电的良导体,而像硫之类的非金属则是良好的非导体,也就是良好的绝缘体。

(4) 实际的热力学系统有许多特点,其中有一些同现在所研究的性能密切相关,有许多是不重要的。还有一些可能有点小作用,或者是我们对它们的作用还不了解。

(5) 制造过程可分为单件生产和大量生产。单件生产就是生产少量的零件,大量生产就是生产大量相同的零件。

(6) 雷达原理是,具有每秒一亿周以上频率的短电磁波能为阻挡其射线的目标物反射回来,有点类似声音产生回响的情形。

Unit 11

Text A

1. Put the following phrases into English.

(1) the International Telecommunications Union (ITU)

(2) broadband wireless access

(3) mobile multimedia service

(4) wideband code division multiple access (W-CDMA)

(5) time division multiple access (TDMA)
(6) the European Telecommunications Standards Institute (ETSI)
(7) frequency division duplex (FDD)
(8) the US Telecommunications Industry Association
(9) time division duplex
(10) World Radiocommunication Conference

2. Put the following phrases into Chinese.

(1) 工作模式
(2) 运行节点
(3) 网络体系
(4) 频率分配
(5) 一套全球统一的标准
(6) 一个基于 CDMA 的标准
(7) 高度的灵活性
(8) IMT-2000 的许可证发放与设备制造
(9) 移动通信网络运营商和设备供应商
(10) 通用移动通信系统陆地无线接入(UTRA)方案

3. Translate the following sentences into Chinese.

(1) 第三代(3G)业务的目的是提供速率达 2 Mbit/s 的宽带无线接入。
(2) IMT-2000 标准以 CDMA 为基础，包括 3 个不同的工作模式。
(3) 每个模式都应当能够工作于 GSM 和 IS-41 的网络体系。
(4) 该决议为希望实施 IMT-2000 标准的国家规定了许多全球范围内可供使用的频带。
(5) 每个国家将根据自身的具体需求确定在其本国范围内实施 IMT-2000 的时机。
(6) 早在 1992 年确定的频带保持不变。
(7) 所有全球范围内供 IMT-2000 使用的频带具有相同地位。
(8) 时分双工模式已被中国的 TD-SCDMA 采用。
(9) 国际电信联盟收到了许多基于时分多址(TDMA)和码分多址(CDMA)技术的方案。
(10) 该决议为运营商们根据市场情况和国情向 IMT-2000 过渡提供了高度的灵活性。

4. Translate the following paragraphs into Chinese.

(1) 中国于 2008 年 5 月宣布，其电信行业重组完成，将在此基础上建成 3 个 3G 网络。中国最大的移动通信运营商——中国移动将保留其 GSM 客户群，采用中国自己的标准——TD-SCDMA 推出 3G 业务。中国联通放弃它的 CDMA2000 客户群，但保留 GSM 客户群，采用全球占主导地位的 W-CDMA (UMTS)标准推出 3G 业务。中国联通的 CDMA2000 客户群划给中国电信，由中国电信根据 CDMA 1xEV-DO 标准推出 3G 业务。这意味着中国将把 3 个主要的第三代移动通信技术标准全部投入商用。

(2) 3G 系统的主要特点如下：具有服务兼容性、小巧的终端设备和全球漫游功能；具备因特网应用、高质量语音和高数据传输的特性；同时 3G 系统提供种类繁多的服务和各式终端。因此，拥有了 3G，你就能享受到生活与工作的便捷。想象一下你可以通过无线电话召开视频会议、通过无线业务查收电子邮件和浏览网页。目前，由于 3G 的强大功能没有任何技术可以与之相比，许多国家将 3G 作为电信发展的极好契机。很多亚洲和欧洲国家增加了在 3G 研究上的投入。他们希望，未来在 3G 方面的领先会给他们的国家带来巨大的效益。

Text B

Mark the following statements with T (true) or F (false) according to the text.

(1) F (2) T (3) T (4) F (5) T (6) F (7) F (8) T (9) F (10) T

Translating Skill 11

Translate the following sentences into Chinese.

(1) 电流不再继续流动,因为电路被绝缘材料隔断了。
(2) 他一进机房,发现灯都开亮了。
(3) 这个工作计划将先由一个特别委员会加以检查。
(4) 电源部分是不许用手指接触的。
(5) 有人看见过他们在修理机床。
(6) 这些资料得到充分利用。
(7) 机器需要定期维修。
(8) 应该简单提一下能量守恒定律。
(9) 应指出这一过程是氧化。
(10) 普遍认为电缆的绝缘电阻与其长度成反比。

Unit 12

Text A

1. Put the following phrases into English.

(1) integrated services digital network
(2) fax machine
(3) local area network
(4) duplex telephone channel
(5) digital subscriber line
(6) analog filter
(7) data stream
(8) echo cancellation
(9) white noise
(10) A/D converter

2. Put the following phrases into Chinese.

(1) 非对称数字用户线
(2) 高速的互联网接入服务
(3) 所购买的 ADSL 服务的等级
(4) 电话和传真机使用的模拟信号
(5) 从互联网送到你的计算机的数据
(6) 双绞线电话线路
(7) 电话线的有效带宽
(8) 时分多路复用
(9) 数字信号处理
(10) 频分多路复用

3. **Translate the following sentences into Chinese.**

(1) 拨号调制解调器方式最快的速率为 57 kbit/s，在良好的工作条件下通常的运行速率是 53 kbit/s。

(2) 由于 ADSL 信号是运行在不同的频率上，电话可以正常使用，即使是在用 ADSL 进行网上浏览时也是如此。

(3) 当电话公司和其他业务服务商在进入新市场以提供视频和多媒体格式信息时，ADSL 将发挥重要的作用。

(4) ADSL 依靠先进的数字信号处理技术和创新算法来将如此大量的信息通过电话双绞线进行传输。

(5) 此外，在变换设备、模拟滤波器和 A/D 转换器方面也需要许多先进技术。

(6) 再利用时分复用技术将下行路径分为一个或多个高速通道以及一个或多个低速通道。

(7) 频分复用将一个频带用于上行数据传输，而另一个频带用于下行数据传输。

(8) 这些新业务的成功却取决于在最近几年就将它们送往尽量多的用户家中。

(9) ADSL 会为电话公司和应用供应商带来市场的活跃并赢利。

(10) 要实现大的动态范围、分离通道和维持低噪声，ADSL 调制解调器的模拟部分工作相当尽力。

4. **Translate the following paragraphs into Chinese.**

(1) ADSL 的工作原理在于话音没有使用标准铜双绞线的所有可用带宽，因此在话音传输的同时可以保持高速数据的连接。为了做到这一点，ADSL 将铜线 1 MHz 的最大带宽分开为多个 4 kHz 通道，只有最低层的 4 kHz 通道用于普通电话、传真和模拟调制解调器数据。其他 256 个可用通道用于并行数字通信。作为非对称方式，192 个 4 kHz 通道用于下行链路，64 个 4 kHz 通道用于上行链路。这样，ADS 可以被看成是简单的采用数字数据的串行数据并将其转换为并行数据串，因此增加了数据吞吐量。

(2) ADSL 采用的调制解调技术称为离散多音(DMT)，编码和解码分别在交换机和用户端完成，这与传统的拨号调制解调器是一样的。被称为无载波幅度相位的早期系统，使用 4 kHz 以上的所有带宽作为单一传输通道，其优势很像速率高于 9.6 kbit/s 的高速调制解调器中使用的正交幅度调制(QAM)技术，并且实现也较便宜。然而，离散多音是一种更可靠、高级和灵活的技术，并成功地成为普遍采用的标准。

Text B

Mark the following statements with T (true) or F (false) according to the text.

(1) F　(2) T　(3) T　(4) T　(5) F　(6) T　(7) F　(8) T　(9) F　(10) F

Translating Skill 12

Translate the following names into Chinese.

(1) 塞缪尔·弗林利·布里斯·莫尔斯
(2) 金岛(澳)
(3) 吉列尔莫·马可尼
(4) 纽波特(新港)(美)
(5) 托马斯·爱迪生
(6) 撒哈拉沙漠
(7) 伊萨克·牛顿
(8) 丰桥(日本)
(9) 阿尔蒙.B.斯特罗杰
(10) 凡城(土耳其)
(11) 乔治.W.科伊
(12) 黄石国家公园(美国)
(13) 小霍华德·甘米奇
(14) 京都(日本)
(15) 本杰明·富兰克林
(16) 约克角(澳大利亚)
(17) 约翰·亨利·史密斯
(18) 丽水(朝鲜)
(19) 乔治·华盛顿
(20) 密执安(美国)

Unit 13

Text A

1. Put the following phrases into English.

(1) emoji
(2) pictogram
(3) bit map
(4) the storage interface
(5) the hard disk
(6) Flash ROM
(7) markup language
(8) push model
(9) pull model
(10) multimedia messaging

2. Put the following phrases into Chinese.

(1) 小型手持设备
(2) 格式争战
(3) 电路交换网络
(4) 分组交换网络
(5) 包含264个象形文字
(6) 存储设备
(7) 无线相机
(8) 简化代码
(9) 慢启动
(10) 重传算法

3. Translate the following sentences into Chinese.

(1) 无线网络是一种新发展起来的激动人心的事物,但它不是唯一的一种。
(2) 基于一些被公认的国际标准,人们曾经期望它是未来移动商务中的重要工具,但是它失败了。
(3) 每一方都从第一代无线网络中学到了一些东西。
(4) 首先,WAP可以被承载在不同类型的网络上。

(5) 第一代使用了电路交换网络,但是分组交换网络是一种选择,即使现在还是这样。
(6) 大家都知道拉模型:客户请求一个页面并且获得该页面。
(7) I-mode 中 emoji 的广泛流行刺激 WAP 联盟也发明了 264 个它自己的 emoji。
(8) 提供一个存储接口并不意味着每部 WAP 2.0 电话都配备一个大硬盘。
(9) 最后,插件能够扩展浏览器的功能,并且 WAP 2.0 还提供了一种脚本语言。
(10) 这些决定最终将结束多年来妨碍无线网络工业成长的标记语言格式之争。

4. Translate the following paragraphs into Chinese.

(1) 尽管 i-mode 在日本取得了巨大的成功,但是目前还不清楚是否在美国和欧洲也能流行起来。在某些方面,日本的环境与西方不同。首先,西方大多数潜在用户(例如十多岁的青少年、大学生和商务人员)的家里已经有了大屏幕的个人计算机,而且几乎肯定有互联网连接,其速率至少 56 kbit/s。而在日本,很少人的家里有与互联网连接的个人计算机,部分原因是因为缺少足够的空间,同时也因为 NTT 过于昂贵的本地电话服务费(安装一条线大约要 700 美元,本地电话呼叫每小时 1.5 美元)。对于大多数用户,i-mode 是他们唯一的互联网连接。

(2) 第二,在西方,人们不习惯每月花费 1 美元仅为了访问 CNN 的网络站点,而为了访问 Yahoo 的网络站点还要花费 1 美元,为了访问 Google 的网络站点再花费 1 美元,如此等等,更不用说每下载 1 MB 还要花费数美元。为了响应用户的要求,西方大多数互联网供应商现在都是每月收取固定的费用,而与实际的使用无关。

(3) 第三,对于许多日本人来说,使用 i-mode 的主要时间是当他们上下班或者上学放学时在火车或者地铁中的那段时间。在欧洲,乘坐火车上下班的人比在日本少得多,在美国几乎没有人这么做。在家里,你在一台配有 17 英寸显示器、1 Mbit/s 的 ADSL 连接以及所有流量均免费的计算机旁边再来使用 i-mode,显然毫无意义。然而,正如当初根本没有人预见到移动电话的广泛普及一样,i-mode 也可能会在西方找到自己的一席之地。

Text B

Mark the following statements with T (true) or F (false) according to the text.
(1) T (2) T (3) T (4) F (5) T (6) F (7) T (8) T (9) F (10) F

Translating Skill 13

Translate the following names into Chinese.

(1) 美国西海岸电报公司
(2) 香港电话有限公司
(3) 日本电话电报公司
(4) 每日广播公司
(5) 首都无线电公司
(6) 有线和无线公司
(7) 遥控科学传输公司
(8) 数据通信公司
(9) 尼内克斯 DPI 公司
(10) 爱立信电信 AB 公司
(11) 第三世界
(12) 国际邮联
(13) 新闻周刊
(14) 山姆大叔
(15) 白宫
(16) 议院(英国)
(17) 三 K 党
(18) 国际电联
(19) 亚太广播联盟
(20) 第一次世界大战

Unit 14

Text A

1. Put the following phrases into English.

(1) wireless LAN
(2) radio transmitters
(3) radio receivers
(4) MAC (medium access control)
(5) LLC (logical link control)
(6) Ethernet
(7) the physical layer
(8) the data link layer
(9) sublayer
(10) 802.11 protocols

2. Put the following phrases into Chinese.

(1) 上网冲浪
(2) 最为实际的一条途径
(3) 短距离无线发射器
(4) 标准分叉现象
(5) 无线局域网标准
(6) 802 标准
(7) 红外线方法
(8) 电视遥控器
(9) 无绳电话
(10) 互联网接入

3. Translate the following sentences into Chinese.

(1) 在第一种情况下，所有的通信都经过基站，按照802.11的术语，基站称为访问点。

(2) 无线局域网正在日渐普及，越来越多的办公楼、机场和其他的公共场合配备了无线局域网。

(3) 甚至高档的咖啡店也在安装802.11。这样顾客在品尝饮料的同时还可以在网上冲浪。

(4) 毋庸置疑，802.11将会在计算机和互联网接入领域引发一场革命。机场、火车站、旅馆、购物商场以及大学都在安装无线局域网。

(5) 这种标准分叉现象意味着，如果一台计算机安装了一个X品牌的无线发射设备，而房间里安装了Y品牌的基站，则这两者相互之间不能协同工作。

(6) 其他两种方法使用短距离的无线电波，所用的技术分别称为FHSS和DSSS。这两种技术都用到了一部分不要求许可的频段(2.4 GHz ISM频段)。

(7) 这项工作很快导致了无线局域网的诞生，并且有一些公司还将产品推广到了市场上。

(8) 这是一个很重要的标准，值得引起人们的注意，所以我们将使用它的正式名称802.11。

(9) 在802.11中，介质访问控制子层确定了信道的分配方式，也就是说，它决定了下一个该由谁传输数据。

(10) 介质访问控制子层上面是逻辑链路控制子层，它的任务就是隐藏802各个标准之间的差异,使得它们对于网络层而言都是一致的。

4. Translate the following paragraphs into Chinese.

(1) 无线网络的下一步发展是无线局域网(WLAN)。在无线 LAN 中有许多计算机,每台计算机都有一个无线电调制解调器和一个天线,通过该天线,它可以与其他的系统进行通信。通常在天花板上也有一个天线,使用的机器都可以与它通话。然而,如果系统之间的距离足够近的话,那么,它们可以按照点到点的对等配置,直接相互之间进行通信。在小型的办公室和家庭中,无线 LAN 正在变得越来越普及,因为这样的环境中,安装以太网太麻烦了。在其他一些地方,比如老式的办公楼、公司的自助餐厅、会议室等,无线 LAN 也在普及。针对无线 LAN 有一个标准,称为 IEEE 802.11,大多数系统都实现了该标准,现在该标准已经非常普及了。

(2) 人们为什么需要无线网络呢？一个常见的理由是移动办公。行走在路上的人们往往希望使用移动设备来发送或者接收电话、传真和电子邮件,或者浏览网络页面、访问远程文件、登录到远程机器上。他们希望在陆、海、空中任何一个地方都能够做到这一点。例如,在如今的计算机会议上,组织者通常在会议区域中建立一个无线网络。与会的人员只要有一个笔记本计算机和一个无线调制解调器,就可以打开计算机并连接到互联网上,其效果就如同他们将计算机接入到有线网络中一样。类似地,有些大学的校园里也安装了无线网络,所以,学生们坐在树下就可以查看图书馆的资料目录或者阅读电子邮件。

Text B

Mark the following statements with T (true) or F (false) according to the text.

(1) F (2) T (3) T (4) F (5) T (6) F (7) T (8) T (9) T (10) T

Translating Skill 14

Translate the following phrases into Chinese.

(1) 从来没有
(2) 决不
(3) 决不
(4) 与……毫无共同之处
(5) 多半,通常
(6) 决不
(7) 一点也不
(8) 远不是,完全不是
(9) 没有什么了不起
(10) 当然,更不用说
(11) 只不过是
(12) 不外是
(13) 不遗余力
(14) 更不用说……了
(15) 毫无结果
(16) 毫无疑问
(17) 没有关系,没有影响
(18) 只不过是

Unit 15

Text A

1. Put the following phrases into English.

(1) computer networks
(2) electronic commerce
(3) on-line auctions
(4) interactive entertainment
(5) access to remote information
(6) person-to-person communication
(7) on-line technical support
(8) telelearning
(9) chat room
(10) instant messaging

2. Put the following phrases into Chinese.

(1) 访问远程信息
(2) 文字处理
(3) 个人之间的通信
(4) 短信业务
(5) 电子跳蚤市场
(6) 直播电视
(7) 家庭购物
(8) 传统电子商务
(9) 在线商品目录
(10) 客户-服务器模型

3. Translate the following sentences into Chinese.

(1) 没有任何理由让每个人家里都拥有一台计算机。

(2) 最初,是为了文字处理和游戏,但是,最近几年情况发生了很大的变化。

(3) 同样是这种思想,一个多人参与的版本是聊天室应用,在聊天室应用中,一组人可以同时输入消息,并且所有的人都可以看到这些消息。

(4) 电子邮件已经成为全世界数百万人日常工作和生活的基础,并且它的使用还在快速地增长。

(5) 因此,大约再过10年,你可能可以选择任何一部电影,或者任何一个国家的电视节目,然后让它立即显示在你的屏幕上。

(6) 直播电视也可能会变成交互式的,观众可以参与智力竞赛节目,选择参赛对手等。

(7) 随着计算机网络变得越来越安全,这种业务肯定会继续增长。

(8) 二手货物的在线拍卖已经变成了一个巨大的行业。

(9) 这些制造商利用计算机网络,就可以根据需要以电子的方式下订单。

(10) 远程医学现在还只是刚刚起步,但是将来可他会变得非常重要。

4. Translate the following paragraphs into Chinese.

(1) 越来越多的公司与其他公司进行电子商务活动,特别是跟供应商和客户公司之间的商务活动。例如,汽车、飞机和计算机的制造商需要从各种不同的供应商购买子系统,然后再将这些部件装配起来。这些制造商利用计算机网络,就可以根据需要以电子的方式下订单。这种实时(即根据需要)下订单的能力大大降低了对于大库存量的需求,并且也提高了效率。

(2) 对那些地理位置极其不便的人来说,计算机网络可能会变得非常重要,因为计算机网络使得他们在访问远程服务的时候与那些住在市中心的人们同样方便。远程学习可能会极大地影响到教育领域,有些高等院校可能会因此变成全国性的或者是国际性的。远程医学现在还只是刚刚起步(例如,远程监控病人),但是将来可能会变得非常重要。但是杀手级应用也许是某一个非常普通的应用,比如在冰箱中使用一个支持网络的小组件,这样你就可以确定是否需要在下班的路上购买一些牛奶。

Text B

Mark the following statements with T (true) or F (false) according to the text.
(1) T (2) F (3) T (4) F (5) T (6) F (7) T (8) T (9) F (10) T

Translating Skill 15

Translate the following sentences into Chinese.
(1) 激光广泛用于制造各种新式武器,是因为它的穿透力很强。
(2) 在许多方面计算机超过人脑,而人却可以控制它。
(3) 当时的解决办法是把许多过滤器放置在系统中,以期获得理想的去污效果。
(4) 但由于数字信号由一组简单脉冲组成,杂音明显,容易发现,因而容易排除。
(5) 安全性是一个范围很广阔的话题,同时也涉及大量的违法犯罪活动。

Unit 16

Text A

1. Put the following phrases into English.
(1) equipment manufacturer
(2) rapid deployment
(3) transmission point
(4) service transference
(5) cross-connections
(6) digital multiplexer
(7) hybrid networking
(8) end-to-end
(9) point-to-point
(10) microwave link

2. Put the following phrases into Chinese.
(1) 低成本
(2) 专用网络

(3) 成本效率
(4) 微波站
(5) 设备级联
(6) 维护成本
(7) 手动连接电缆
(8) 数字配线架
(9) 光配线架
(10) 信息互通

3. Translate the following sentences into Chinese.

(1) 微波通信描述了一个传统的传输技术,这个技术受益于固有的强大的生命周期。

(2) 设置新的、高效的和符合成本效益的微波传输网络,来为英国电信有效地节省成本。

(3) 为了支持多业务传输,微波室内单元继承了 MSTP 平台的先进和成熟的优势。

(4) 在新兴的网路化的微波系统中,微波链路被视为光传输设备的线路和支路,这根除了点到点微波传输系统的弱点。

(5) 更高的调制效率、更大的带宽、更长的传输距离和增强的可靠性表明,不断进步仍然是根本的市场驱动力。

(6) 模拟微波通信系统,起源于 20 世纪 50 年代,并历经随后的几十年的发展,其发展见证了从模拟到数字以及从 PDH 到 SDH 的演进。

(7) 因此,华为开发网路化的微波的新概念,在网路化的微波中,在微波设备内进行交叉连接。

(8) 如果传统的点至点微波被网路化,这些问题都可以迎刃而解。

(9) 这些措施引起额外的建设和维护成本的损害。

(10) 对传统的微波技术而言,蓬勃发展的消费需求既是机遇又是挑战。

4. Translate the following paragraphs into Chinese.

(1) 与传统的点至点微波相比,网路化的微波提供以下技术优势:一个单一的室内单元支持多种微波方向,从而消除了手动电缆连接在中继或汇聚节点的需要。混合组网可以通过微波无线和有线传输的整合来实现。业务的衔接和疏导可以通过嵌入式分插复用器来执行。

(2) 微波传输指的是使用无线电波来传输信息或能量的技术,其波长恰好用厘米来度量,这些被称为微波。微波被广泛用于点到点的通信,因为小波长允许大小适宜的天线,用直接指向接收天线的狭窄光束来指引其传输。

Text B

Mark the following statements with T (true) or F (false) according to the text.

(1) F (2) T (3) T (4) F (5) F (6) F (7) T (8) T (9) T (10) F

了效率。

(2) 对那些地理位置极其不便的人来说,计算机网络可能会变得非常重要,因为计算机网络使得他们在访问远程服务的时候与那些住在市中心的人们同样方便。远程学习可能会极大地影响到教育领域,有些高等院校可能会因此变成全国性的或者是国际性的。远程医学现在还只是刚刚起步(例如,远程监控病人),但是将来可能会变得非常重要。但是杀手级应用也许是某一个非常普通的应用,比如在冰箱中使用一个支持网络的小组件,这样你就可以确定是否需要在下班的路上购买一些牛奶。

Text B

Mark the following statements with T (true) or F (false) according to the text.
(1) T (2) F (3) T (4) F (5) T (6) F (7) T (8) T (9) F (10) T

Translating Skill 15

Translate the following sentences into Chinese.
(1) 激光广泛用于制造各种新式武器,是因为它的穿透力很强。
(2) 在许多方面计算机超过人脑,而人却可以控制它。
(3) 当时的解决办法是把许多过滤器放置在系统中,以期获得理想的去污效果。
(4) 但由于数字信号由一组简单脉冲组成,杂音明显,容易发现,因而容易排除。
(5) 安全性是一个范围很广阔的话题,同时也涉及大量的违法犯罪活动。

Unit 16

Text A

1. Put the following phrases into English.

(1) equipment manufacturer (6) digital multiplexer
(2) rapid deployment (7) hybrid networking
(3) transmission point (8) end-to-end
(4) service transference (9) point-to-point
(5) cross-connections (10) microwave link

2. Put the following phrases into Chinese.
(1) 低成本
(2) 专用网络

(3) 成本效率
(4) 微波站
(5) 设备级联
(6) 维护成本
(7) 手动连接电缆
(8) 数字配线架
(9) 光配线架
(10) 信息互通

3. Translate the following sentences into Chinese.

(1) 微波通信描述了一个传统的传输技术,这个技术受益于固有的强大的生命周期。

(2) 设置新的、高效的和符合成本效益的微波传输网络,来为英国电信有效地节省成本。

(3) 为了支持多业务传输,微波室内单元继承了 MSTP 平台的先进和成熟的优势。

(4) 在新兴的网路化的微波系统中,微波链路被视为光传输设备的线路和支路,这根除了点到点微波传输系统的弱点。

(5) 更高的调制效率、更大的带宽、更长的传输距离和增强的可靠性表明,不断进步仍然是根本的市场驱动力。

(6) 模拟微波通信系统,起源于 20 世纪 50 年代,并历经随后的几十年的发展,其发展见证了从模拟到数字以及从 PDH 到 SDH 的演进。

(7) 因此,华为开发网路化的微波的新概念,在网路化的微波中,在微波设备内进行交叉连接。

(8) 如果传统的点至点微波被网路化,这些问题都可以迎刃而解。

(9) 这些措施引起额外的建设和维护成本的损害。

(10) 对传统的微波技术而言,蓬勃发展的消费需求既是机遇又是挑战。

4. Translate the following paragraphs into Chinese.

(1) 与传统的点至点微波相比,网路化的微波提供以下技术优势:一个单一的室内单元支持多种微波方向,从而消除了手动电缆连接在中继或汇聚节点的需要。混合组网可以通过微波无线和有线传输的整合来实现。业务的衔接和疏导可以通过嵌入式分插复用器来执行。

(2) 微波传输指的是使用无线电波来传输信息或能量的技术,其波长恰好用厘米来度量,这些被称为微波。微波被广泛用于点到点的通信,因为小波长允许大小适宜的天线,用直接指向接收天线的狭窄光束来指引其传输。

Text B

Mark the following statements with T (true) or F (false) according to the text.

(1) F (2) T (3) T (4) F (5) F (6) F (7) T (8) T (9) T (10) F

Translating Skill 16

Translate the following sentences into Chinese.

(1) 根据因特尔公司估计,在一两年之内,美国家庭使用的个人计算机数将达到 5 000 万台,而到 1995 年年底或者 1996 年年初,个人计算机产量将超过电视机。

(2) 如果面向阳光,就看不见自己的影子。

(3) 将来的电话将更加机动,能完成多种任务,不但如此,还将成为用途广泛的信息网络的一部分。

(4) 错误的东西在所难免,但并不可怕。

(5) 一个部门对专用计算机需求很少,而专用方式不能很好地完成其他任务。

(6) 以太网使用总线拓扑结构,且依靠所谓的 CSMA/CD 访问方式来调节主通信线路上的交通。

参考文献

[1] 刘玉芝,游建青,等.英汉电信缩略语词典.北京:人民邮电出版社,1994.
[2] 人民邮电出版社.英汉电信技术词典.北京:人民邮电出版社,1993.
[3] 清华大学外语系《英汉科学技术词典》编写组.英汉科学技术词典.北京:国防工业出版社,1996.
[4] Tanenbaum A S.计算机网络(4版).潘爱明,译.北京:清华大学出版社,2004.
[5] 张筱华,石方文.通信英语(5版).北京:北京邮电大学出版社,2008.
[6] 徐秀兰.计算机与通信专业英语(修订3版).北京:北京邮电大学出版社,2003.
[7] 李霞,杨英杰.电子与通信专业英语.北京:电子工业出版社,2007.
[8] 王琳,夏怡.电子与通信专业英语.北京:北京理工大学出版社,2007.
[9] 马宪庆,常晓东.计算机英语.北京:人民邮电出版社,1995.
[10] 郭著章,李庆生.英汉互译实用教程.武汉:武汉大学出版社,1988.
[11] 邮电中专英语教材编写组.英语(第3册).北京:人民邮电出版社,1992.
[12] 骆如楠.英汉对照现代电信科技读物选.北京:人民邮电出版社,1994.
[13] 邮电部中专教学指导组.电信英语.北京:人民邮电出版社,1994.
[14] 高廷健,何体侨,王文博,等.专业基础英语.北京:人民邮电出版社,1998.
[15] 刘兆毓.计算机英语.北京:清华大学出版社,1997.
[16] 刘乃琦.计算机专业英语.北京:电子工业出版社,1998.
[17] 李鄂强.通信专业英语.北京:电子工业出版社,2000.
[18] 刘艺.计算机英语.北京:机械工业出版社,2001.
[19] 韩定定,赵菊敏.信息与通信工程专业英语.北京:北京大学出版社,2006.
[20] 常义林,任志纯.通信工程专业英语.西安:西安电子科技大学出版社,2001.
[21] 赵淑清.电子信息与通信专业英语.哈尔滨:哈尔滨工业大学出版社,2007.
[22] 黎楷模.通信与网络技术专业英语.北京:电子工业出版社,2003.
[23] 高艳萍.电子信息类专业英语.北京:中国电力出版社,2007.
[24] 况常兰.通信工程专业英语.成都:电子科技大学出版社,2006.
[25] 曹玲芝.电子信息工程专业英语.武汉:华中科技大学出版社,2006.
[26] 王颖.电子与通信专业英语.北京:人民邮电出版社,2006.
[27] 朱一伦.电子技术专业英语.北京:电子工业出版社,2006.
[28] 宋宏.前沿科技英语阅读文选.北京:国防工业出版社,2007.
[29] 杨泽清.通信英语.北京:外语教学与研究出版社,2007.
[30] 贾杰,金郁.电子技术专业英语.成都:电子科技大学出版社,1999.
[31] 李白萍,等.电子信息类专业英语.西安:西安电子科技大学出版社,2003.
[32] Anon. Circuits[EB/OL].[2008-06-28]. http://www.doctronics.co.uk/circuits.htm.

[33] Anon. Resistors[EB/OL]. [2008-06-28]. http://www.doctronics.co.uk/resistor.htm.

[34] Anon. Digital Logic Circuit [EB/OL]. [2008-06-28]. http://library.thinkquest.org/C006657/electronics/digital_logic_circuit.htm.

[35] Anon. Power Supply [EB/OL]. [2008-06-28]. http://en.wikipedia.org/wiki/Power_supply.

[36] 佚名. 面向未来的CNCnet [EB/OL]. [2008-06-28]. http://www.ccw.com.cn/htm/net/viewp/01_1_5_3.asp.

[37] Anon. GSM [EB/OL]. [2008-06-28]. http://en.wikipedia.org/wiki/GSM.

[38] Anon. Introduction to CDMA [EB/OL]. [2008-06-28]. http://www.cdg.org/technology/cdma%5Ftechnology/a_ross/Intro.asp.

[39] Anon. Code Division Multiple Access [EB/OL]. [2008-06-28]. http://en.wikipedia.org/wiki/Code_division_multiple_access.

[40] Anon. CDMA IS-95 Digital Mobile Telephone Standard [EB/OL]. [2008-06-28]. http://www.mobilecomms-technology.com/projects/cdma_is95.

[41] Anon. IMT-2000 Global 3G Standard [EB/OL]. [2008-06-28]. http://www.mobilecomms-technology.com/projects/imt2000.

[42] Anon. 3G [EB/OL]. [2008-06-28]. http://en.wikipedia.org/wiki/3G.